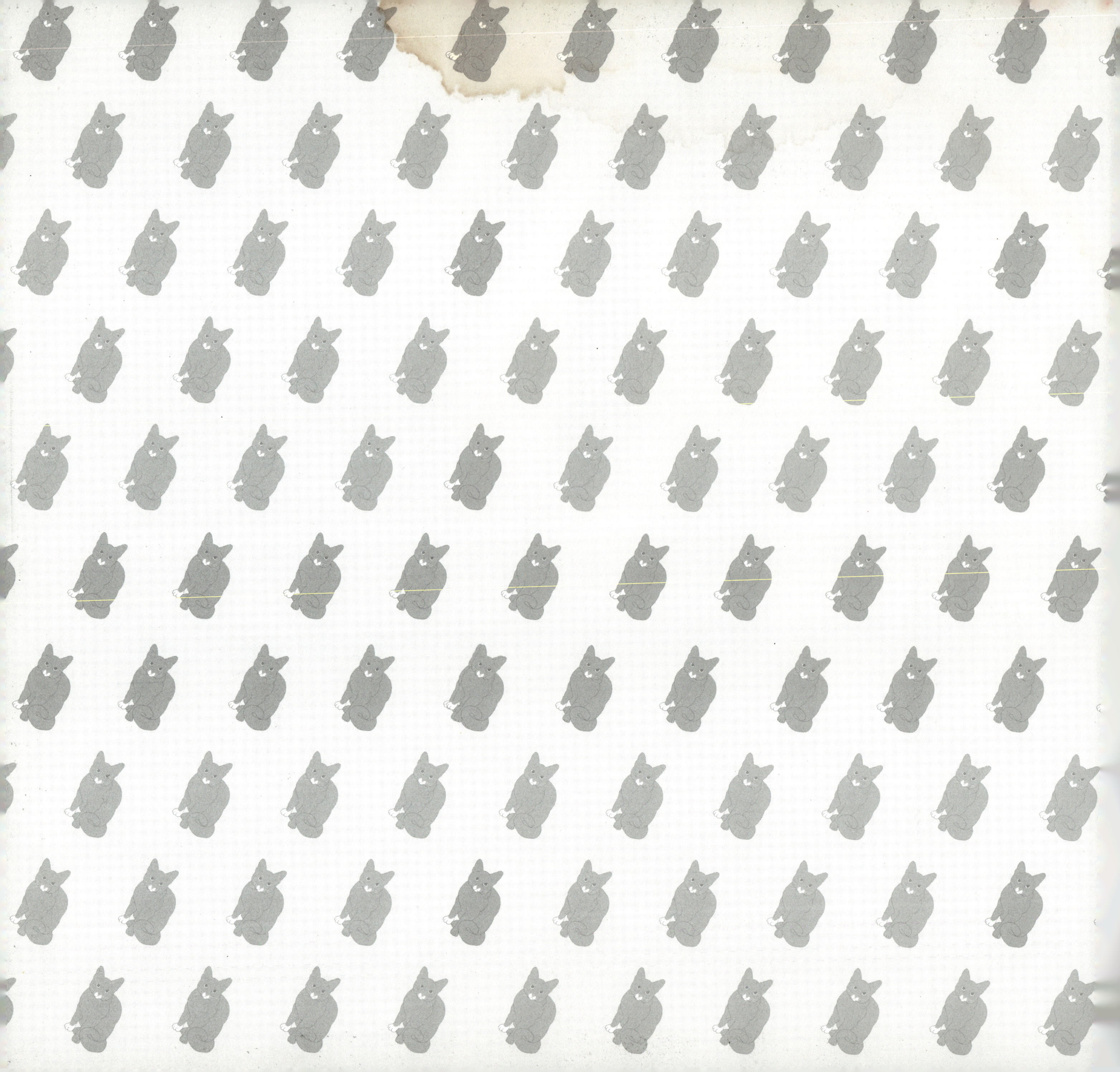

Charlie the Red Cat

Charlie the Red Cat

JIM TWEEDY

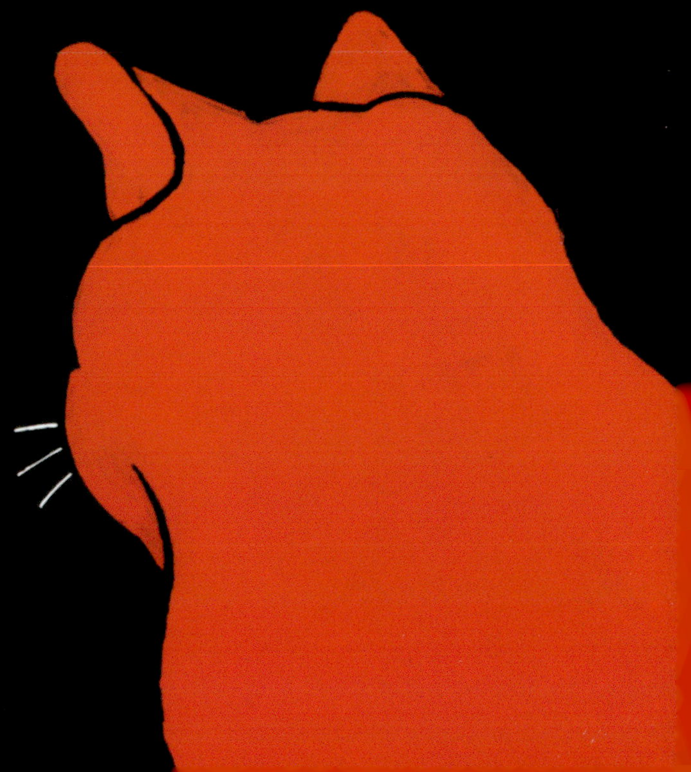

Front cover painting: "Family Reunion" by Jim Tweedy
Back cover painting: "Charlie's Tribute to the June Taylor Dancers" by Jim Tweedy

Published by:
Crane Hill Publishers
www.cranehill.com

Visit the home of Charlie the RedCat:
Richard Russell Gallery
641 Royal Street
New Orleans, Louisiana 70130
800/536-0533
www.charlietheredcat.com

Book design by Carla Coker and Bob Weathers
Printed in Singapore

Library of Congress Cataloging-in-Publication Data
Tweedy, Jim, 1958-
Charlie the RedCat / by Jim Tweedy.
p. cm.
Includes index.
ISBN 1-57587-110-6
1. Cats—Caricatures and cartoons. 2. American wit and humor, Pictorial. I. TITLE. II. TITLE: Charlie the Red Cat.
NC1429.T79A4 1999
741.5'973—dc21 99-10568
CIP

10 9 8 7 6 5 4 3 2 1

*For my wife Robyn, my three children,
Mark Ellen, Mackenzie, and Sean, and
my mother, Katherine.*

PLATES

ACKNOWLEDGMENTS

This book and all these Charlie the RedCat paintings exist not just because I've been sitting in a corner and painting them for seven years. (Although, that does have a lot to do with it.) Encouragement and support from so many people have been just as important.

I want to especially thank Richard Russell, who gave me my first big break when he stepped on my hand. To make up for it, he let me show my Charlie paintings in his gallery in the New Orleans French Quarter. In fact, he also works as my agent and we've become great friends. Richard has believed in my artwork since the beginning and he shares my vision of a RedCat for every home in America. Call him up and bother him.

Special thanks also go to Richard's brilliant and beautiful wife, Janis, and everyone on the Richard Russell Gallery staff—Matt, Rebecca and Angela, I'm their biggest fan; to my assistant, Alison Evans, for keeping me organized, if that's at all possible; to all the Charlie the RedCat owners out there—from t-shirts to original paintings, you fuel the RedCat fire and I never forget that; to Art Nisle, you're my hero; to Ken Olsho, the man who showed me how Picasso would really see Charlie and then how to train my cat; to Shelley DeLuca, who dreamed up this book, lobbied for it, got most of my jokes, and helped me every step of the way; to Ellen Sullivan, world traveler, publishing authority, and an expert at knowing a good thing when she sees it—you da woman; to my other RedCat business associates who help me get Charlie into so many homes and without whose continued help RedCat fever would be impossible—Kathleen, Ricky, Holly, Marguerita, Gene, Kendra, David, and Linda, you da galleries!

In a special category is my family: Thank you to my mother Katherine who has always had absolute confidence in me; my in-laws, Mark and Jaye, who give me never-ending support and encouragement; my children and my real inspiration, Mark Ellen, Mackenzie, and Sean, without whom I wouldn't know so much about Winnie the Pooh (or just poo-poo in general), and most of all my wife Robyn, who convinced me to break away from advertising art and focus on painting. She has always had faith in me and my ability to make this dream of mine into a real business. Our life together seems busier than ever lately. Me with my growing business and she with our growing family. She managed to care for our three small children, oversee the building of our new home, and still make time to listen and talk with me about this book.

Oh yeah, and thanks to Charlie for being able to hold still longer than anyone I have ever known.

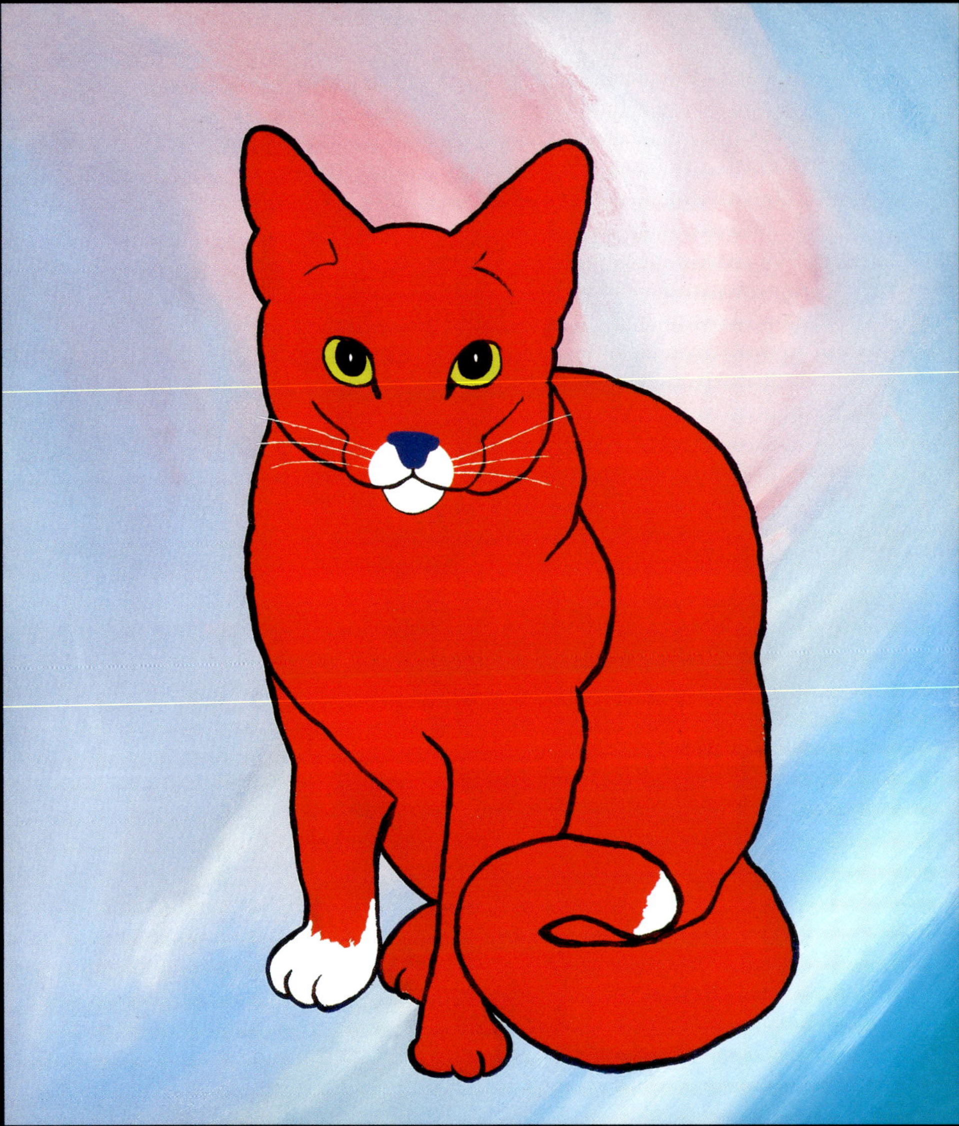

This is the first painting of Charlie the Redcat.

INTRODUCTION

The funniest thing about Charlie the RedCat is that the original painting was meant to be the one and only. It was done as a spoof. I figured if a guy could paint a picture of his dog blue, why couldn't I paint a portrait of my cat red?

My focus up until that time had been on sports art, and I had developed a steady following. But a funny thing happened on the way to the easel. The calls kept coming in for Charlie the RedCat.

In fact, the day after I painted that first RedCat a lady came into the gallery and "just had to have one!" She commissioned a smaller version. The very next day it happened again. Another commission! I told my wife: "I think I'm on to something."

That was an understatement. Nearly seven years and more than four hundred Charlie the RedCat paintings later, I hardly have time to watch sports on television—let alone create sports art.

I may have painted the original RedCat as a spoof, but that's where the similarities end. Charlie himself is definitely one of a kind in personality and in looks. In reality, Charlie is a big gray tabby. He still lives in my studio and remains my inspiration. If I'm ever at a loss for ideas, a little Charlie-watching gets my creative juices flowing.

The real Charlie tears around the house chasing a flashlight beam. He leaps high into the air to catch a rolled up pair of socks. Also, he is forever getting into trouble in my studio. One of Charlie's favorite hobbies is standing behind my easel and watching me paint. The little indentations my brush makes on the backside of the canvas drive him crazy until he loses all self-control and attacks. On more than one occasion I've had to drop my brush and catch a flying canvas inches from my face.

On canvas I portray Charlie red because it is the perfect color for him. His personality is fun and feisty. Another reason is that Charlie's home (my studio) is in the world-famous New Orleans French Quarter. Everything about New Orleans can be described as being red-hot and spicy—the food, the climate, the music, and even the local people.

Charlie's nose, however, is a different story. It's blue because whenever you touch it (and I would encourage you to do so), it is always ice-cold. His paw is white to symbolize the fact that he's always got one foot into trouble. The white tip on his tail is there because, well, his tail really does have a white tip.

The increase in demand for Charlie the RedCat paintings provided me with the opportunity to become very creative in my scenarios and titles. I could finally do more than just put him on plain backgrounds, which is what my early commissions wanted. The RedCat became my alter ego. He was cool where I was not. Charlie needed to be the central figure of some very cool and funny situations. I also made him travel to the most exciting places. With just a stroke of my brush (or sometimes a whole lot of strokes) Charlie could go places I had never been and probably will never have time to see.

Although Charlie the RedCat paintings are often designed to be funny, collectors take Charlie very seriously. One of them told me that his RedCat is hanging between his Max and his Warhol (sounds like he ought to see a doctor). To be in that company is more than even Charlie himself could imagine.

My father, who was a Walt Disney animator in the 1930s, was my favorite cartoonist when I was a child. In fact, his old drawings are still my favorites. Dad gave me my first art lessons. I can remember back when I was three years old. He would fill an entire page with ovals to represent heads, and I would spend hours filling them with faces. He was a wonderful teacher, always helping me when I had questions. I remember both of us sitting at the kitchen table drawing cartoons. We were trying to create funny characters but never came up with anything we were crazy about. Dad would have loved Charlie the RedCat because Charlie is that fantastic idea we were always looking for. Somehow, I know my father is watching all of this and he's enjoying every brushstroke.

Welcome to Charlie's world ... and it's a funky place.

For Charlie the RedCat, music isn't part of the world, but rather, the world ***is*** *music. Living and working in the French Quarter makes it impossible to avoid music. In fact, Charlie's first job was a four-year stint as the official mascot of the Baton Rouge Blues Festival. And almost every night he's out there caterwauling and trying to get gigs in various music clubs. I worry about him a bit, but then again, he's forty-nine in human years.*

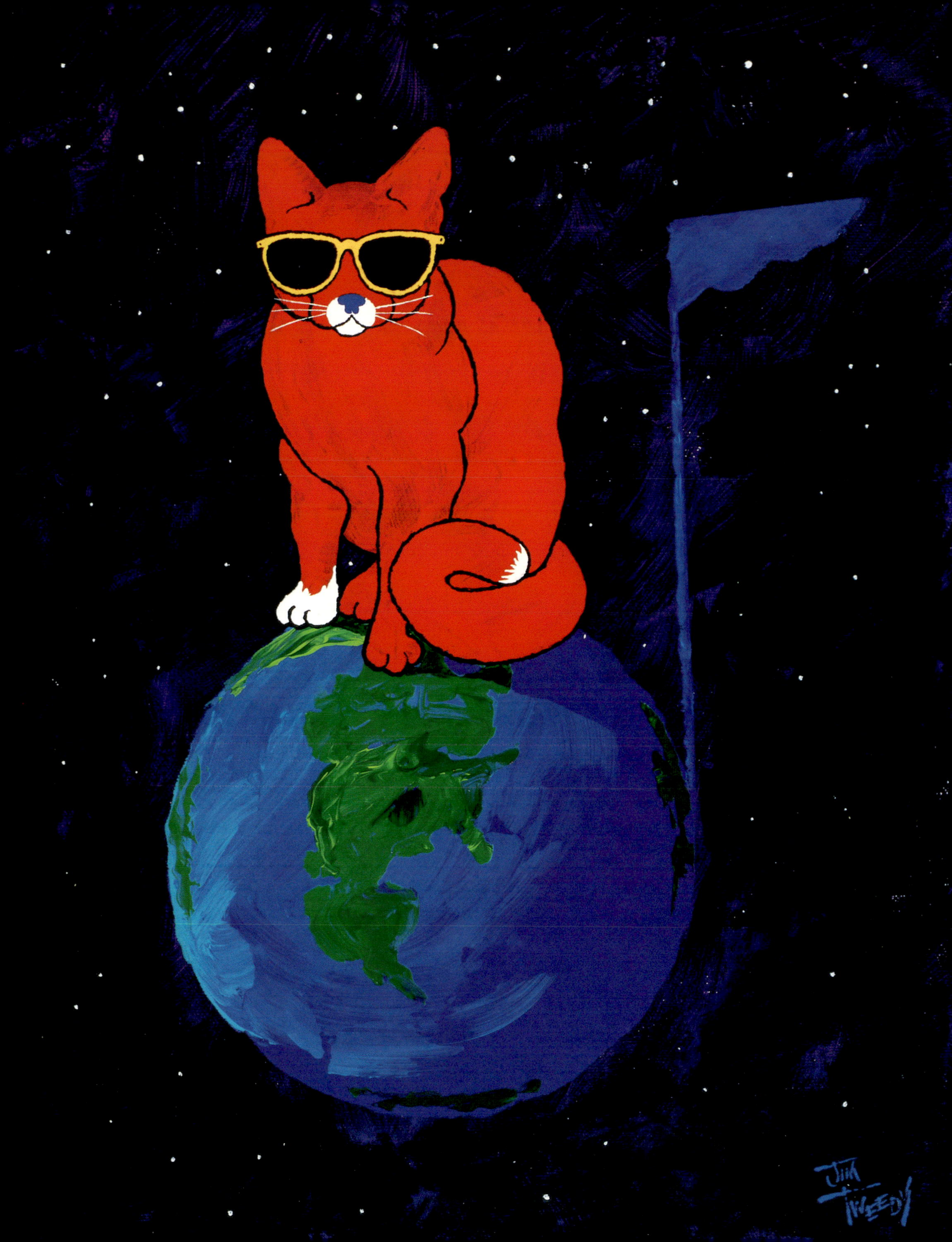

Charlie's World
... and It's a
Funky Place

My cat Charlie is always "crowning around." I guess that's because in his world, cool is king.

Ever since we got that Walt Disney video, "The Lion King," for the kids, Charlie's been wearing this thing and insisting I refer to him as Kunta RedCat.

Crowning Around

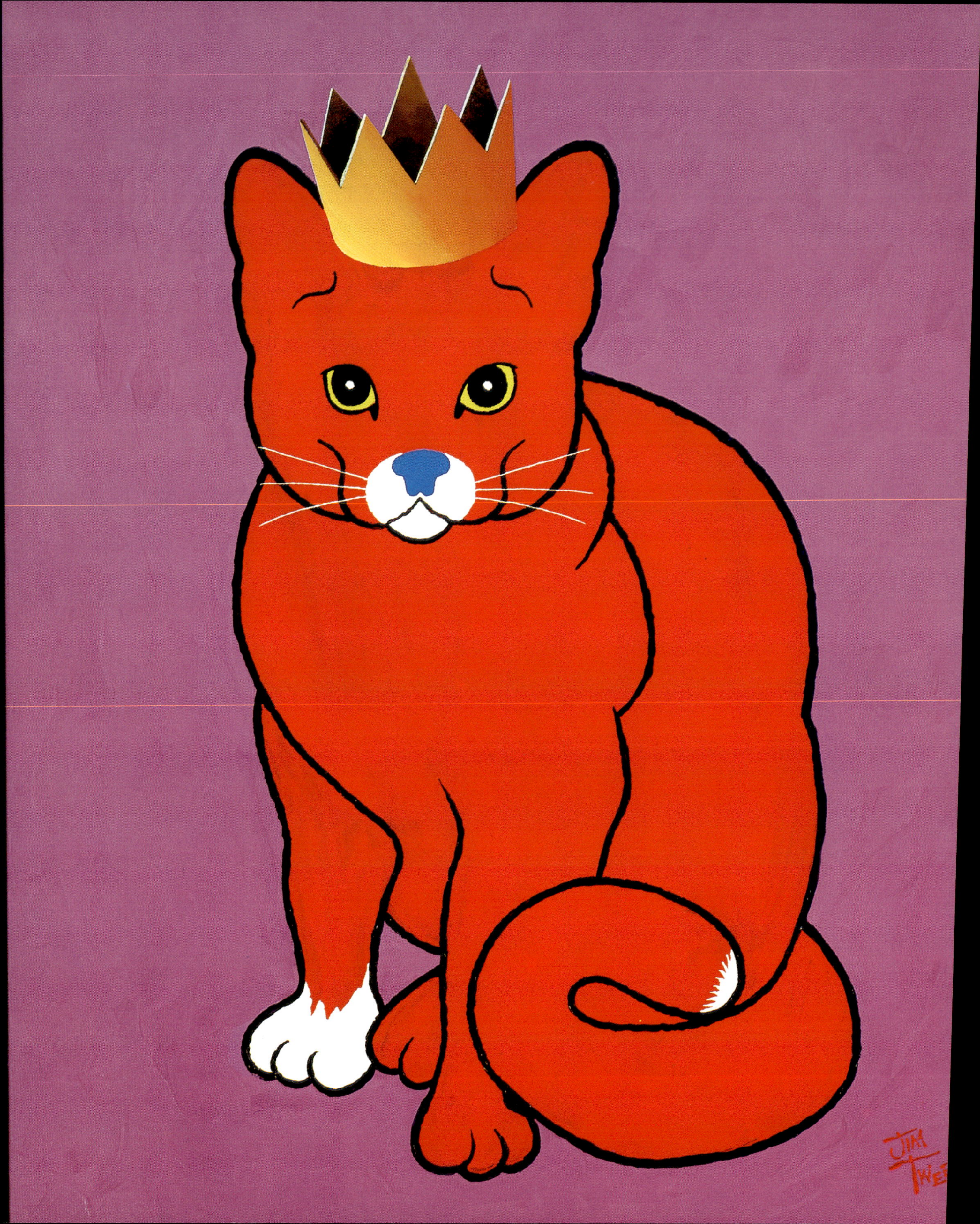

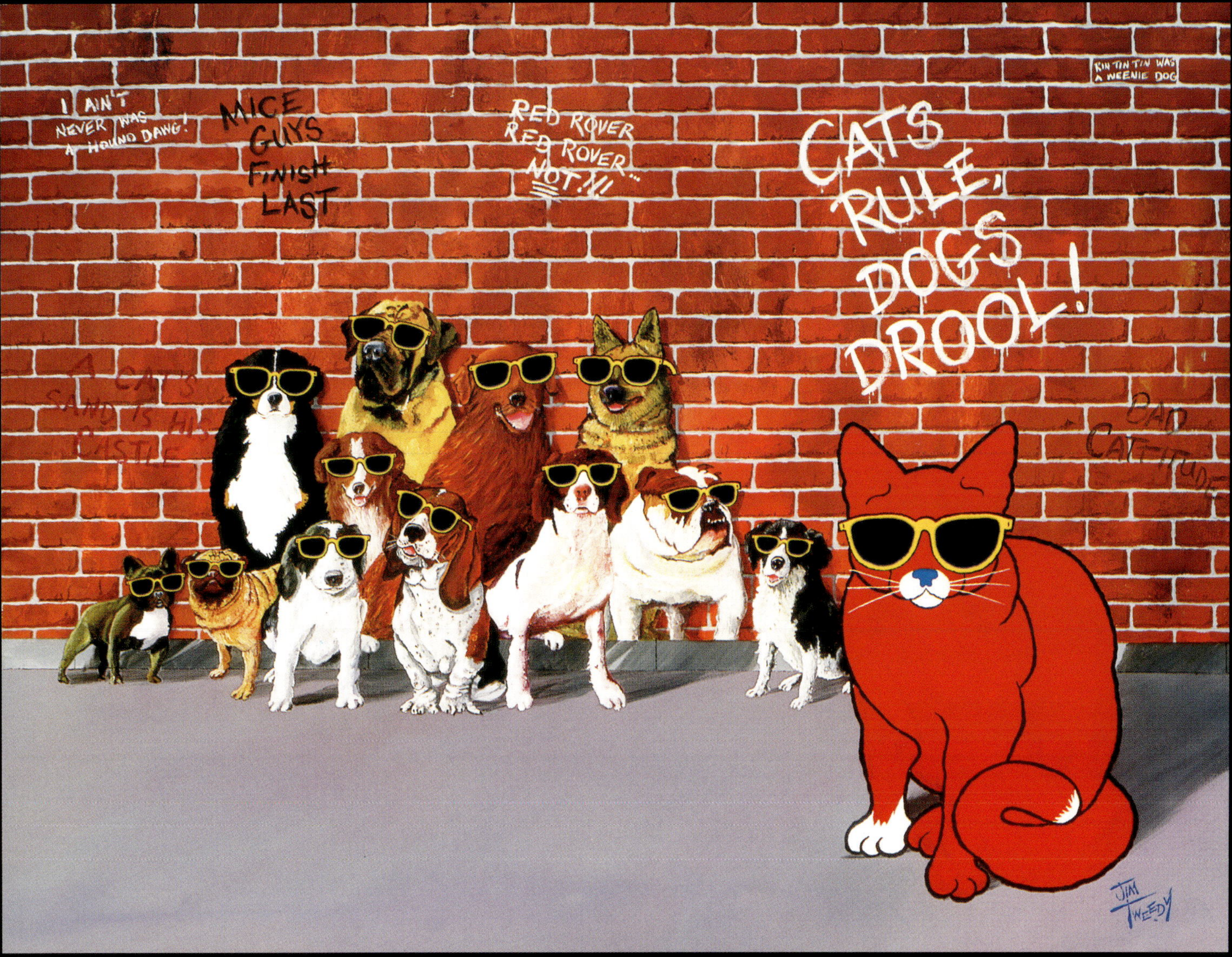

And as for man's so-called best friend? Well they've got a lot to learn. But it's nothing a little crash course at Cool School can't handle.

The problem with dogs is they need a dose of cool and they need it now. So Charlie the RedCat has hung out his shingle. From the looks of things, this proud and suave-looking pack of graduates has seen the writing on the wall.

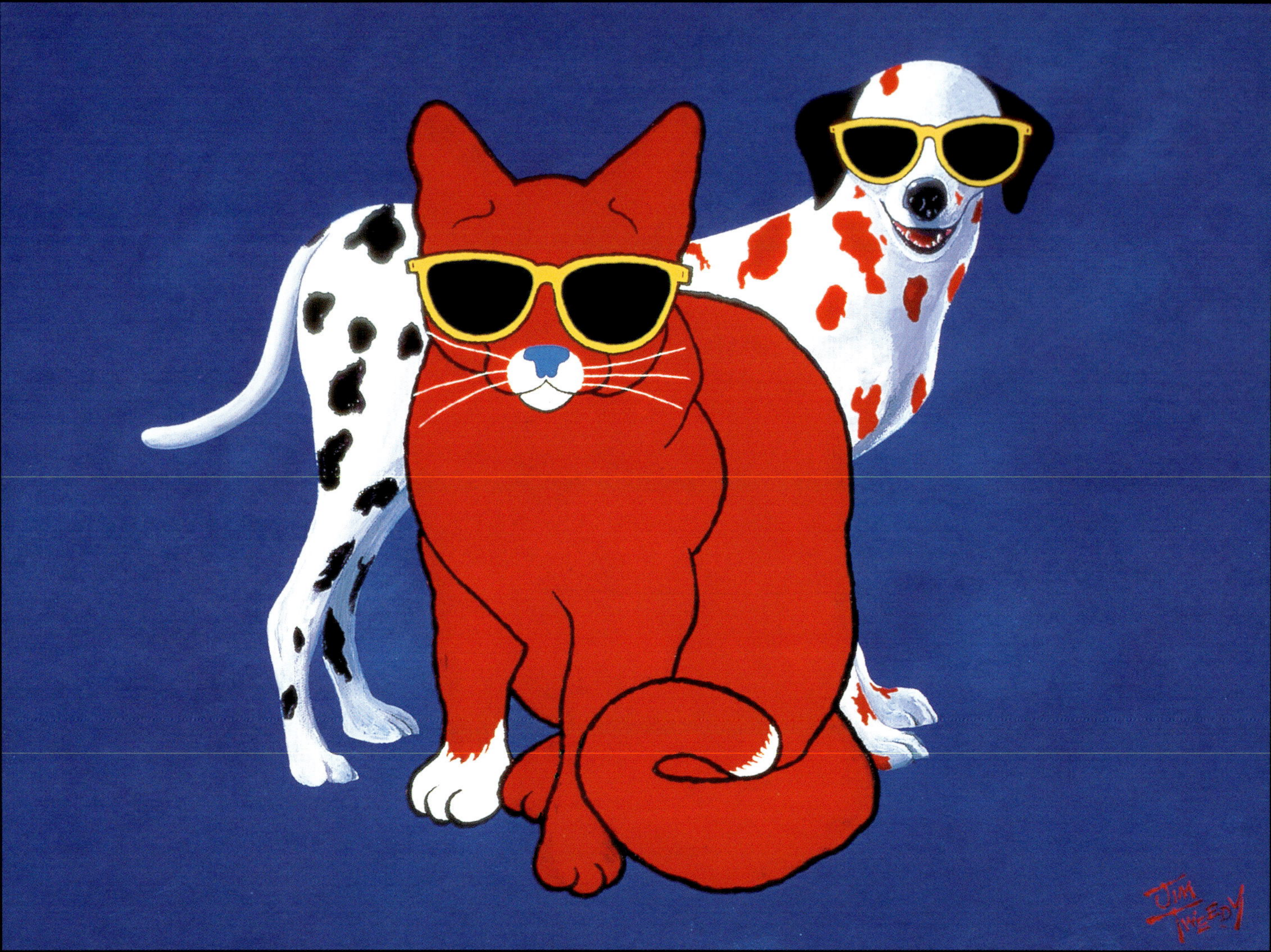

Of course, there's no denying the power of Red.

Legend has it that a RedCat possesses powers far beyond those of an ordinary kitty cat.

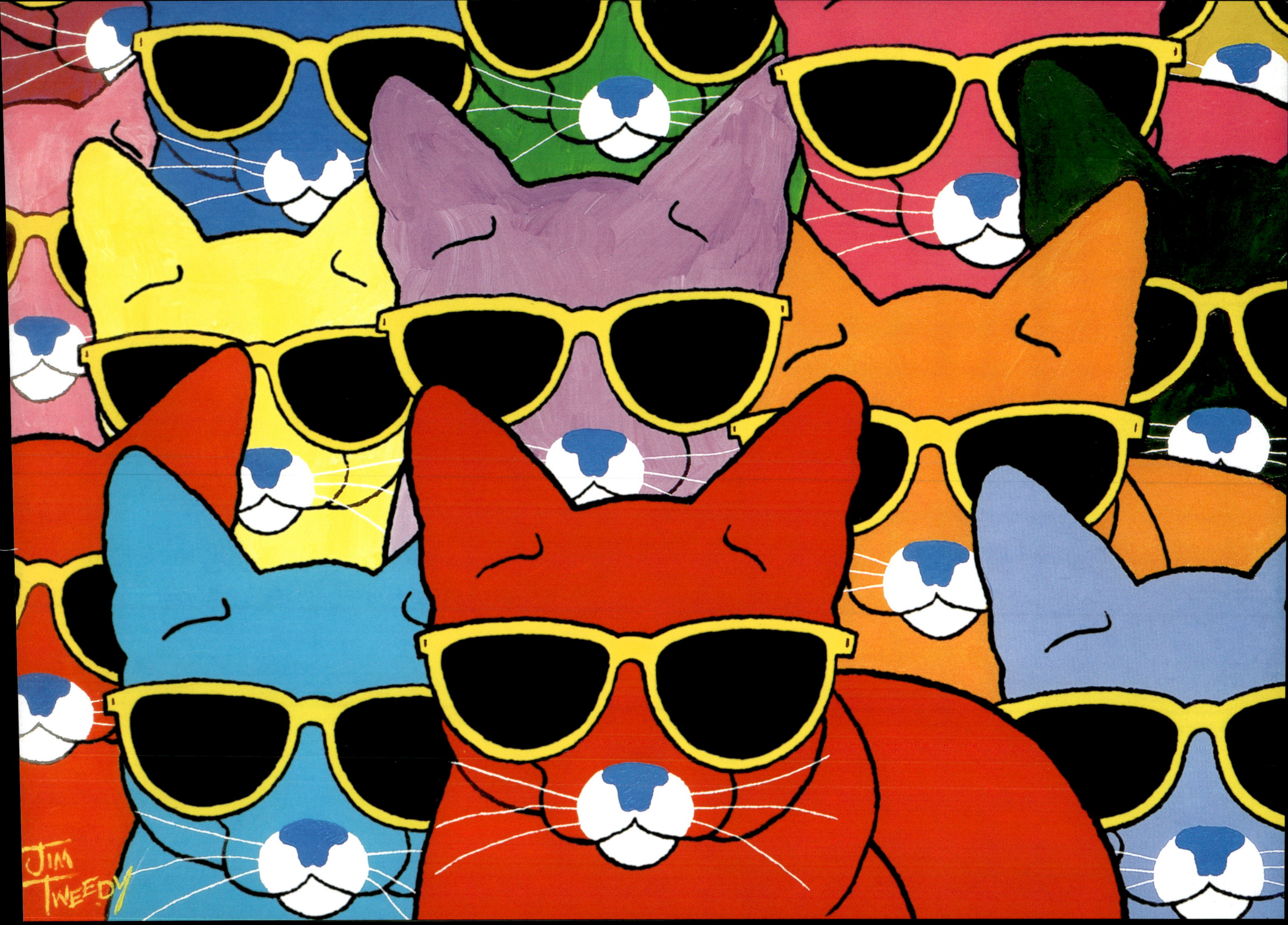

Everybody Wants to Get into the Act

The power of Red makes everybody want to get into the act.

You know, it seems that every time I look up, some other oddly coloRedCat is stopping by my studio trying to audition for a part. But it's more than a funny color thing. It's more than a red thing. It's a cool thing.

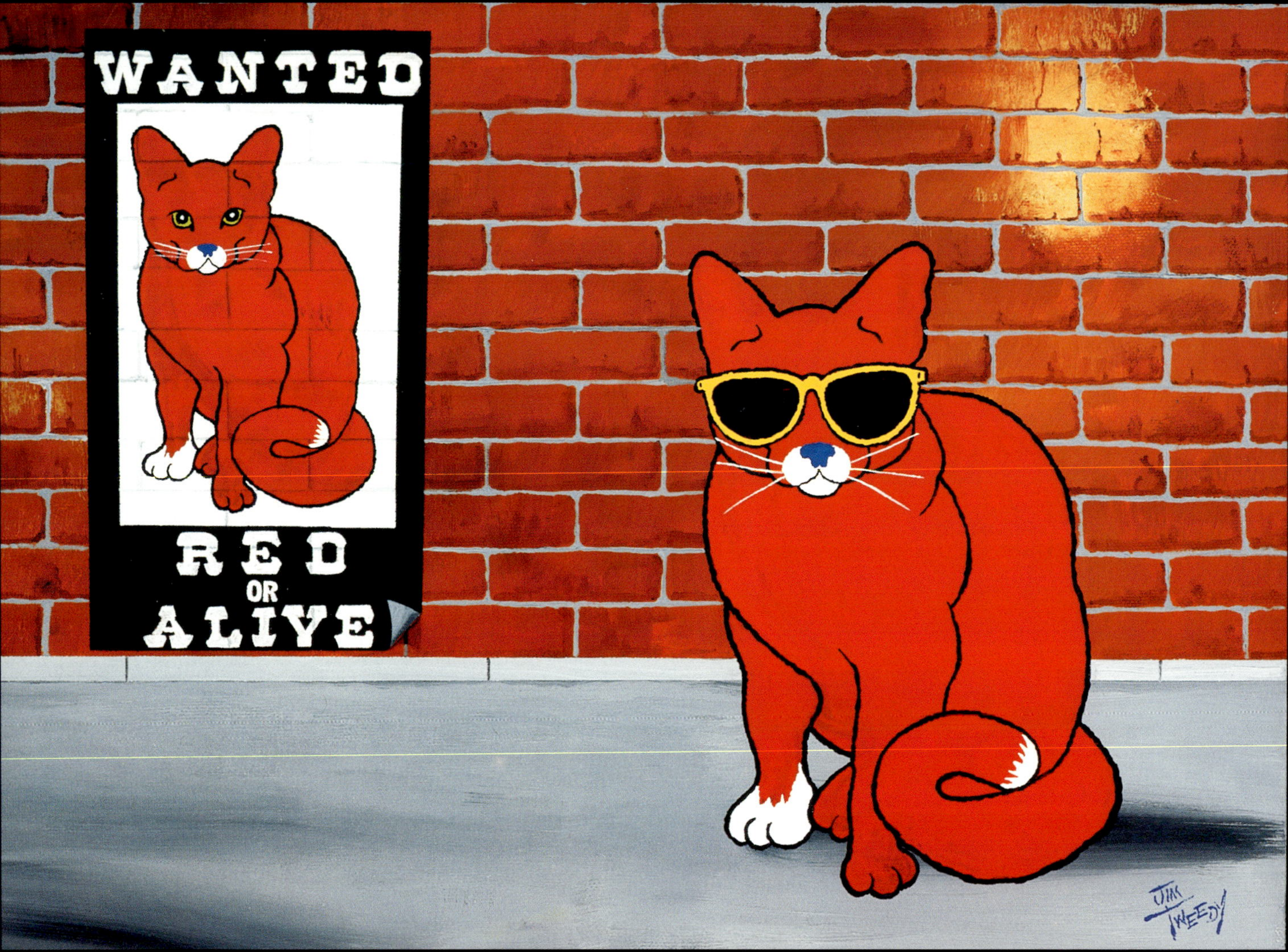

Charlie developed a brilliant disguise.

So simple, yet so effective. Charlie's not like that super guy in the comics with the ordinary glasses. Who could hide behind those?

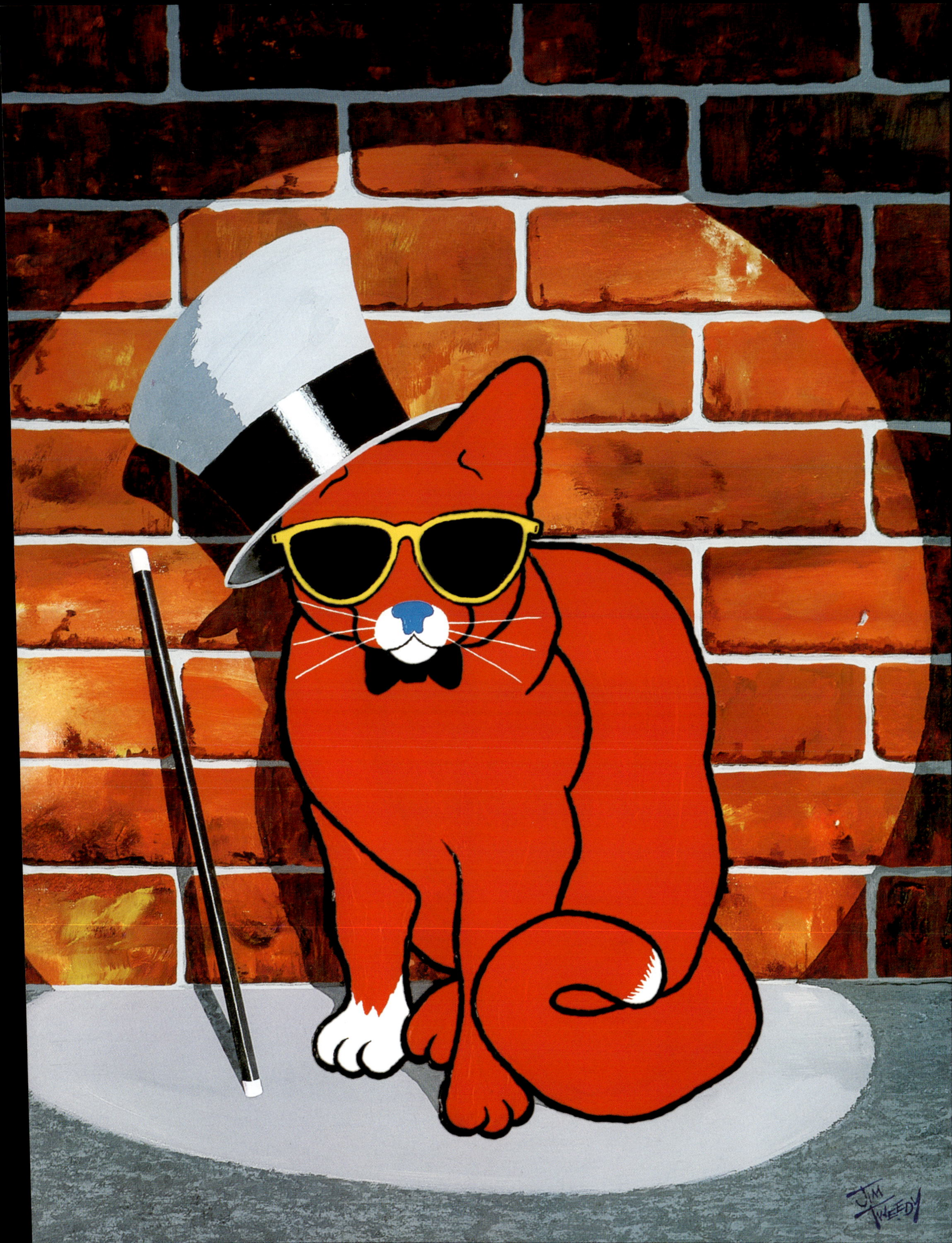

But his disguise apparently didn’t work because he was caught in the act.

There’s nothing a tomcat loves more than a good night of caterwauling. Charlie the RedCat always seems to carry things just a little too far.

Caught in the Act

Charlie managed to get away and attend the annual family reunion.

It's always fun to attend family reunions to see how the little ones have grown and see if you can spot the family resemblance. Charlie's pretty easy to find here.

This may be my all-time favorite RedCat image.

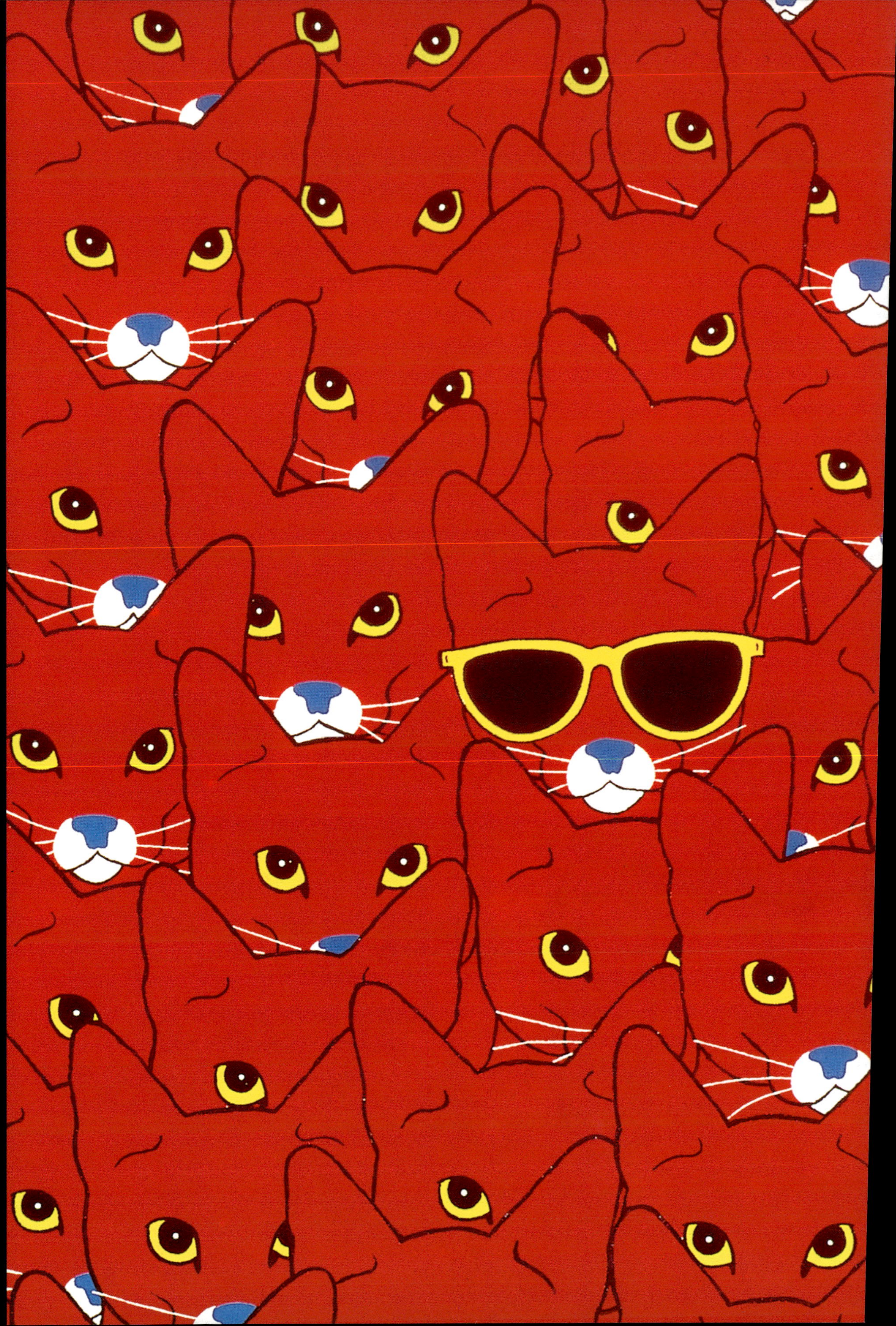

Family Reunion

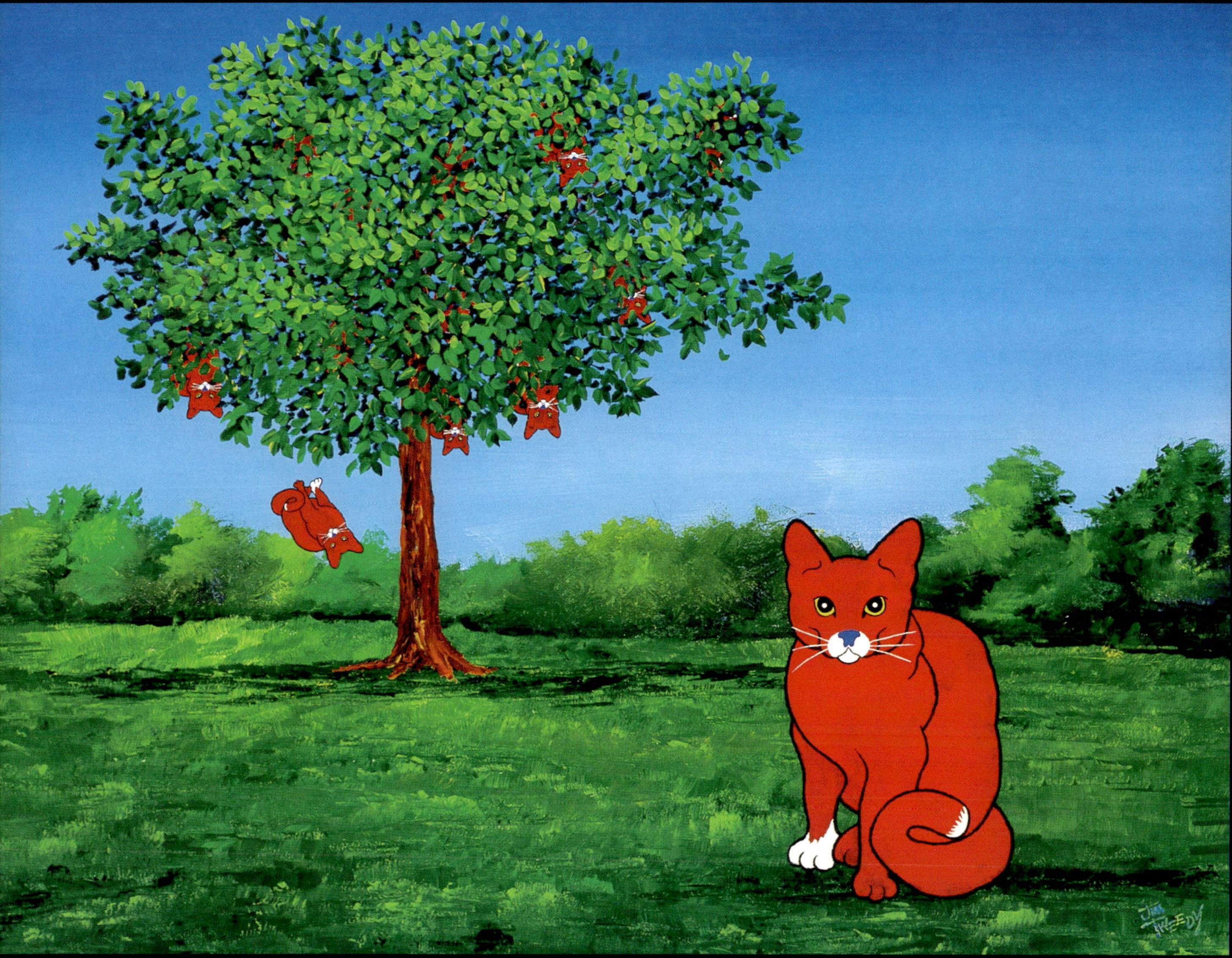

Reunions are especially fun for Charlie because he can look up his family tree.

I feel it's important that everyone knows just how a RedCat comes into the world. He lands on his head.

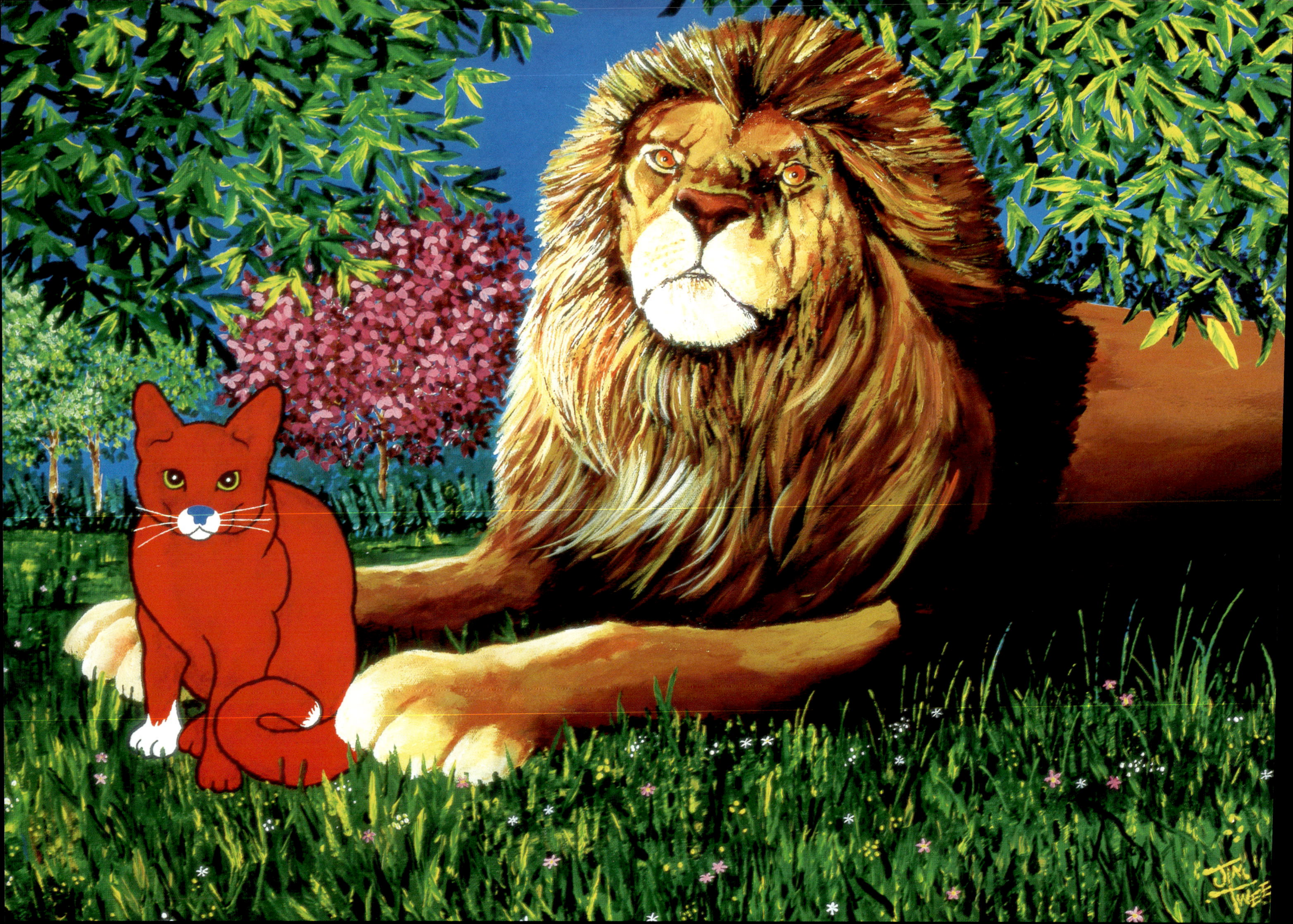

A Visit with Uncle Leo

While at the family reunion Charlie enjoys a visit with Uncle Leo . . .

Charlie's proud to be a member of the cat family. This painting was an effort to document some of the similarities between the proud, noble King of the Beasts and the proud, noble King of the Fridge.

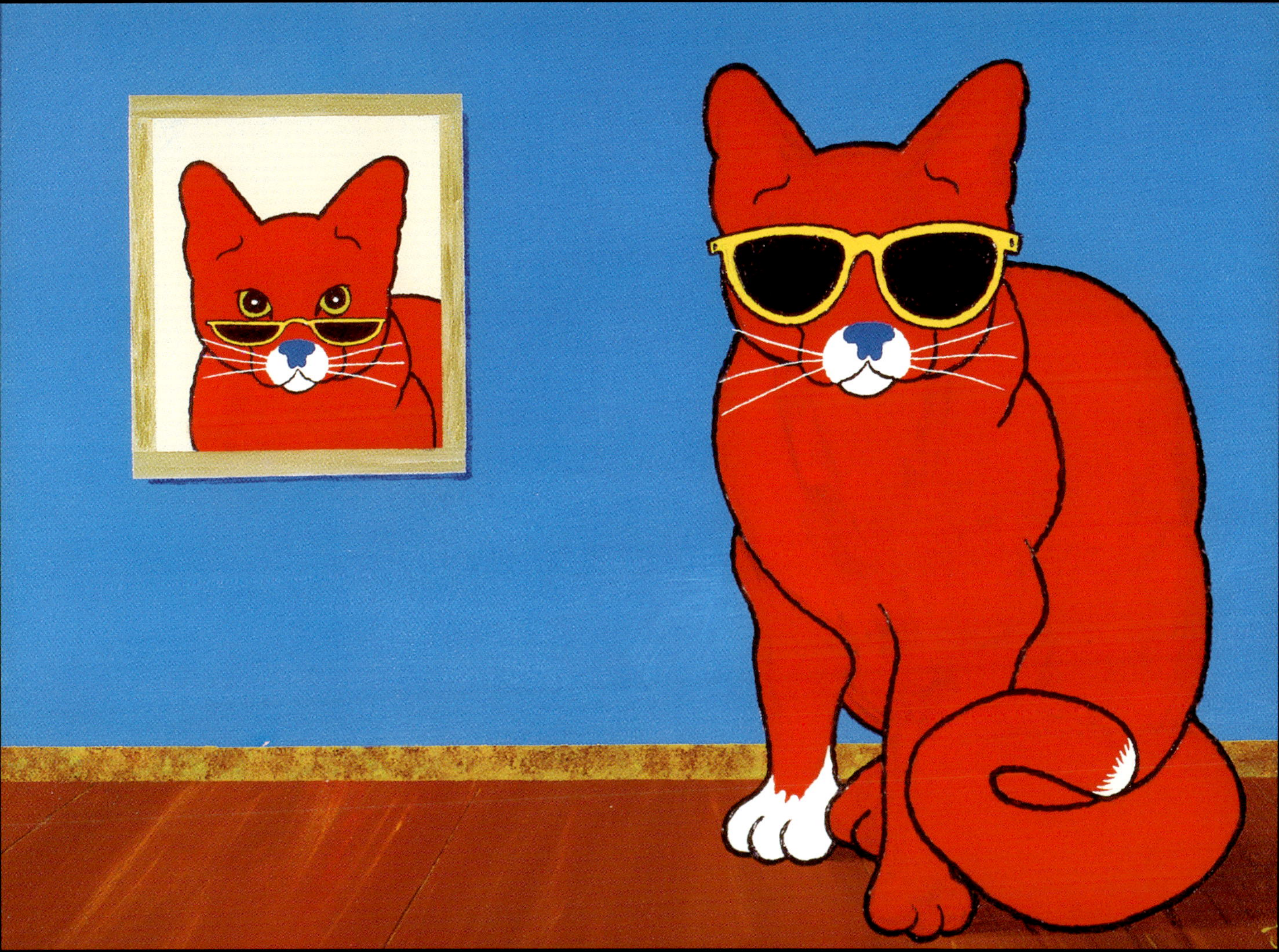

... and spends a little time with Mom.

When I look closely at Charlie and then at this portrait of his mom, I think most everyone would have to agree that this cool thing is something you are born with. It's not just a lifestyle choice.

Later it will be time to enjoy a sundae in the park . . .

Summer in New Orleans can get pretty darn hot. Charlie's developed some fairly unorthodox ways to beat the heat.

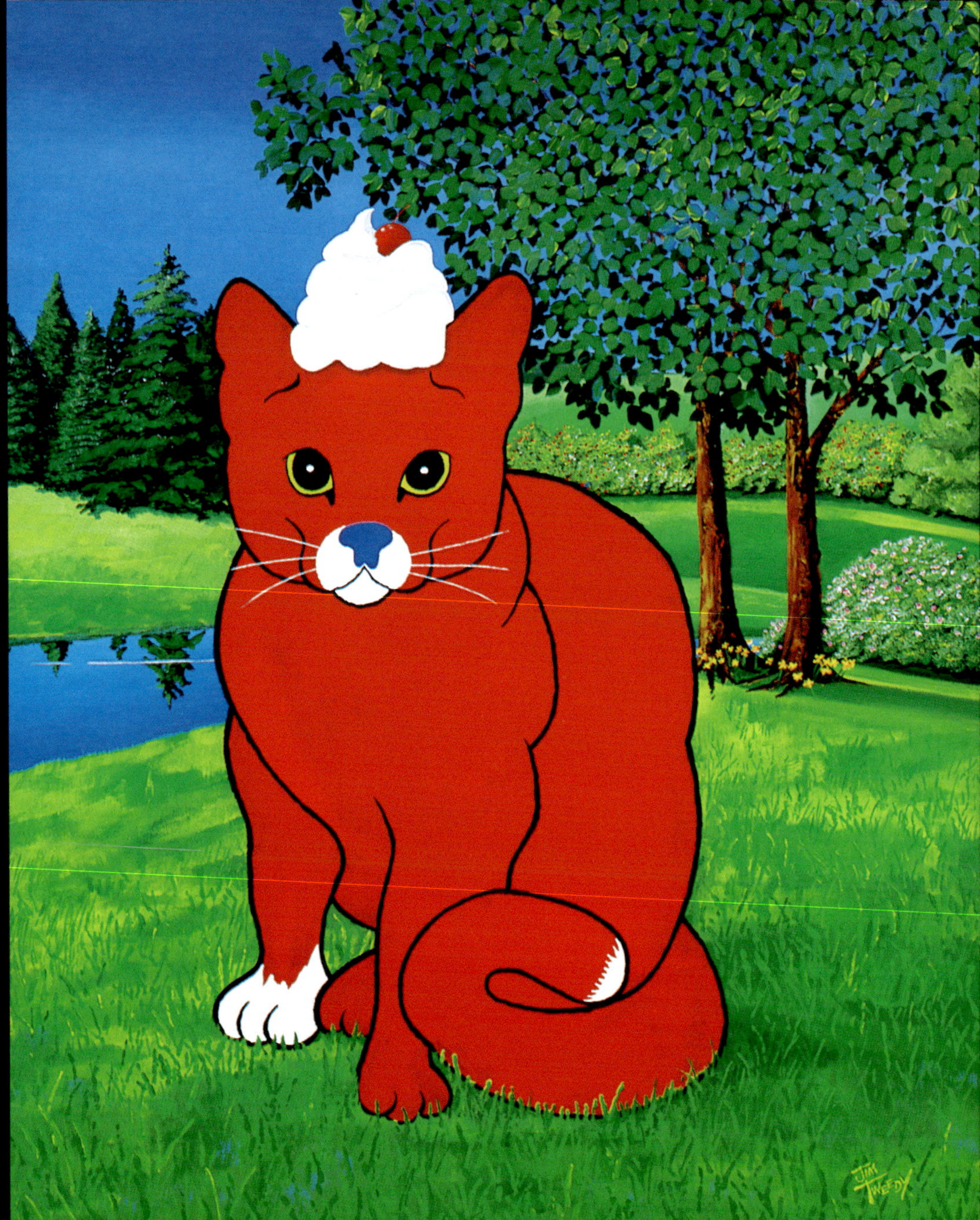

Sundae in the Park

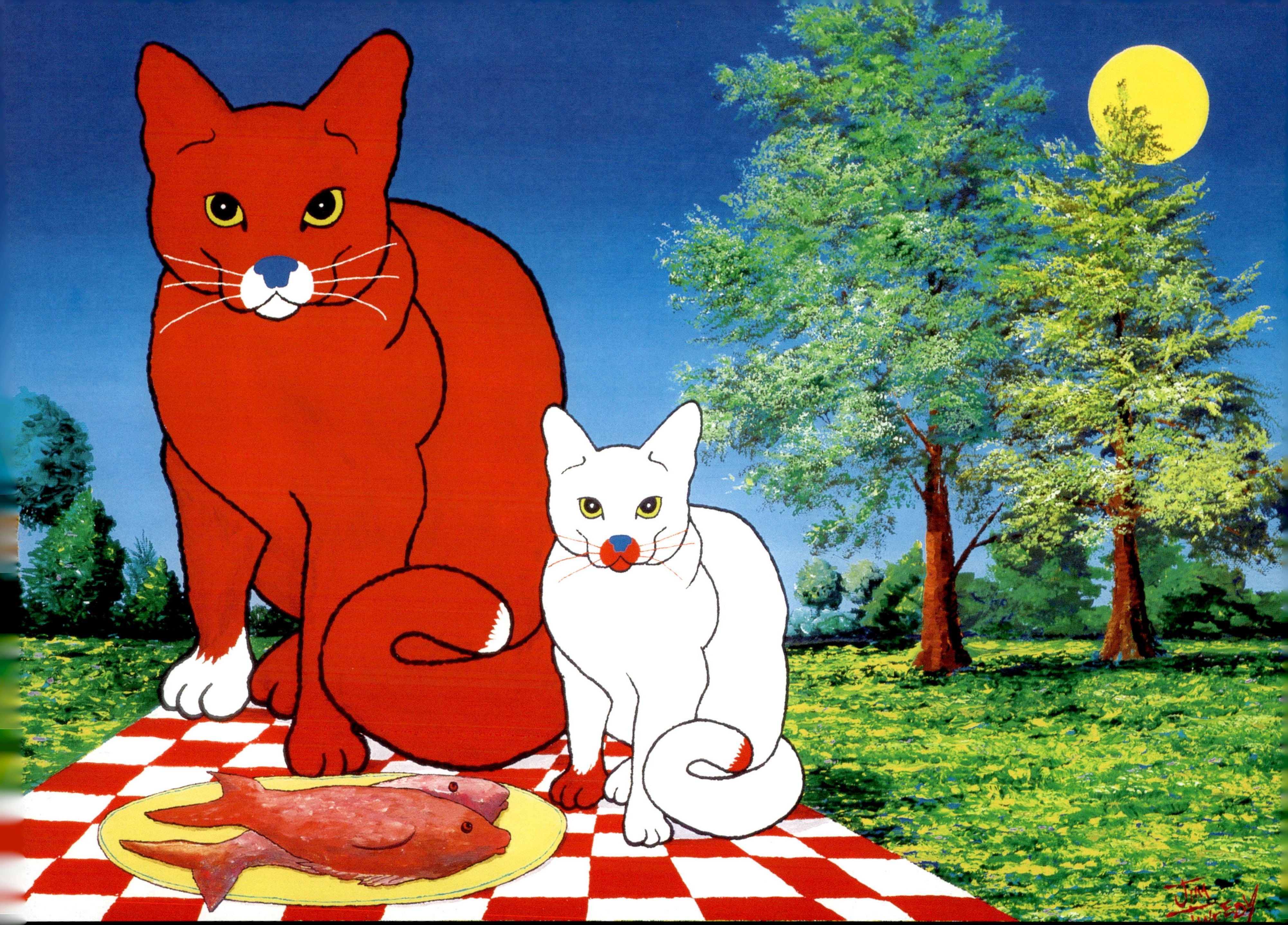

Father and Son Picnic

… and have a father and son picnic

On rare occasions Charlie's son, Chip, makes an appearance. I painted this touching scene during the annual company outing we have at RedCat Enterprises.

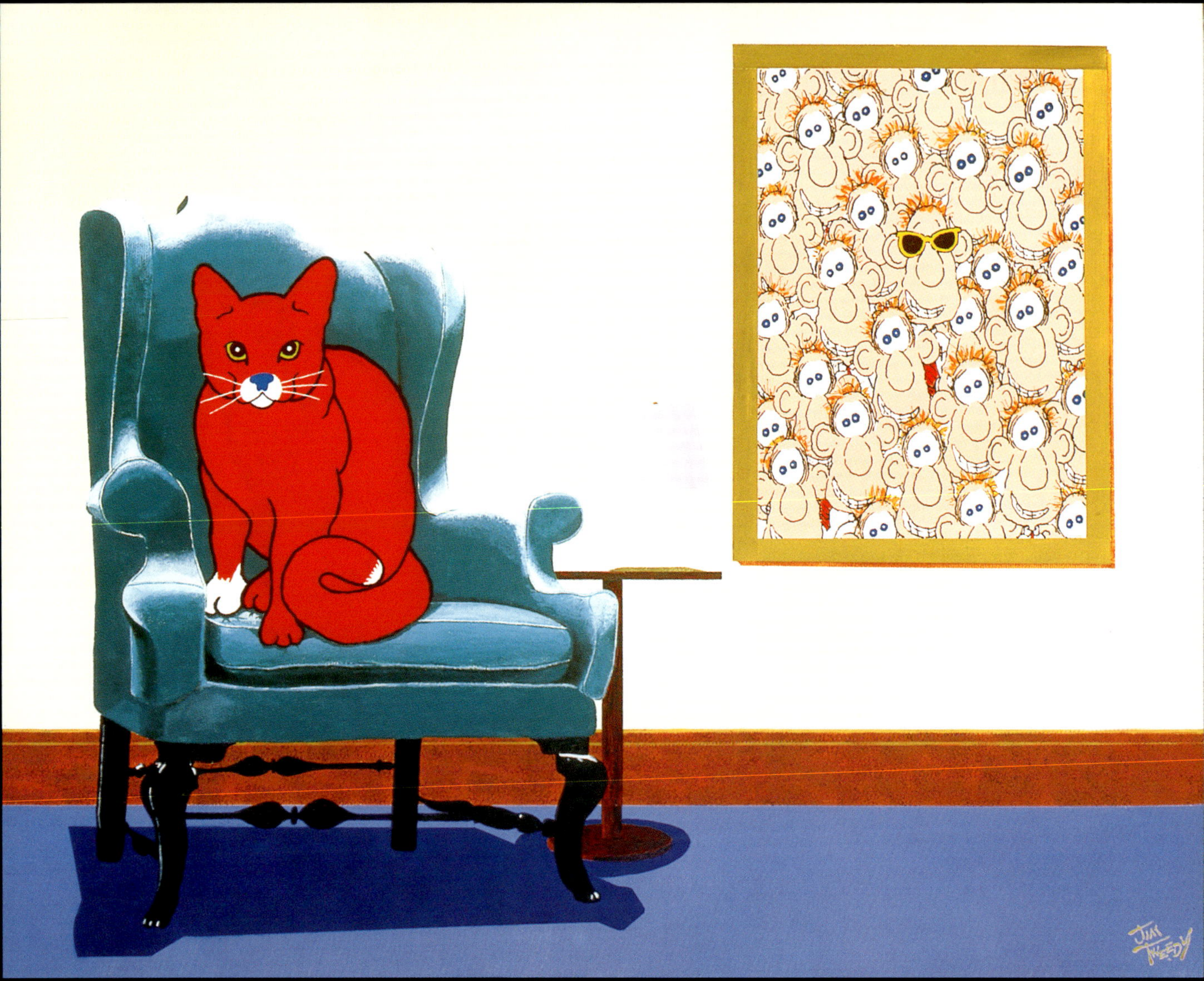

As the day comes to a close, I find myself at home with Charlie.

Everybody seems to want a peek into the private lives of celebrities. Here's a scene shot by the paparazzi! Over Charlie's shoulder is an example of his own artwork.

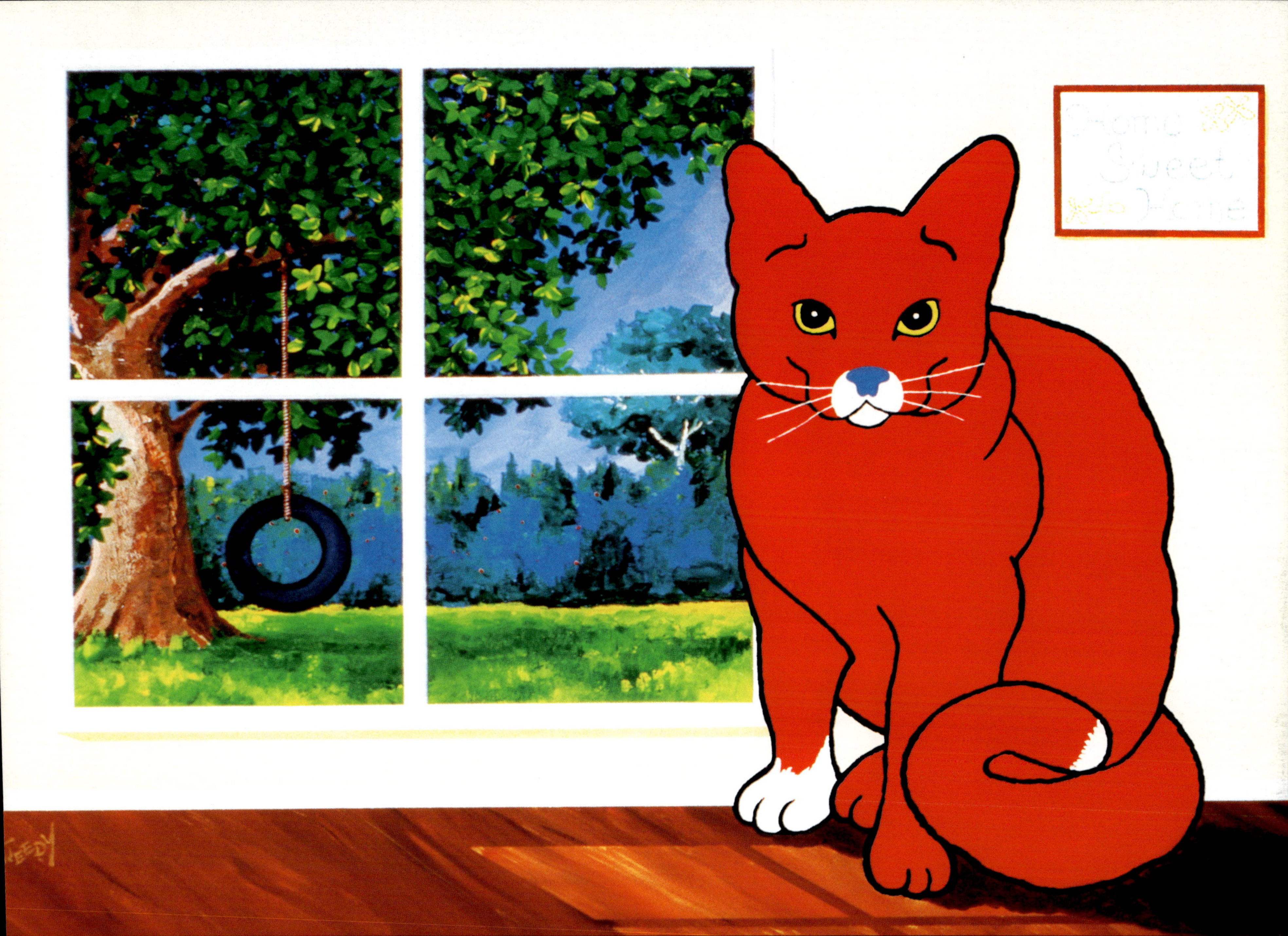

The Tire Swing

In the evening Charlie likes nothing better than playing on the tire swing.

As a kitten, before becoming a cosmopolitan kind of guy, Charlie actually grew up in the country. His happiest childhood memories took place on this very tire swing. However, he doesn't miss the yapping weenie dog living next door.

After all the day's exercise Charlie enjoys winding down with a little catnip next to his hidden lake.

When Charlie visits the country, he loves to stop and smell the roses, and he knows where all the best fishing spots are. On this warm spring day he paused just long enough for me to sketch this scene.

Charlie's Hidden Lake

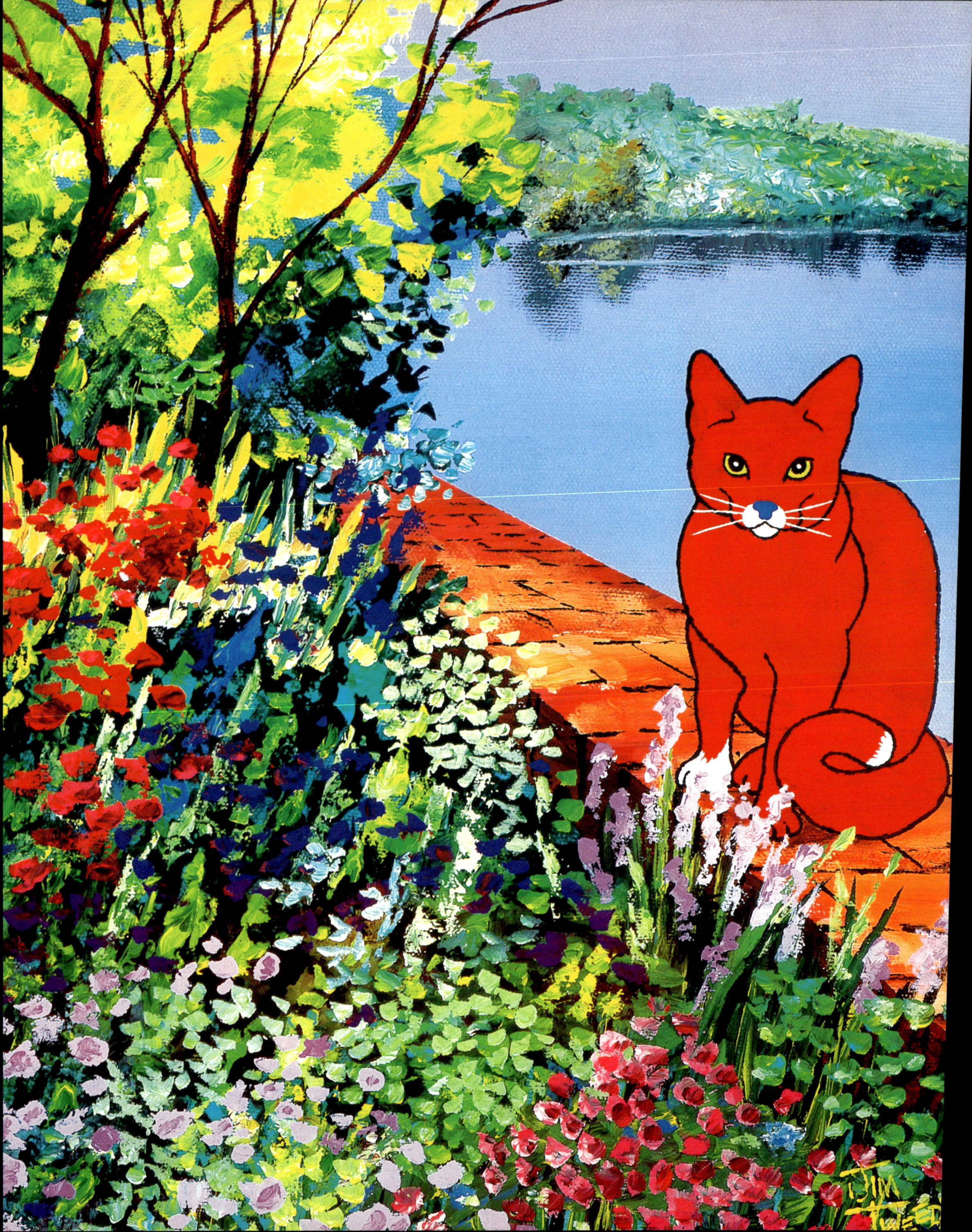

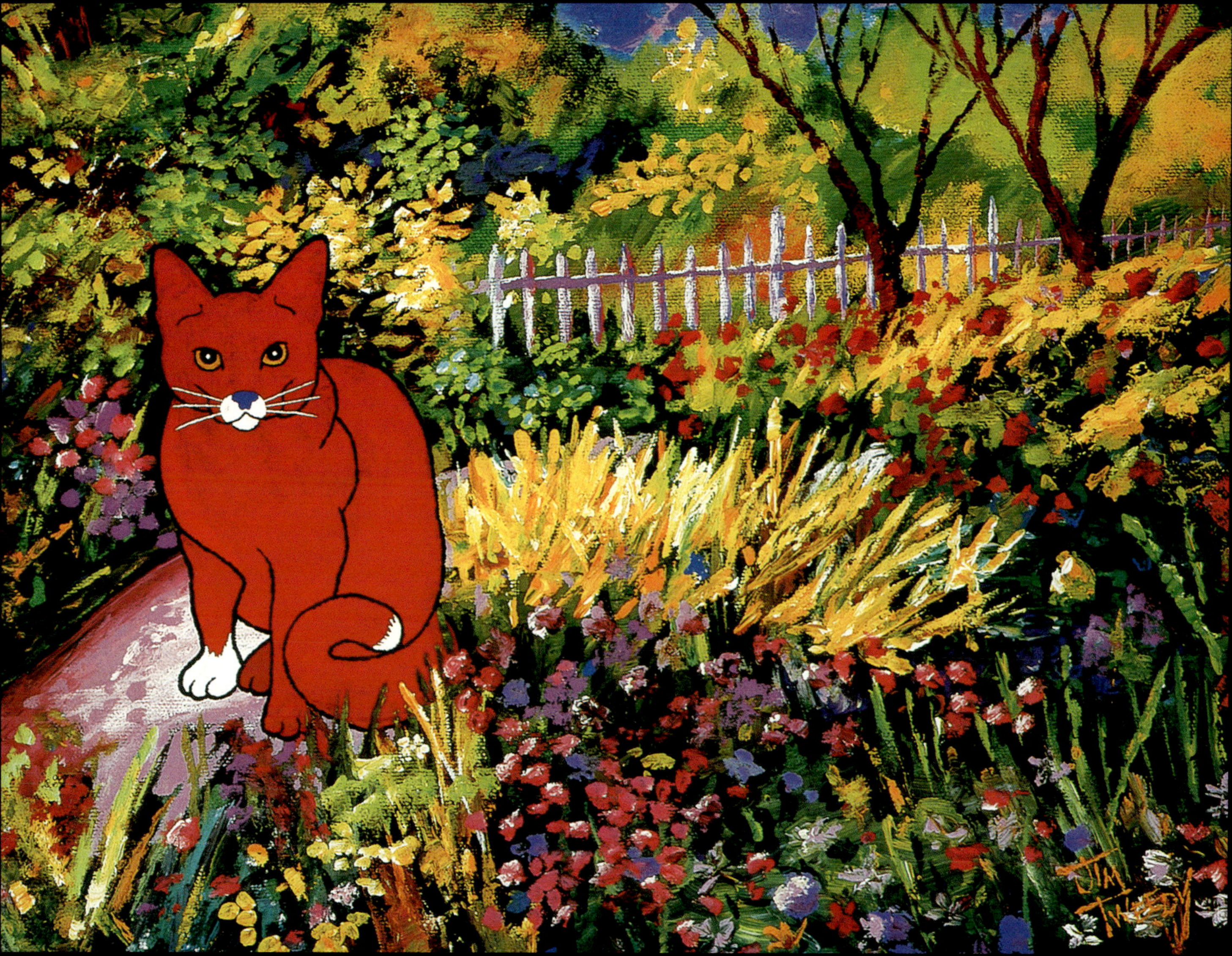

Finally, Charlie watches the sun set from the privacy of his secret garden.

We all need a special secret place to get away and ponder life's little mysteries, like: Why is catnip so good? Charlie's no different than you or I in this regard. This little garden in our French Quarter patio is his favorite getaway.

This is one of the first RedCat paintings I made. Over time, Charlie's image has evolved some. He's become a little rounder and softer—both on canvas and in real life.

Charlie the RedCat is a pretty tough guy. Stronger than the average alley cat, he's known by his fellow felines as more of an Oak Alley Cat.

One of the most popular things to do while visiting New Orleans is to see the beautiful antebellum homes along the Mississippi River. Most popular is the famous Oak Alley

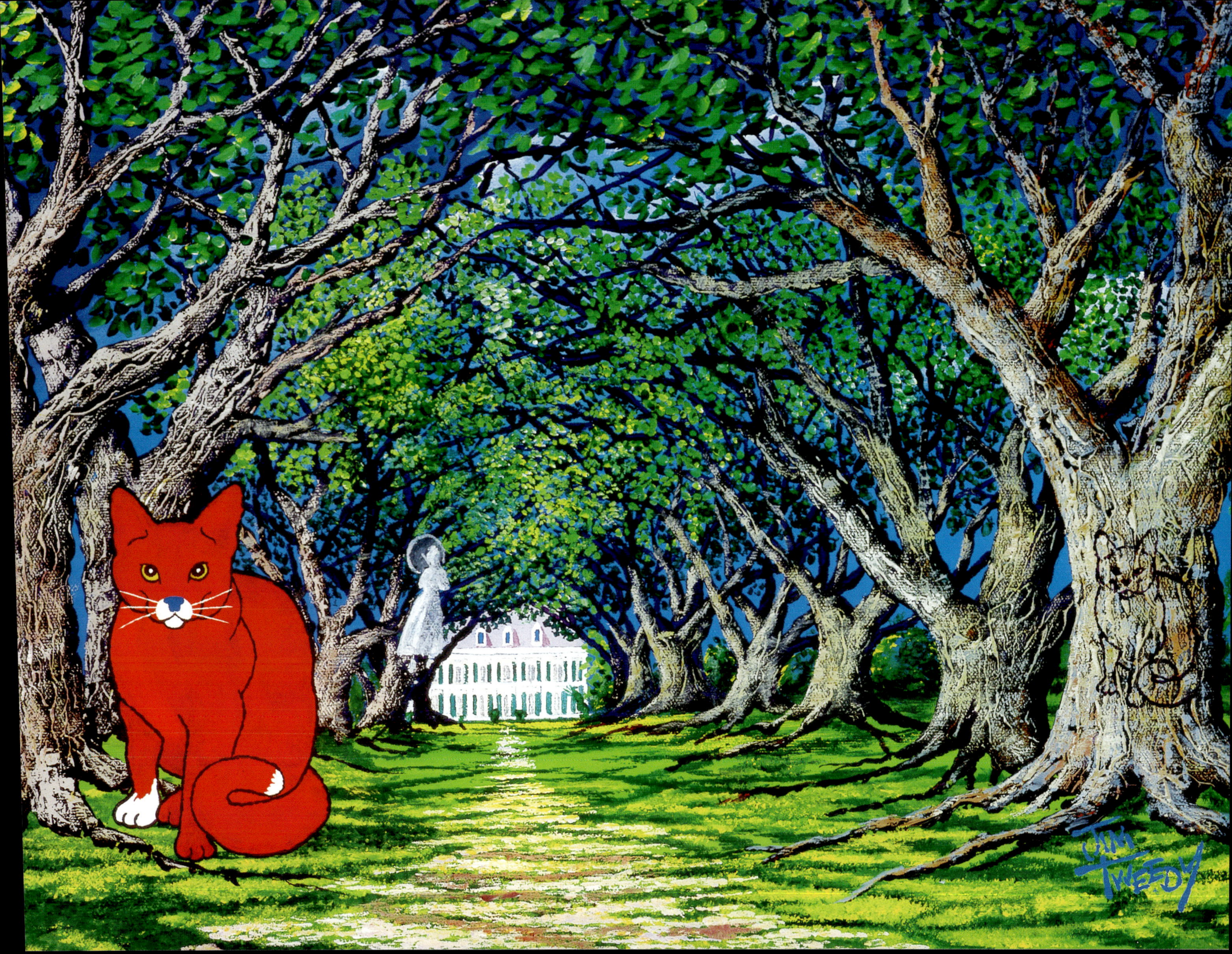

Oak Alley Cat

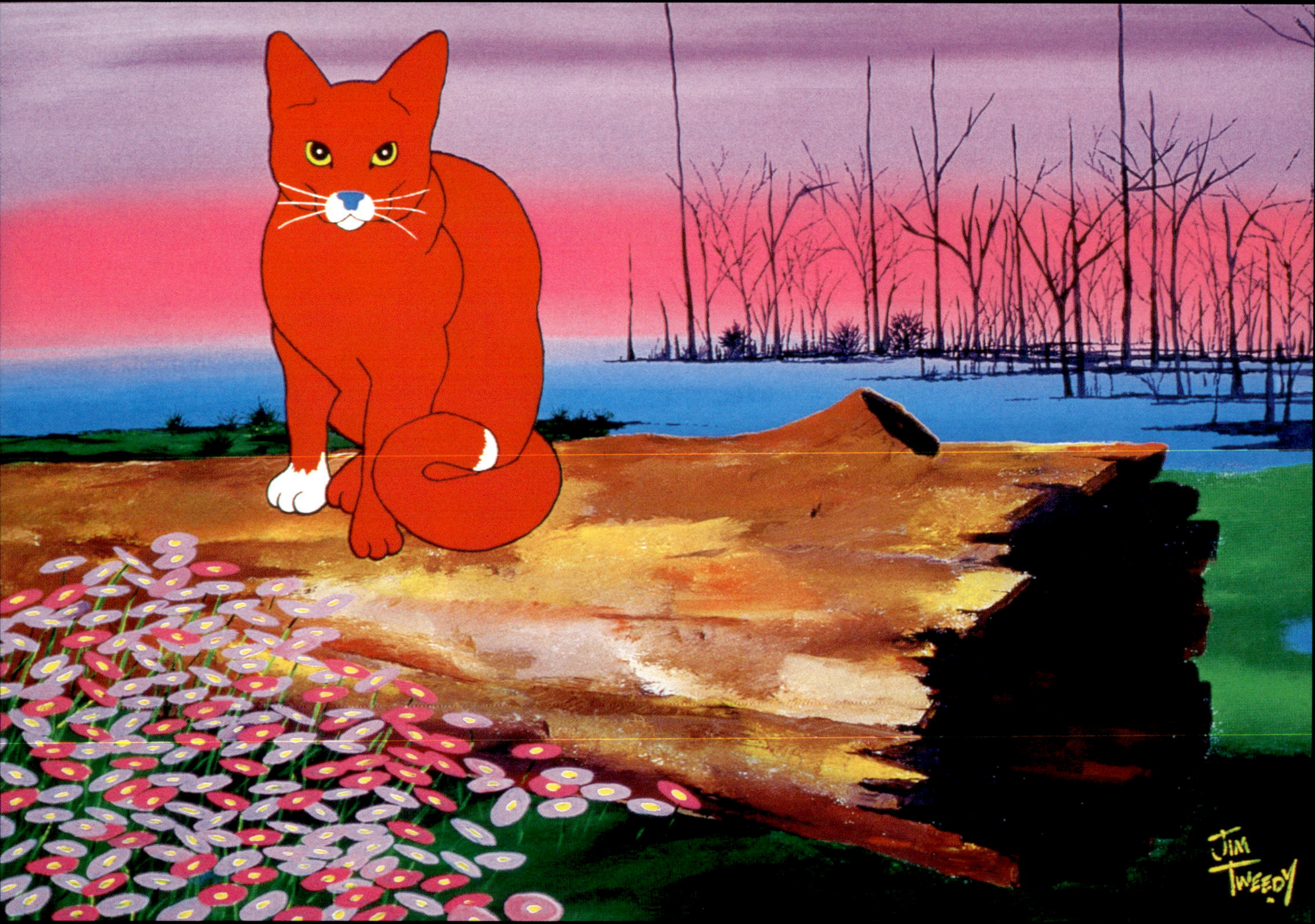

Although Charlie is tough, this bayou RedCat is not without a sensitive side.

Louisiana has thousands of bayous. Charlie rarely ventures into them because he's scared of snakes; on the other hand, he can't resist fresh fish. It's the classic case of brain versus stomach.

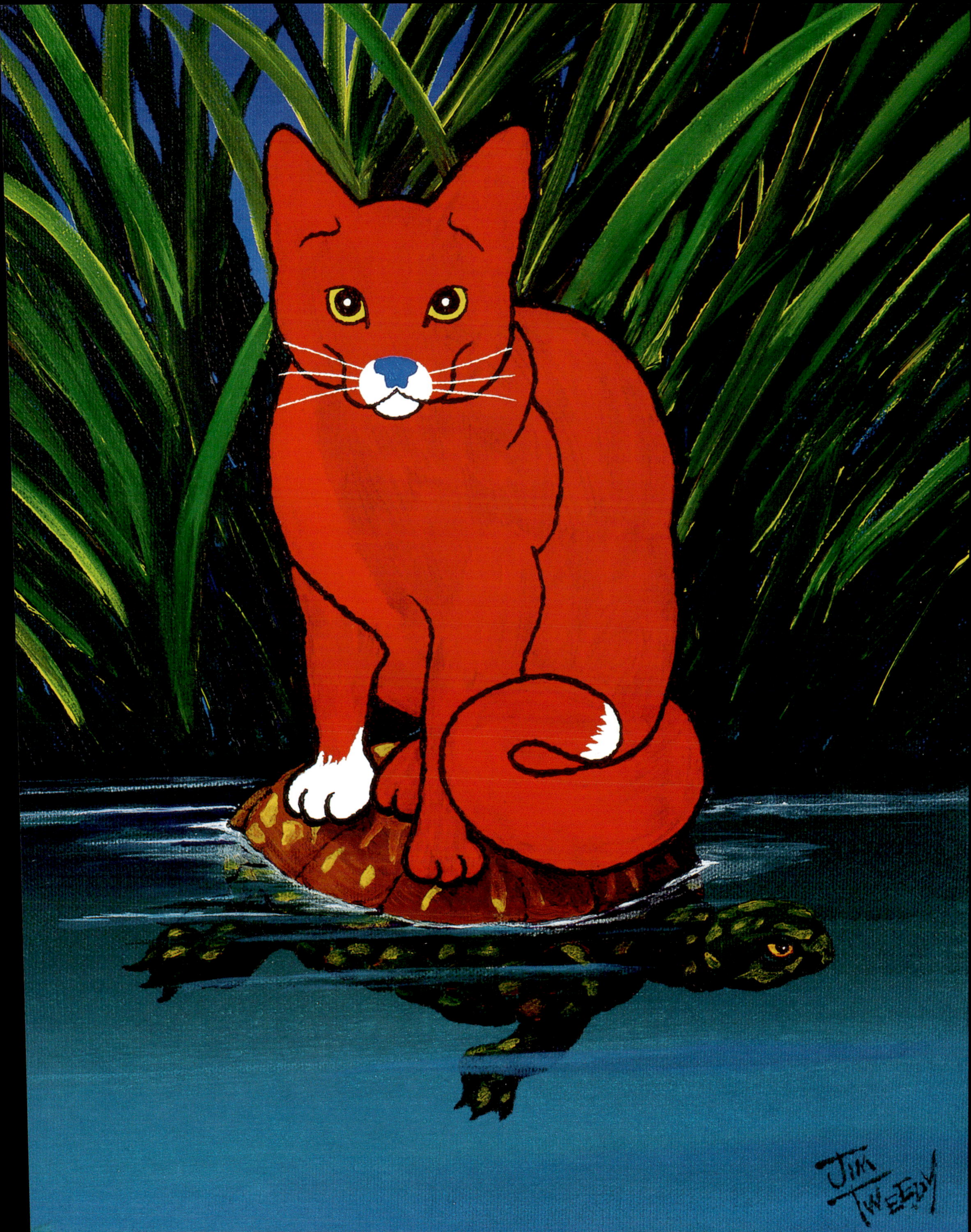

When Charlie visits his bayou buddies he gets tickled red.

It never ceases to amaze me. Everyplace I go, Charlie the RedCat knows somebody. This turtle, who Charlie swears had a bit part in the first Rocky *movie, came along just in time for Charlie to avoid the dreaded—getting his feet wet.*

Bayou Buddies

Charlie thinks one of the best things about living in New Orleans is Fat Tuesday.

Charlie's home, New Orleans, is known for Mardi Gras and great food.

Fat Tuesday

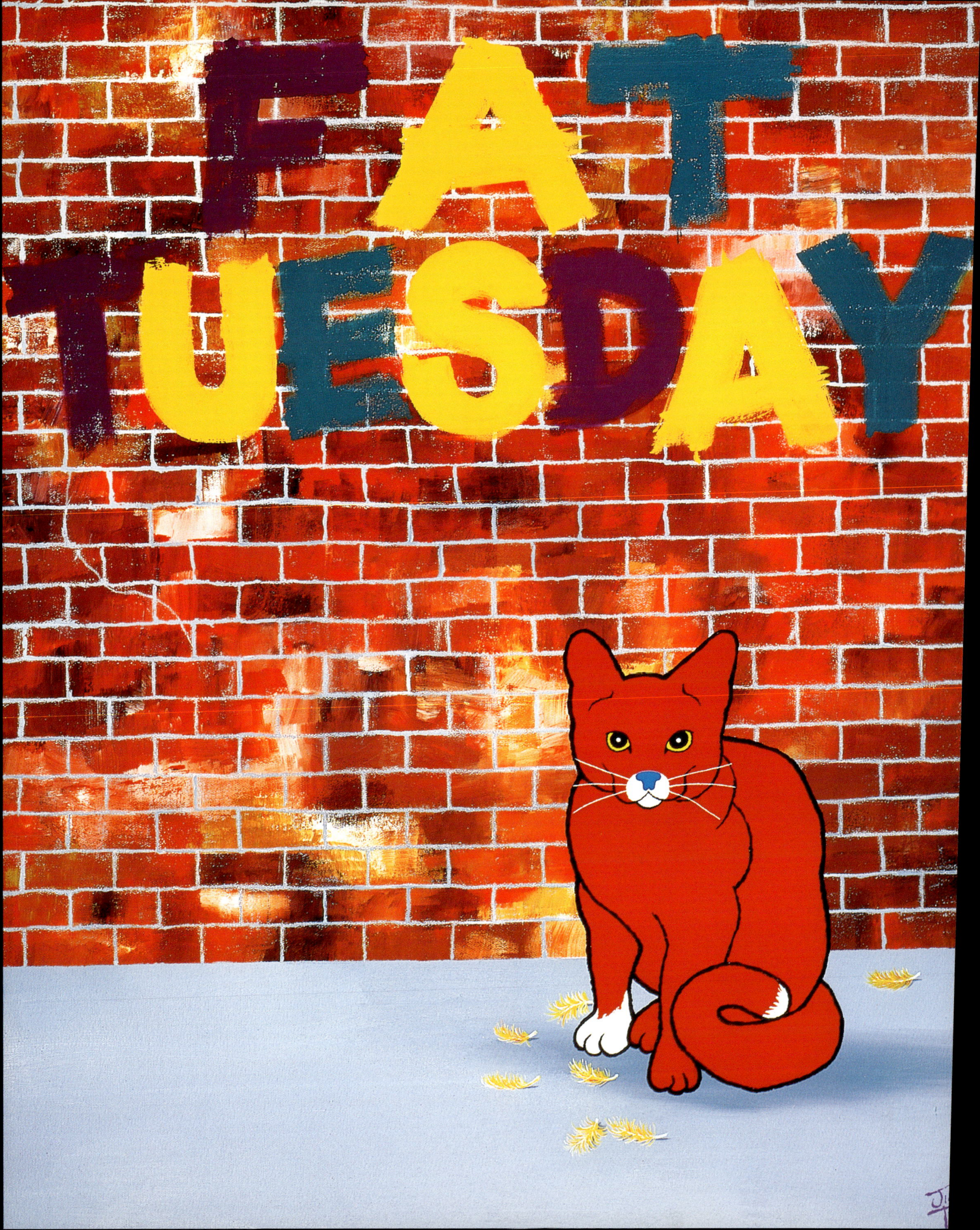

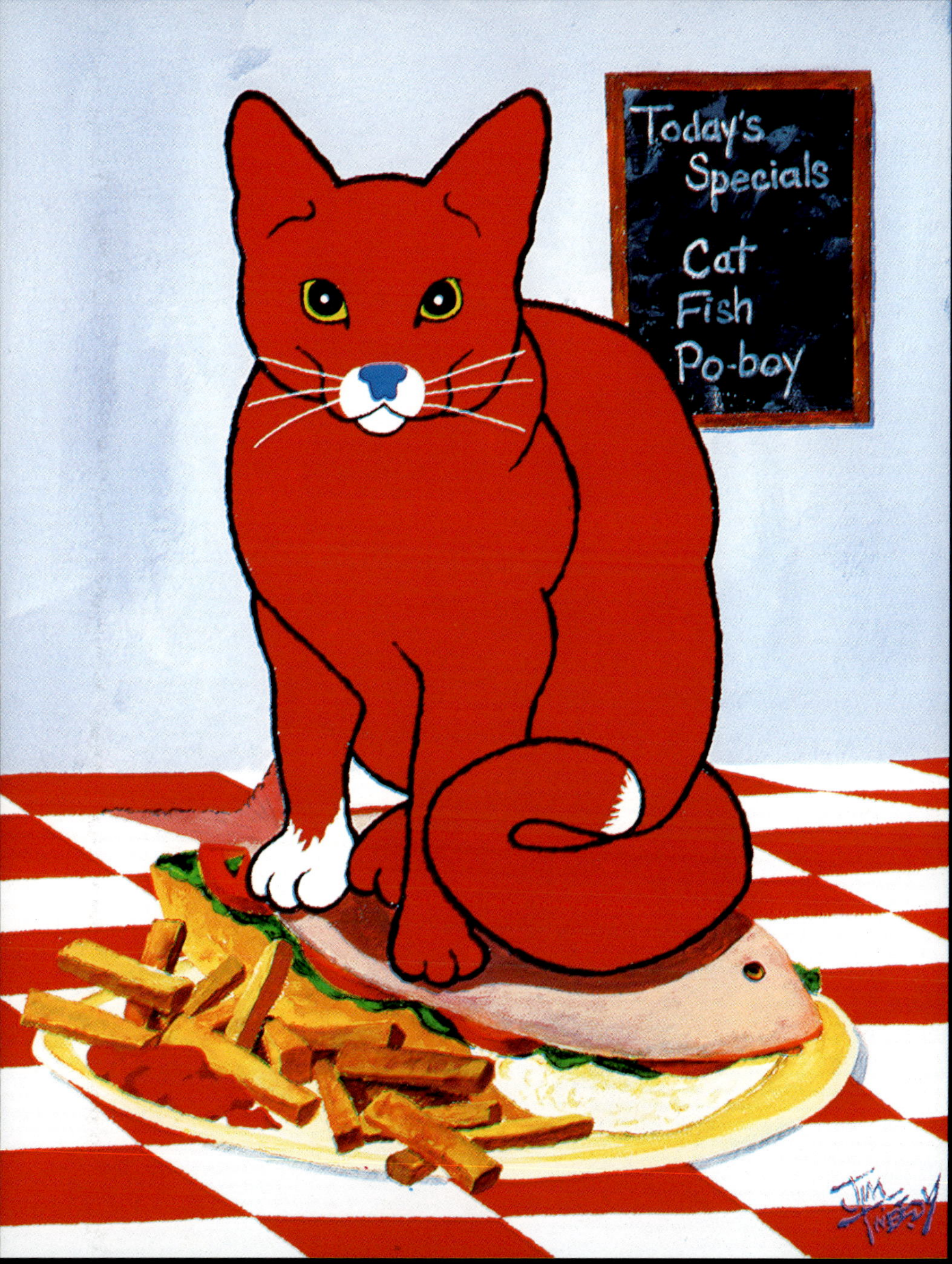

Cat, Fish, Po-Boy

Charlie has a Fat Tuesday tradition of dining on a catfish po-boy.

The po-boy sandwich, a New Orleans specialty, has never been so appealing to Charlie.

One of this year's Mardi Gras parades, the Krewe la Rouge, ...

Mardi Gras is a special time of the year in New Orleans. On Fat Tuesday, when it's time to wear masks, a celebrity like Charlie can go out and have fun with the other cats while remaining incognito.

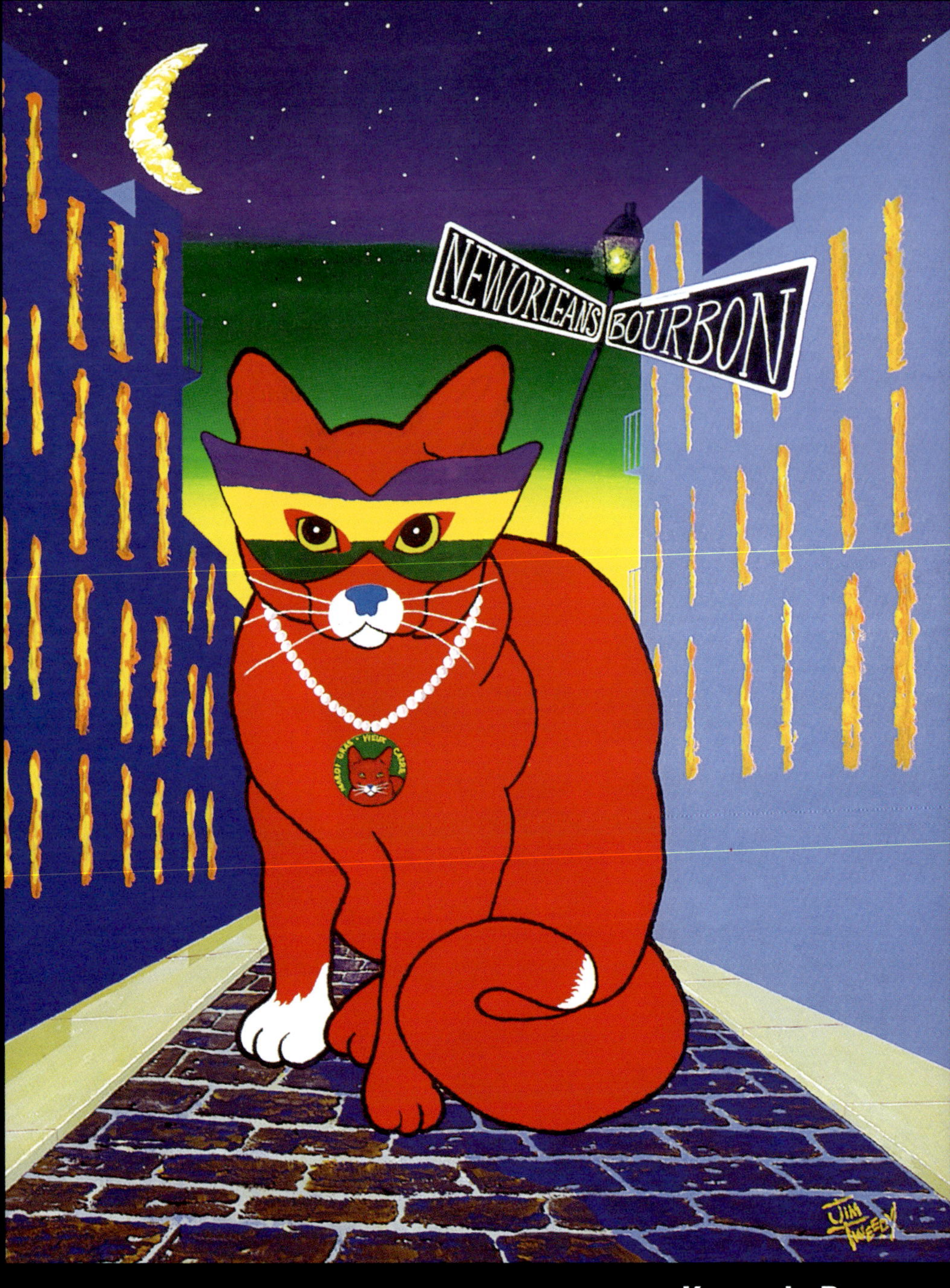

Krewe la Rouge

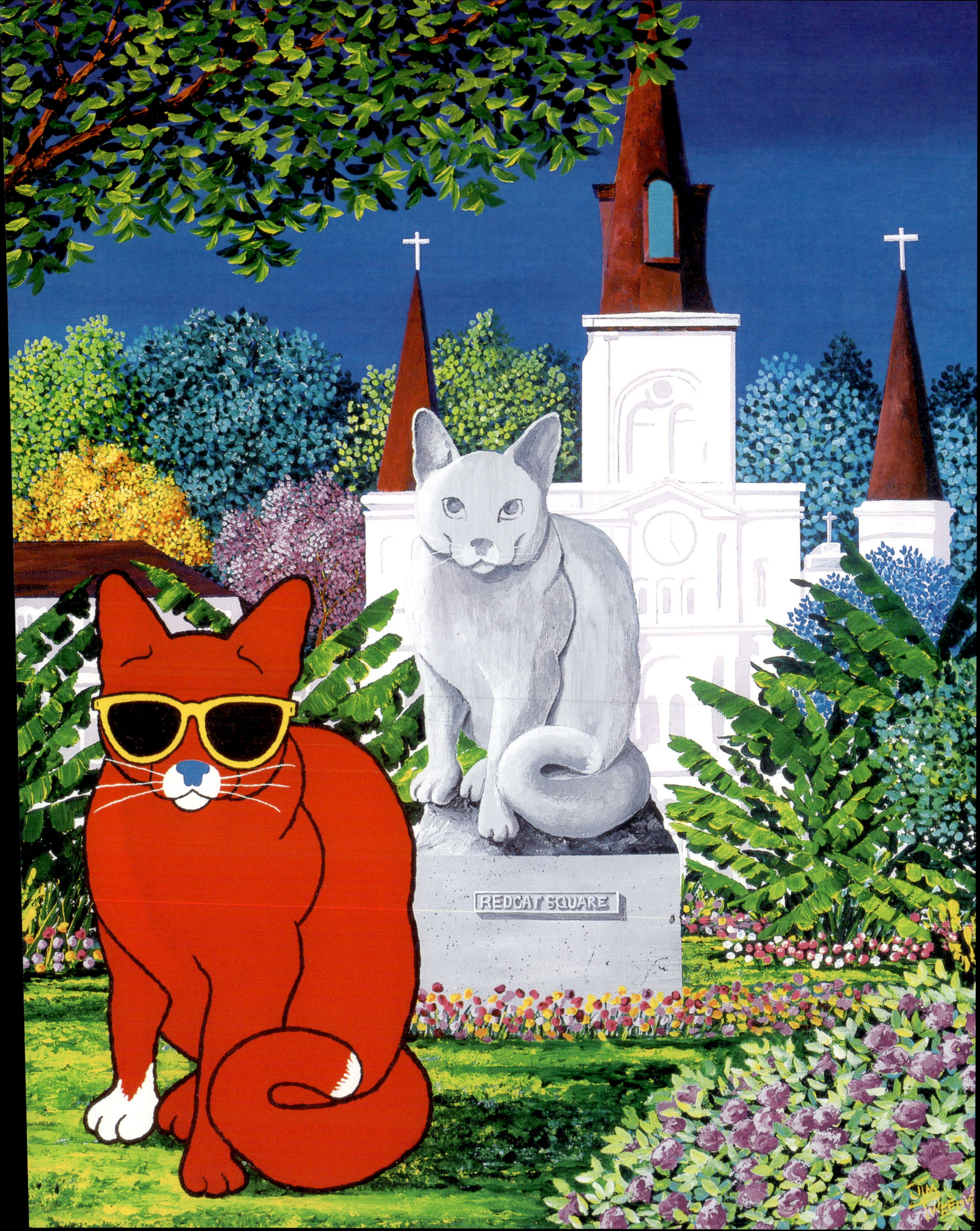

… will be forming at RedCat Square.

Charlie thought New Orleans' most famous landmark, Jackson Square, needed a new look. After all, Andrew Jackson has been on that horse for more than a century. So we submitted this idea to the city council. We're still waiting for a reply.

RedCat Square

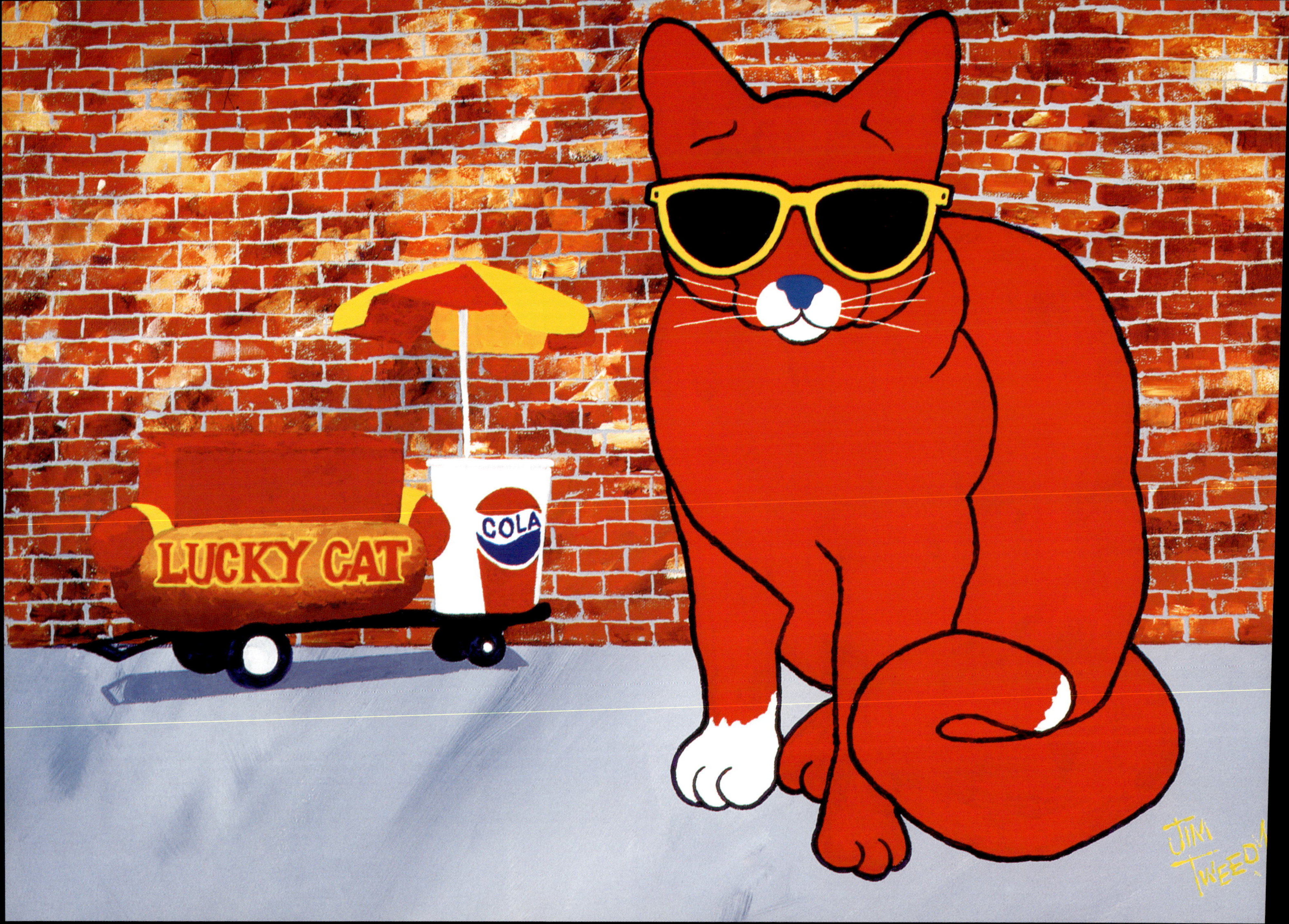

Lucky Cat

Living in New Orleans sure makes Charlie feel like a lucky cat.

A typical French Quarter street corner has guys selling hotdogs out of these machines. But if, as Charlie says, "nothing's hotter than the RedCat," then a name change is certainly in order.

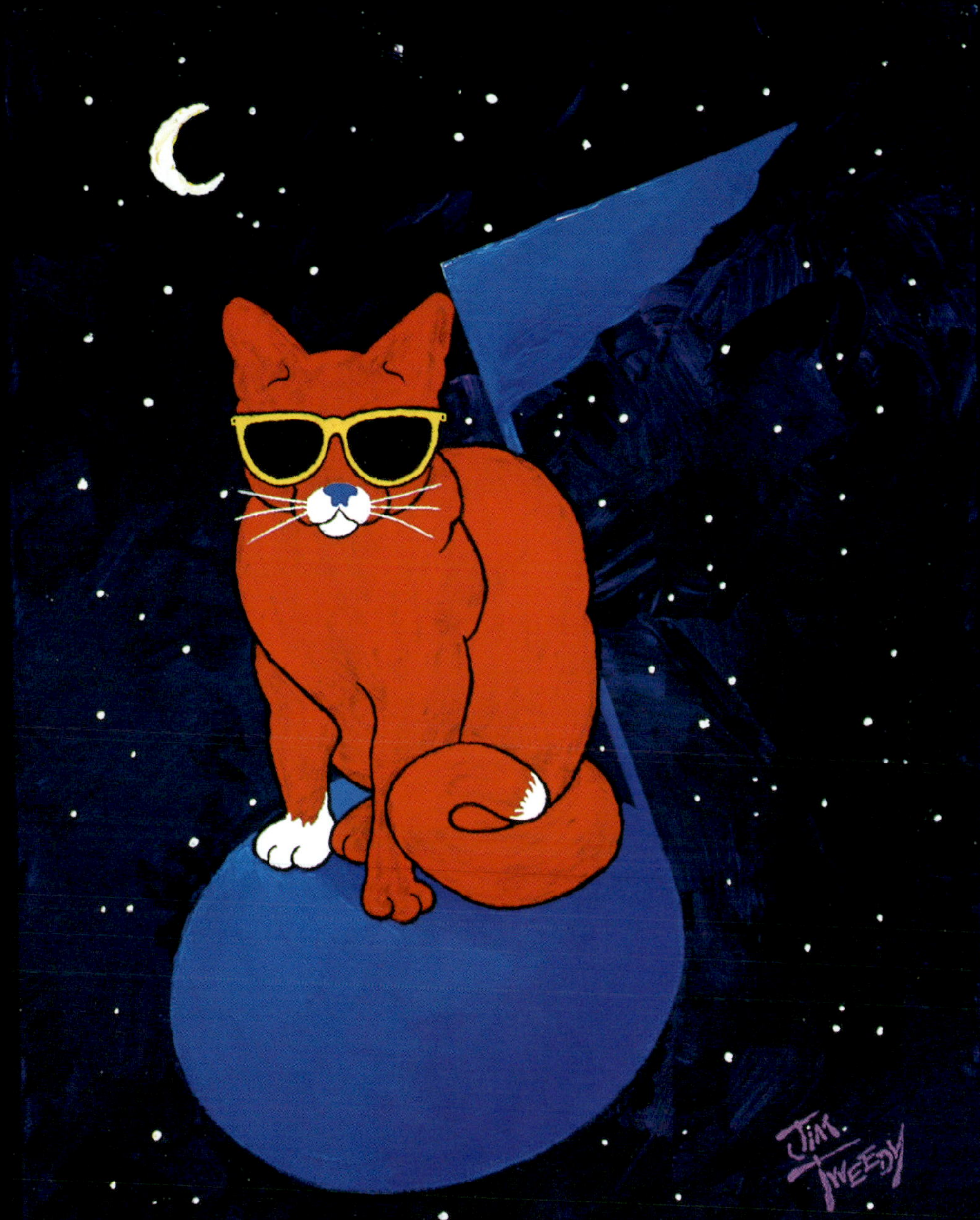

Charlie's favorite aspect of New Orleans is the music. There's nothing quite like enjoying a blues cruise with the heppest cat in town.

Charlie's taste in music is simply out of this world, and half the time he acts like he's from another planet. That makes this one of my favorite ways to portray him. It's a great way to sum up his life and his personality.

Charlie loves to take a cruise on a Mississippi River paddlewheel boat during any of the four seasons.

Winter, spring, summer, or fall, um ... Charlie really doesn't do anything.

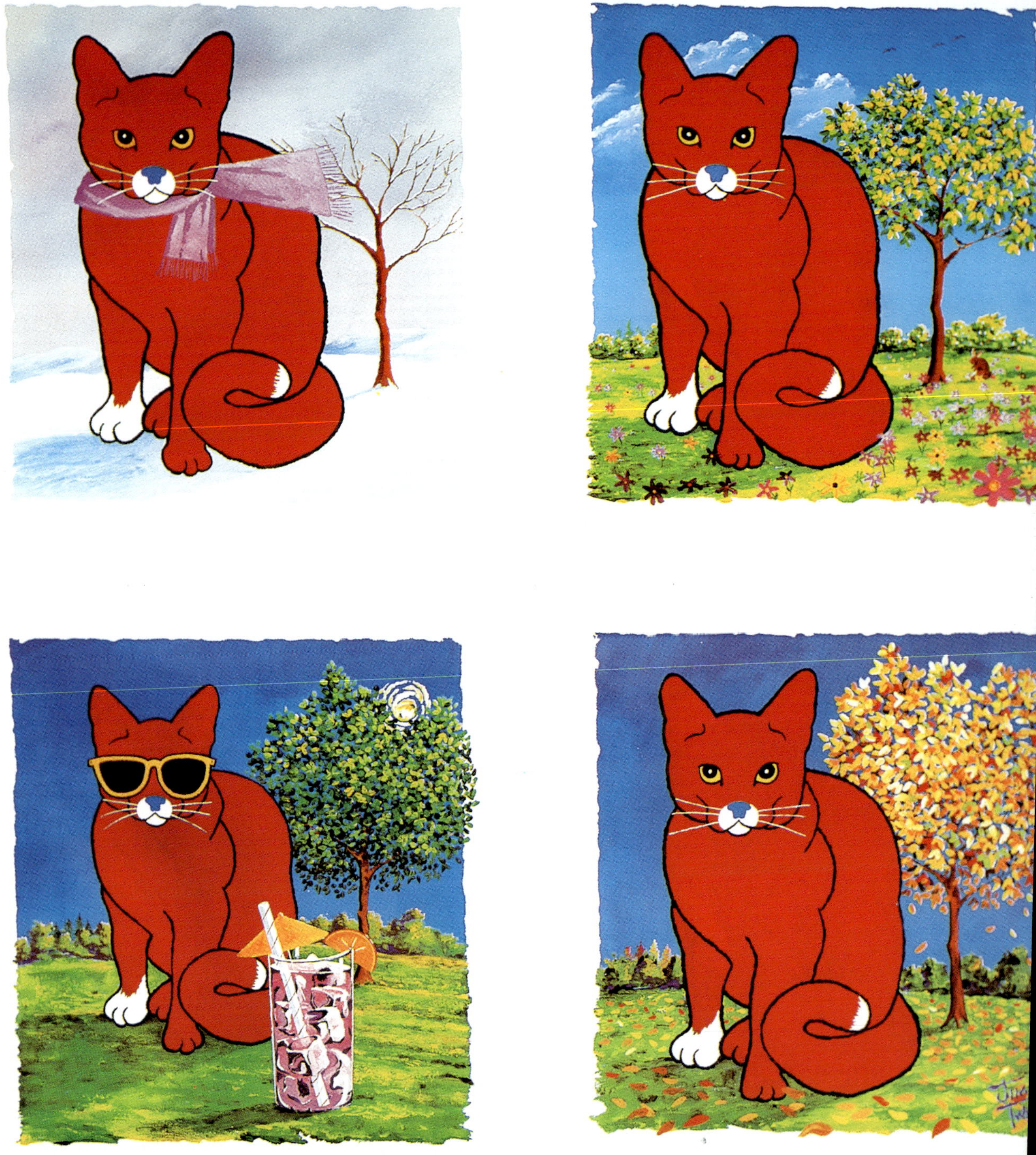

The Four Seasons

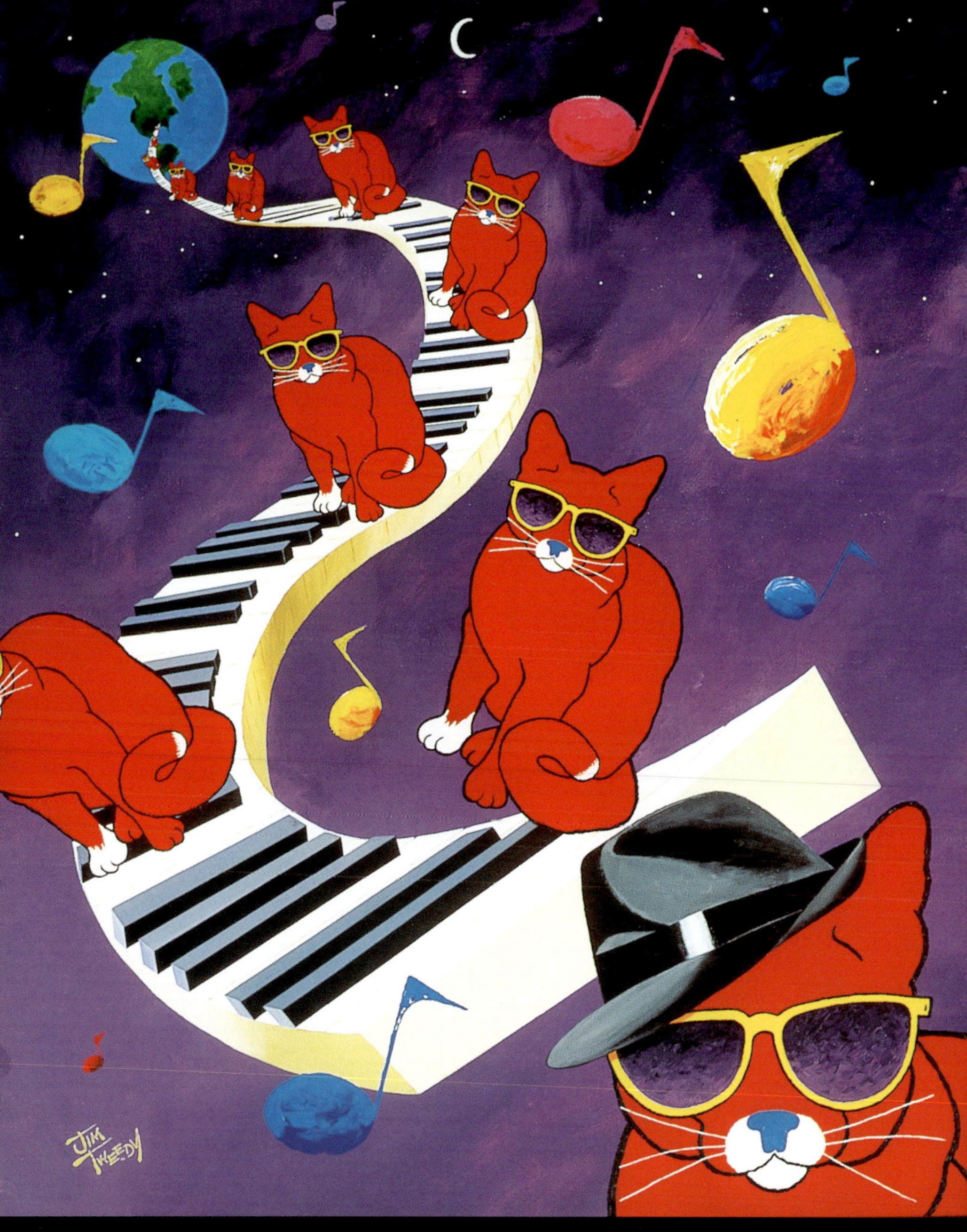

The band might even strike up a little RedCat jazz if you mention Charlie's name.

Charlie is a man, I mean a cat of the world. But he lives in the French Quarter, which means the sound of jazz echoes through my studio—his home—most of the day and night. (I know, I could close the windows.)

I couldn't help but wonder what Charlie dreams of at night. I noticed that he taps his tail when he sleeps, and so, through a bizarre series of meows and purrs, he expressed to me the visions in his little head when he slept. This is my interpretation of Charlie's dream.

RedCat Jazz

RedCat Jazz has become quite popular since Charlie's first gig at the Baton Rouge Blues Festival.

This was Charlie the RedCat's first big break—his first gig! Mascot for the Baton Rouge Blues Festival was a position he held proudly for four years.

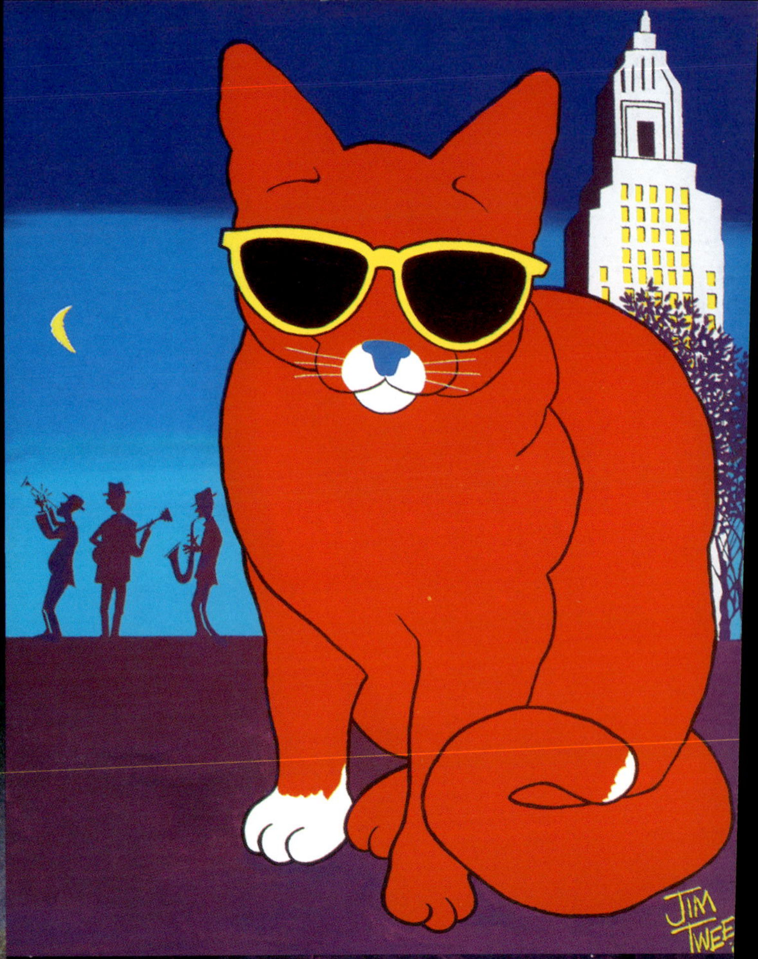

1992 Baton Rouge Blues Festival

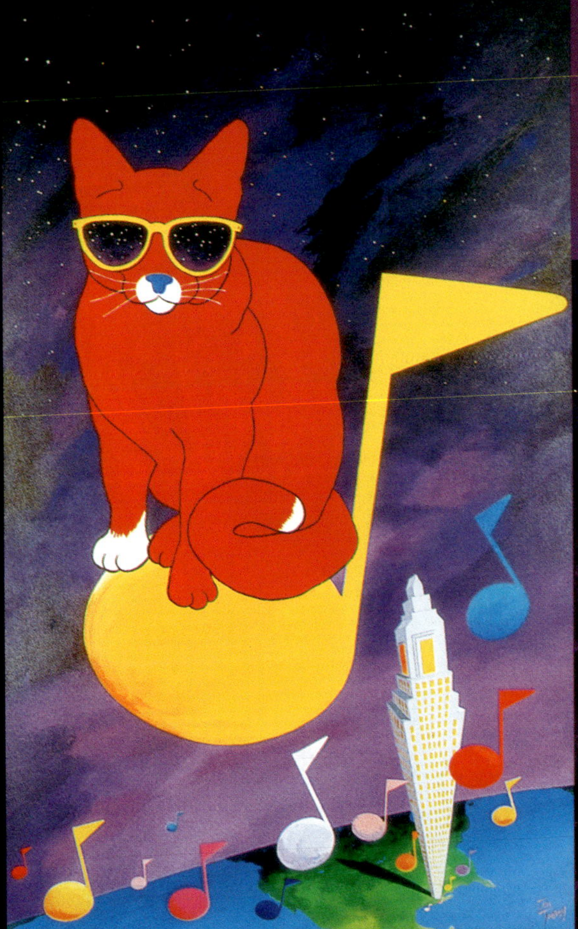

RedCat Blues Over Baton Rouge
1994 Baton Rouge Blues Festival

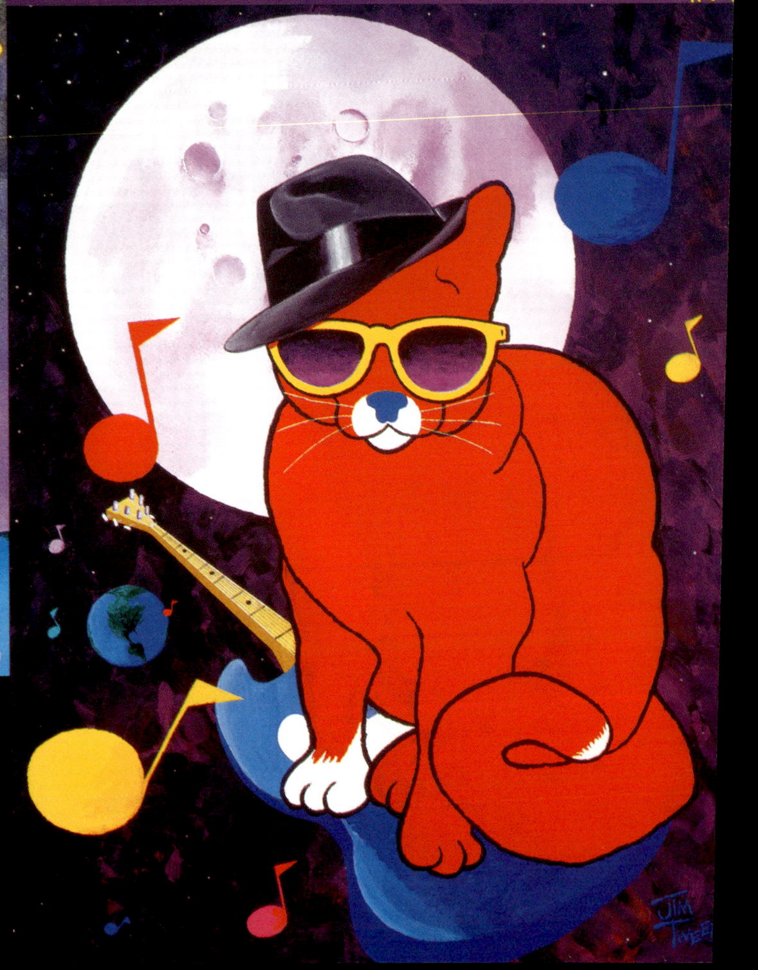

The Rouge Brother
1995 Baton Rouge Blues Festival

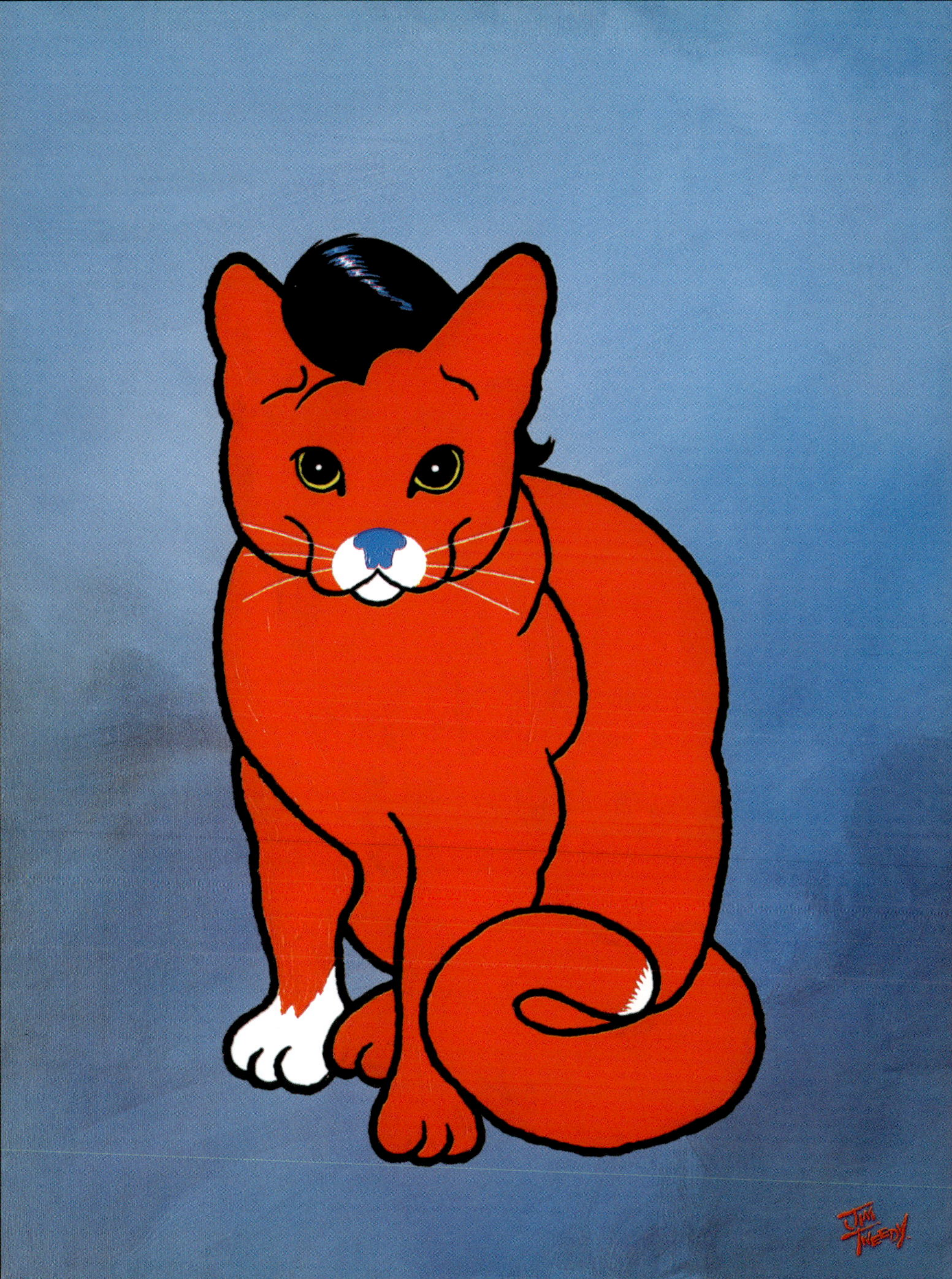

I Ain't Never Was a Hound Dog

At the festival Charlie performed his smash hit, "I Ain't Never Was a Hound Dog."

Always one who prefers to express his feelings with music, Charlie believes this old Elvis tune said it all and said it proudly.

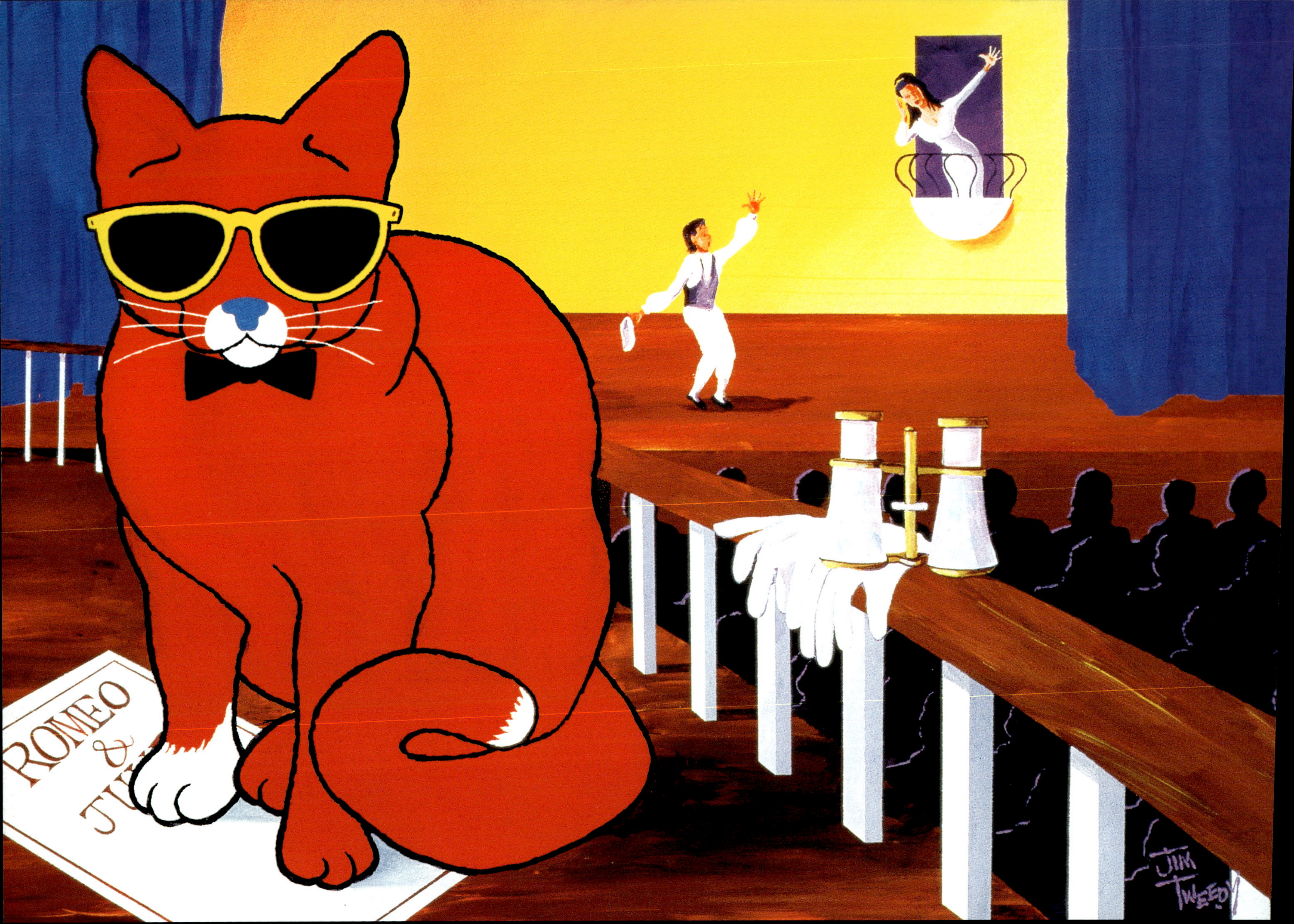

A Night at the Opera

Those who heard Charlie sing at the Baton Rouge Blues Festival said it was just like a night at the opera.

Any kind of music is Charlie's kind of music. However, at one point during this performance, the woman hit a high note and Charlie thought somebody had put iodine on an open wound. To this day when Charlie's in the mood for a little culture he grabs a bottle of iodine and heads for Bourbon Street.

After it was over, Charlie read, "Hey Diddle Diddle, the RedCat and the Fiddle" for all the little ones in attendance.

At an auction five years ago I bought a first-edition book of nursery rhymes. Now this was a very old book, and wouldn't you know it? It was a <u>*Red*</u>*Cat and the fiddle. In subsequent editions the* word red *had been deleted, dropped, overlooked, and other wise poo-pooed.*

The next night Charlie and I grabbed a fiddle and staked out an old oak tree in Audubon Park in New Orleans. As soon as a cow jumped over the moon I sketched like a mad man. At long last, a great injustice was righted.

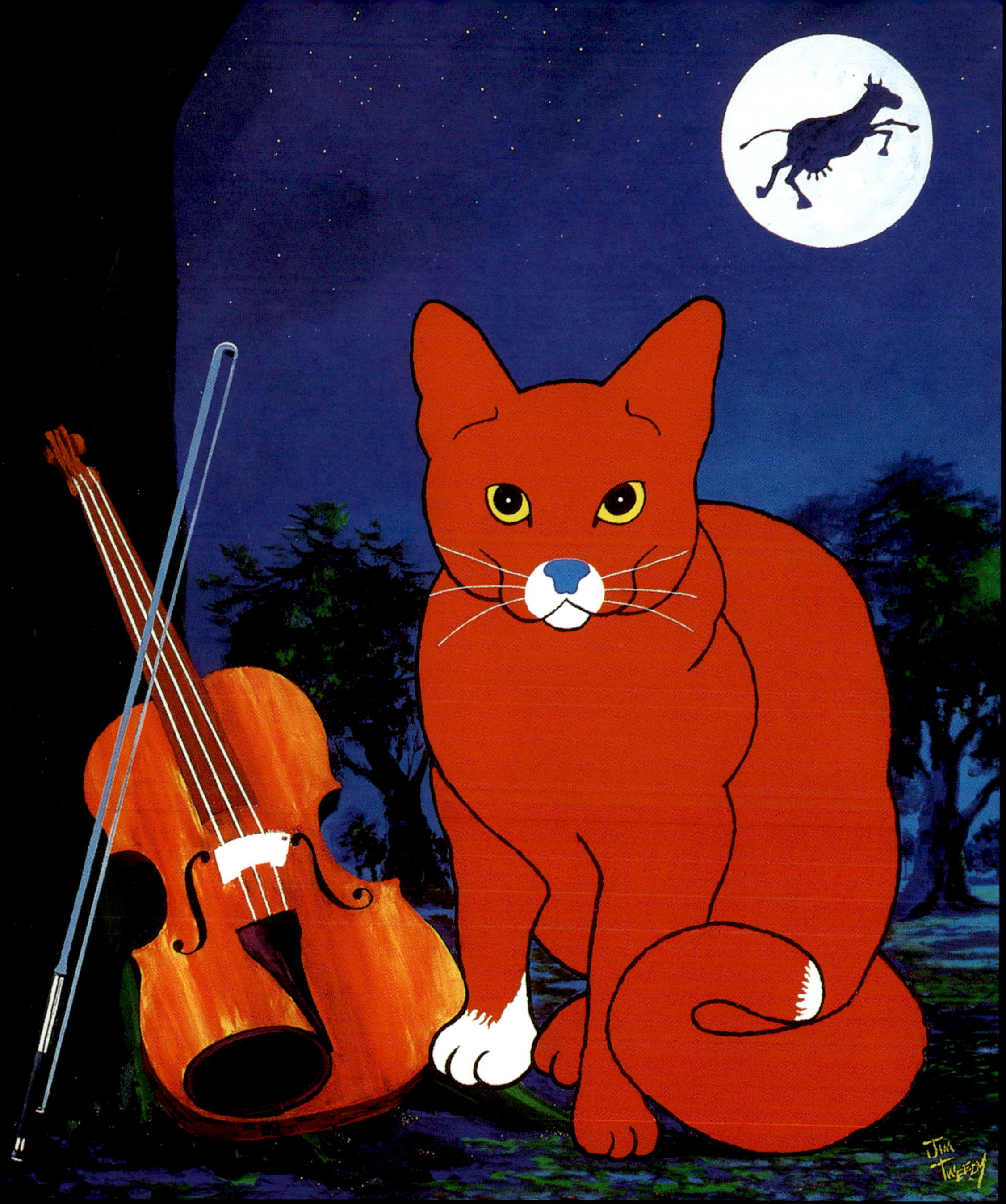

Hey Diddle Diddle, The RedCat and the Fiddle

RedCats have taken up with artists for generations. One can only imagine what "Whistler's RedCat" might have looked like.

This shocking discovery occurred when movers were cleaning out Whistler's mother's attic.

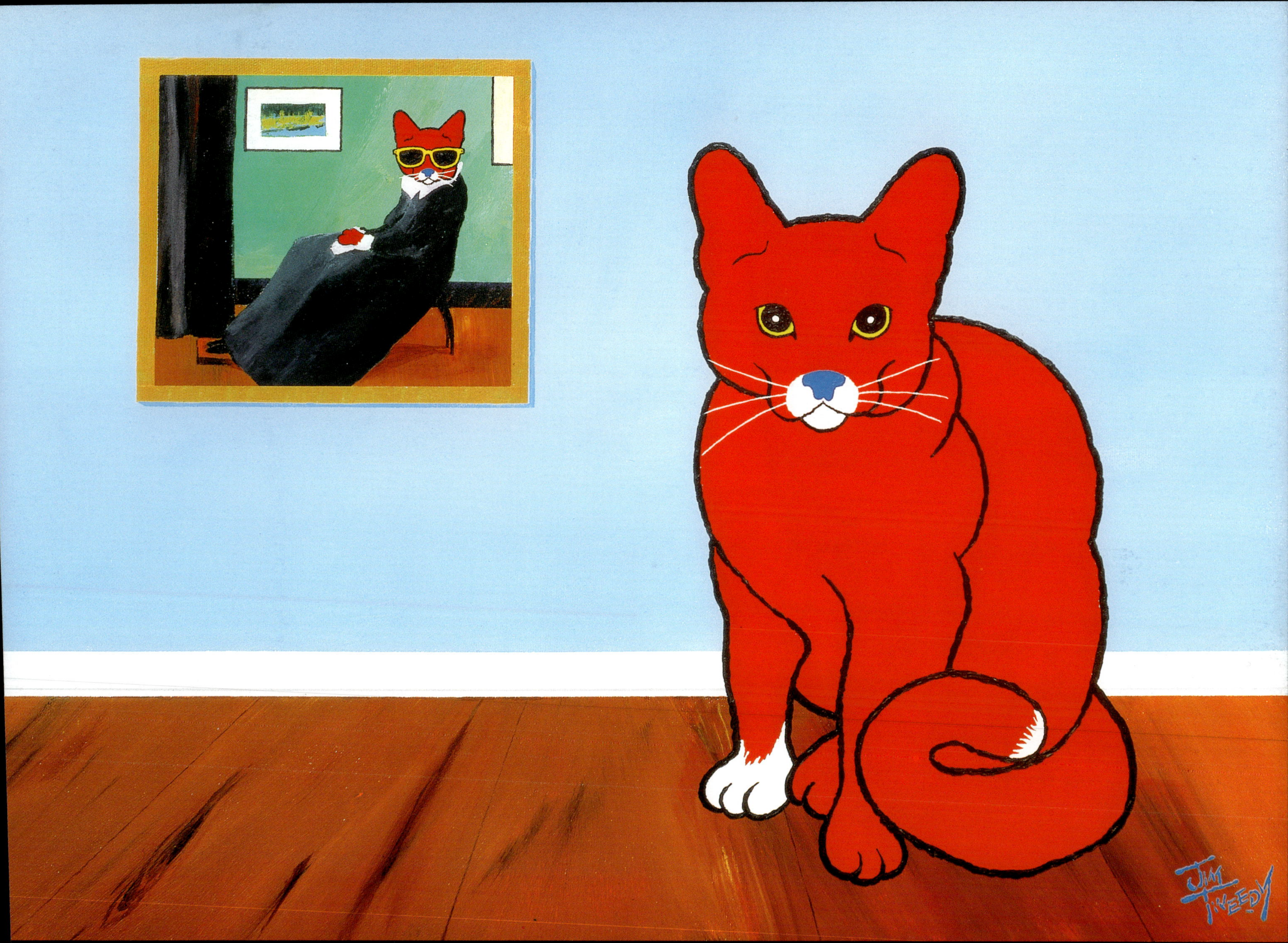

Whistler's RedCat

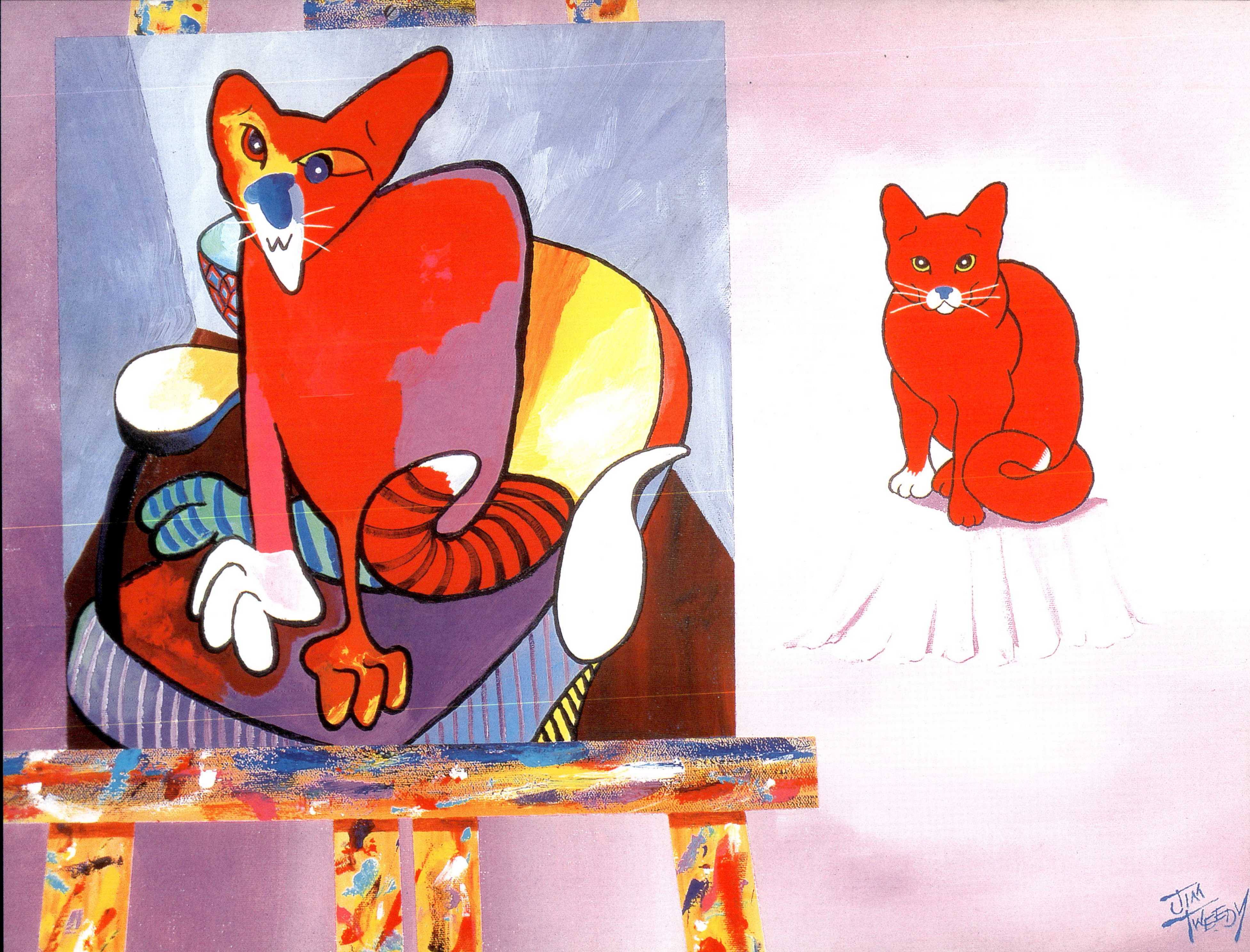

How Picasso Saw Charlie

It's not hard to imagine how Picasso would have seen Charlie.

This painting was created some years back when a certain famous artist stopped by a young Jim Tweedy's studio for some pointers. He soon became drunk with laughter and couldn't paint a straight line. The rest is history.

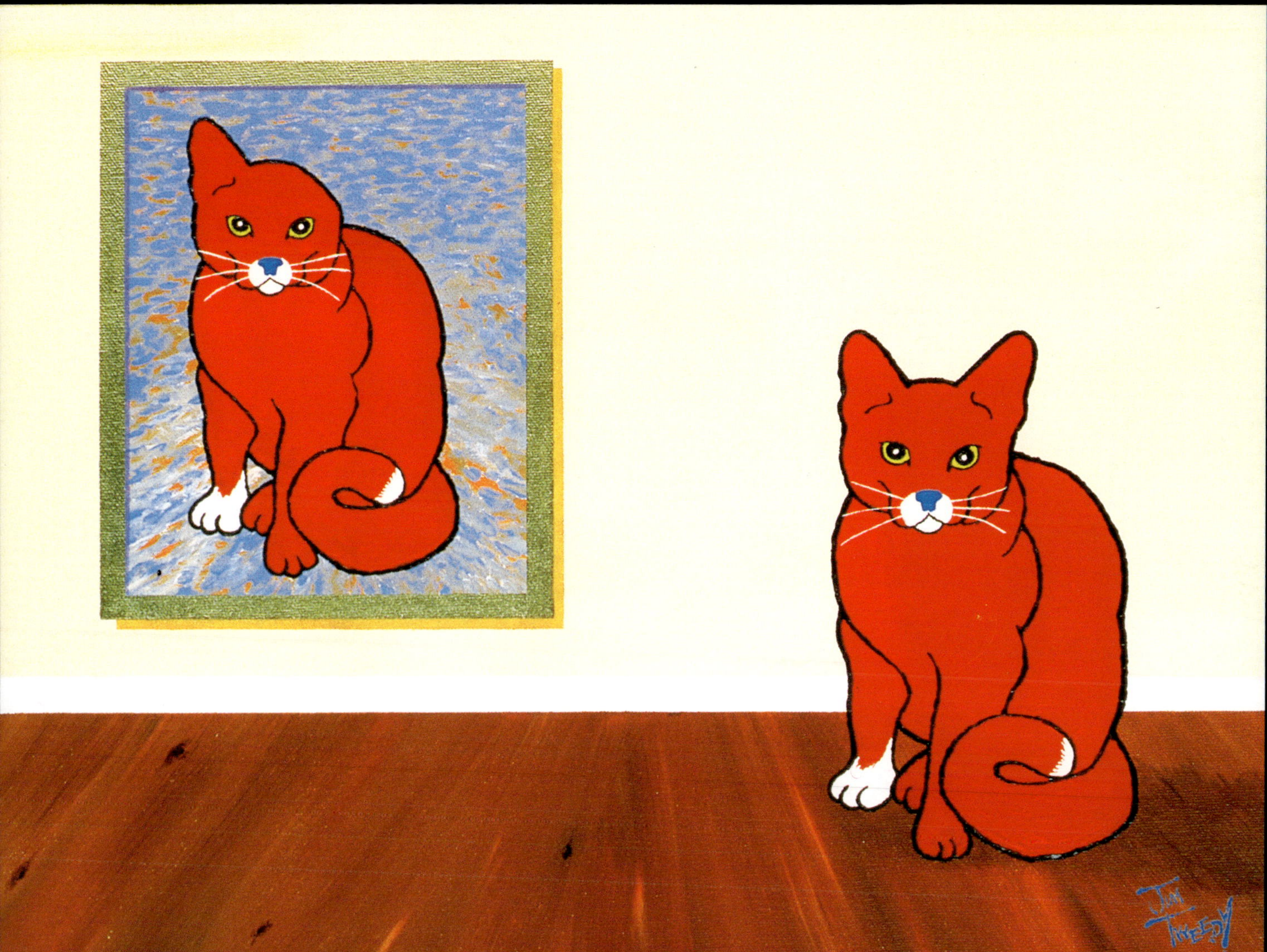

Rumor has it that Van Gogh was so enamored with his Vincent van RedCat that he styled his own appearance after the cat.

In Paris in the 1800s a certain artist named Vincent owned a RedCat who had his appearance altered in a cat-fight. The girl cats took pity on Little Vinnie, while the boy cats saw his injury as a badge of honor. Vincent became consumed with jealousy. Then one morning as he was shaving, it dawned on him. As he and Little Vinnie stared at each other in the mirror, the painter realized this could be his ticket to finally get the attention he so desired from that girl next door, plus it might help him sell some of them swirly paintings too. The rest, of course, is art history.

Have you ever seen Vincent van Gogh's self-portraits? That red hair was no coincidence.

Graffiti has gotten out of control in our major cities.

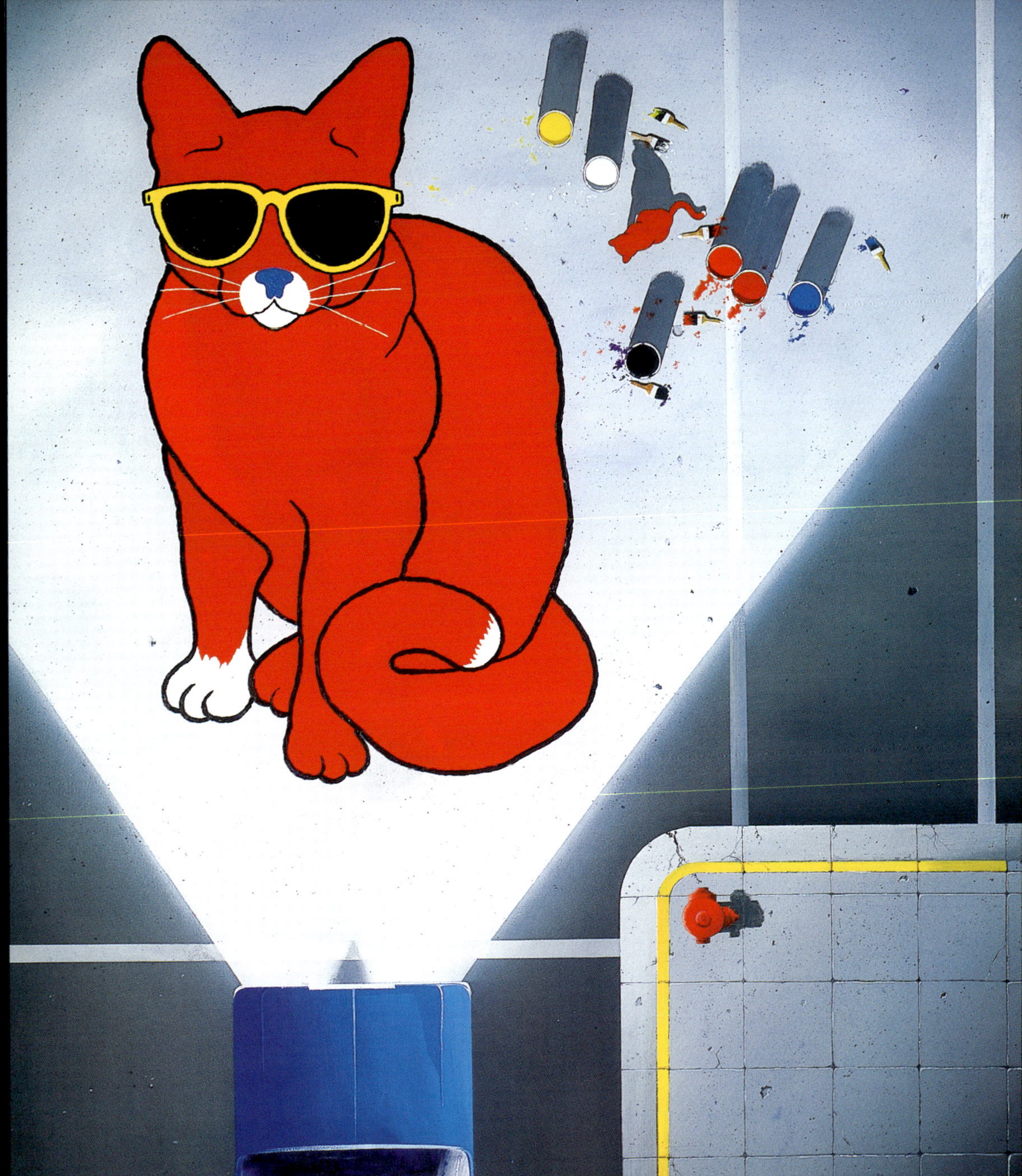

Self Portrait

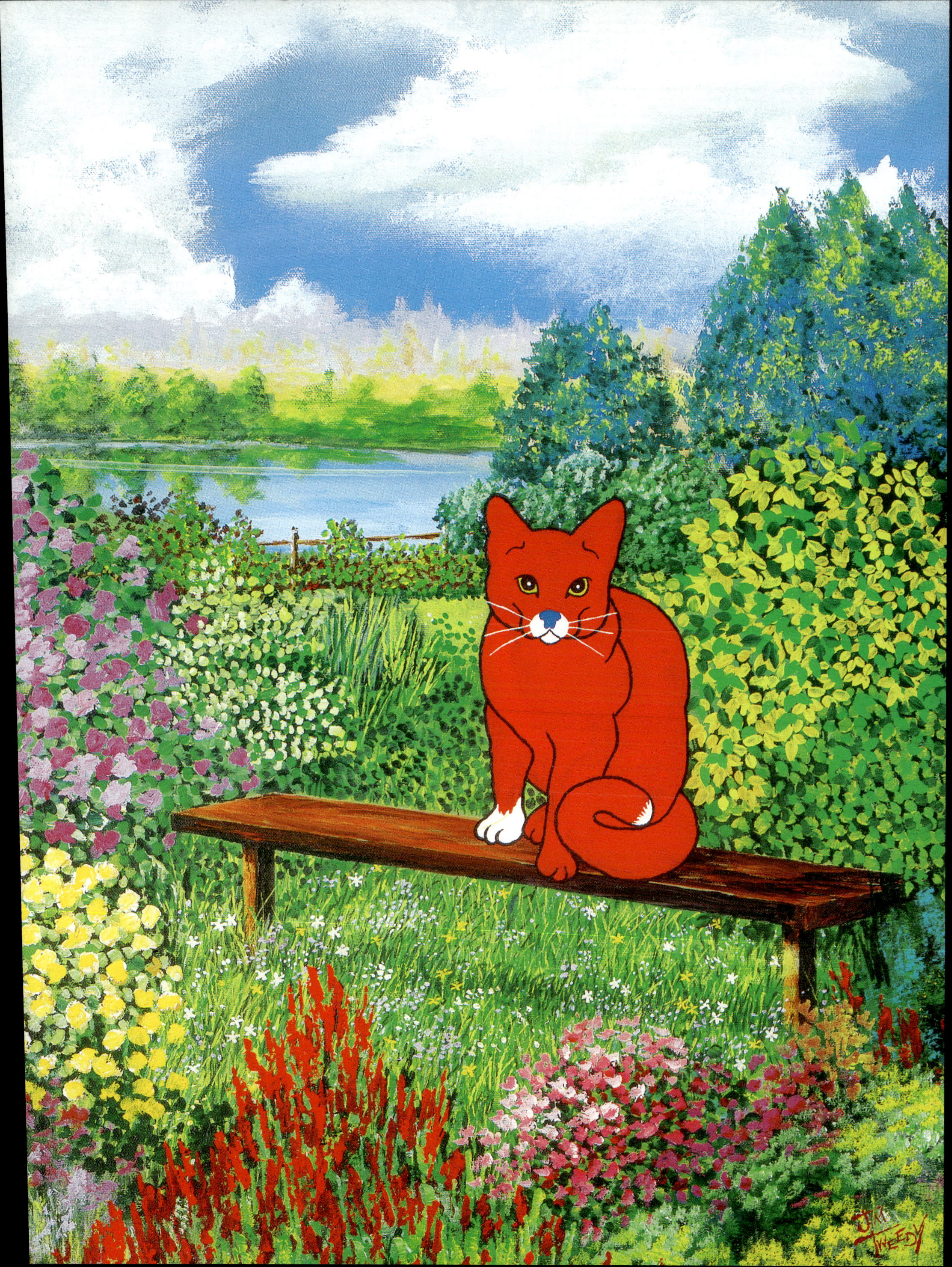

Monet painted "Charlie Giverny" and then covered it with one of those lily pad paintings so it wouldn't be stolen.

If a RedCat believes in one thing, it's stopping to smell the roses ... or the daisies ... or really anything that doesn't stop to smell him first. So what better place to find him than in the legendary Giverny gardens? Monet drew inspiration from his RedCat here until finally giving in to his own desires and drawing the RedCat himself.

Charlie Giverny

Charlie began to make his presence known on the silver screen after filming the motion picture Cat Kong.

This shot is from the original movie, which was not the one released in movie theaters. The original version is available only on home video.

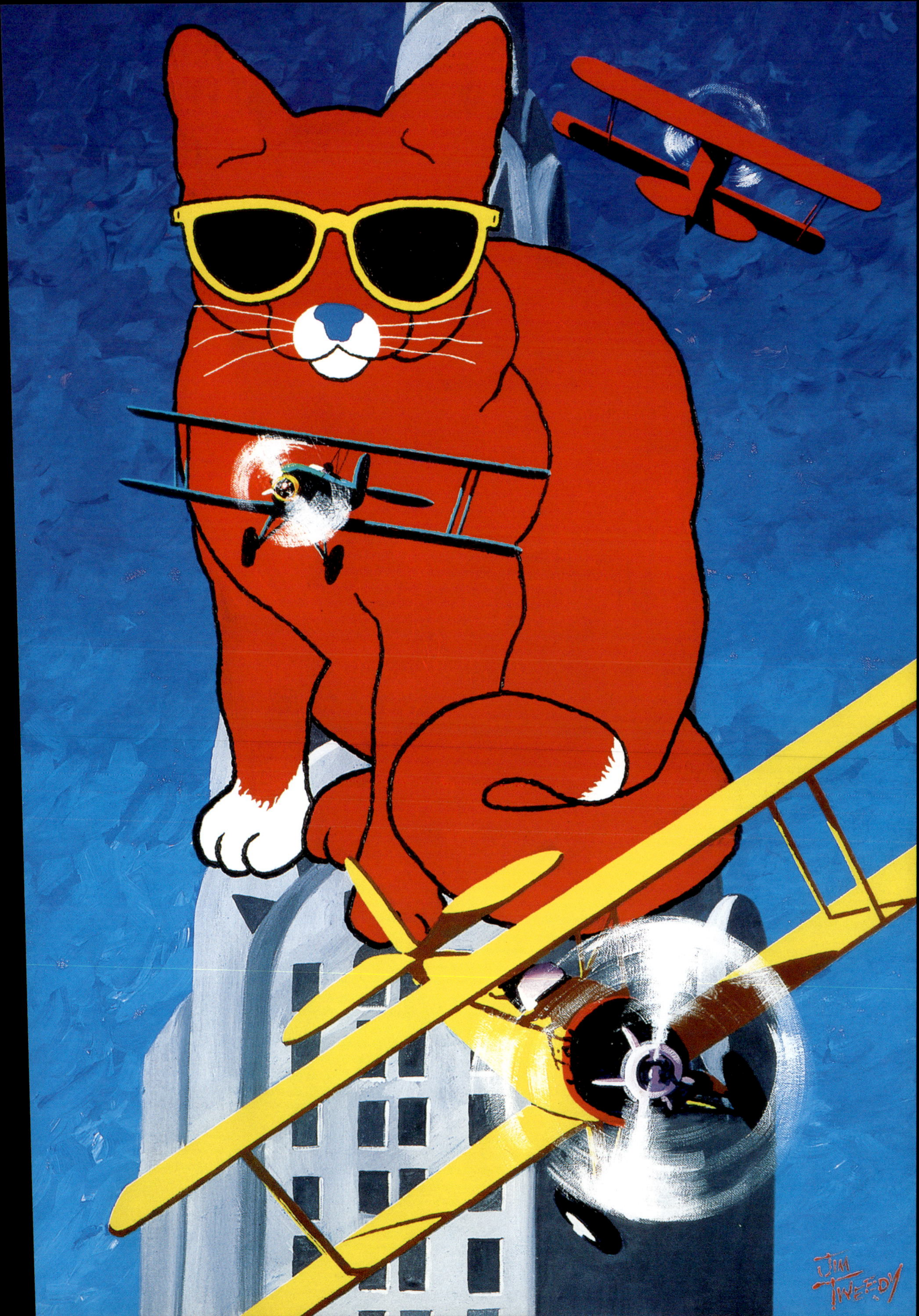

Cat Kong

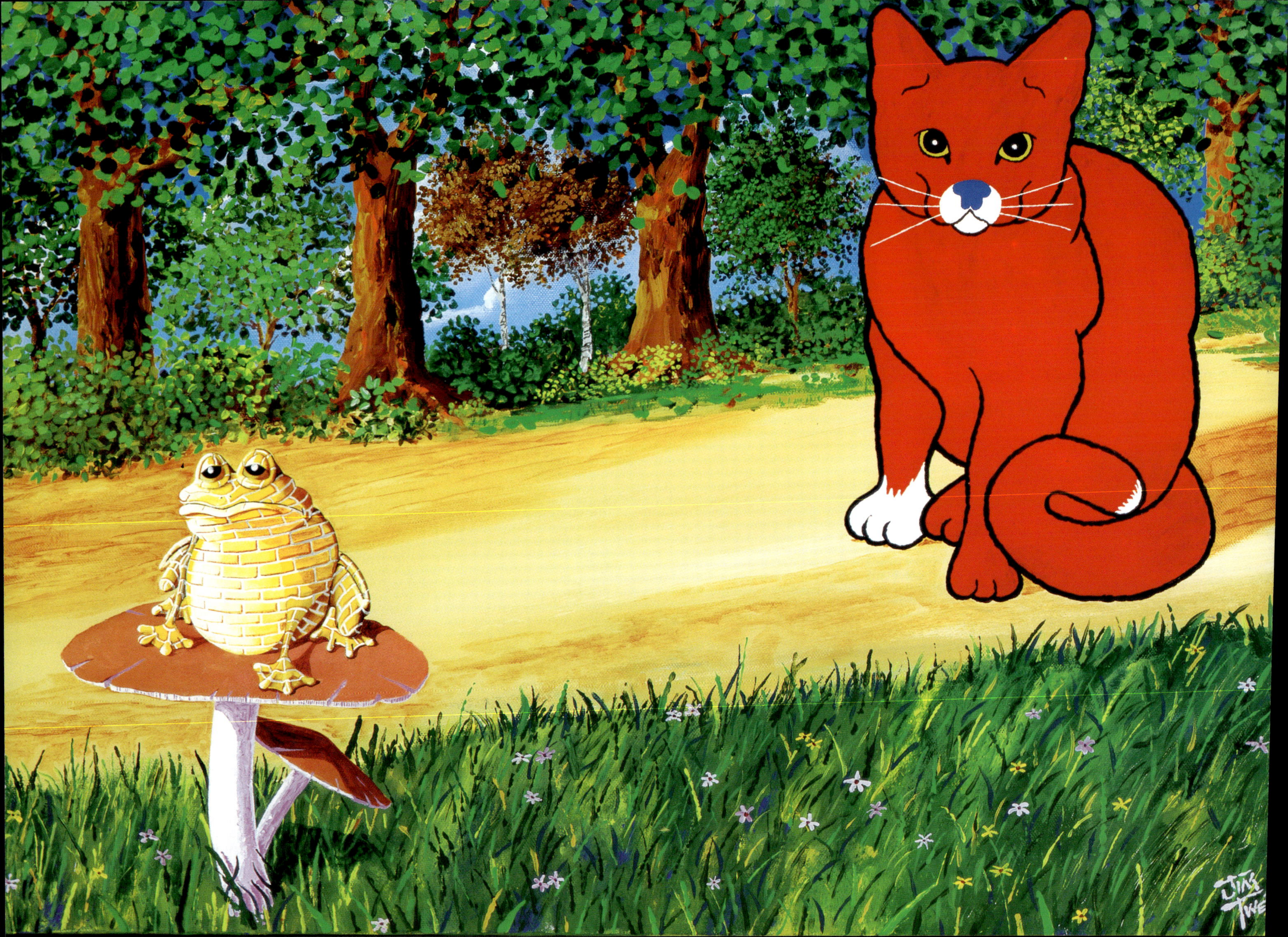

Due to a Grievous Error, Charlie Never Made It to Oz

Charlie was up for an even bigger role after filming Cat Kong, but due to a grievous error, Charlie never made it to Oz.

How was Charlie supposed to know that little Munchkin guy said road?

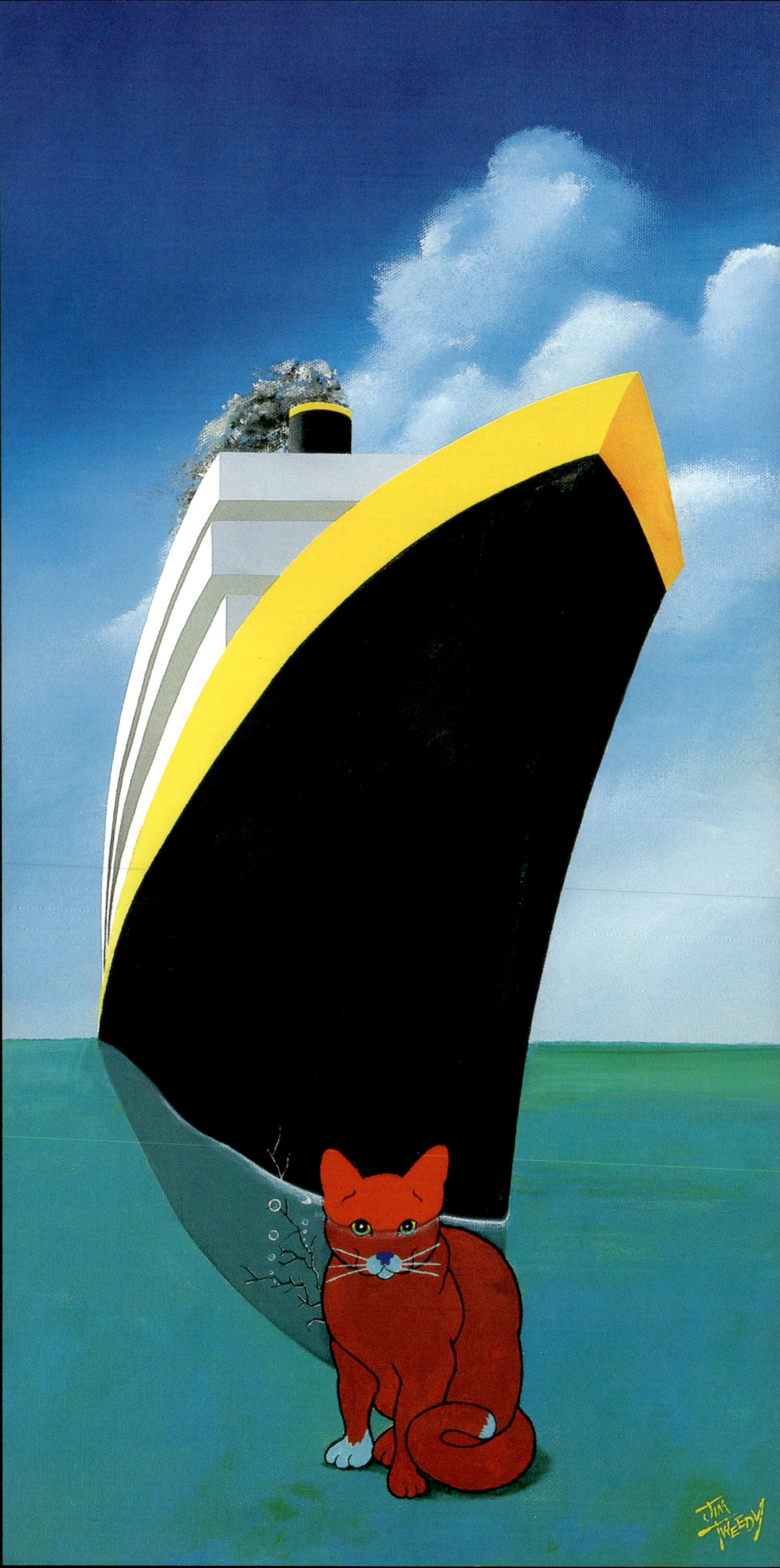

Things were not the same after Charlie's fall from stardom, and no one ever learned the truth about the Titanic.

Thanks to that movie, a whole lot of heretofore unknown facts have been unearthed.

The Truth About the Titanic

Television presented a whole new creative avenue for Charlie to showcase his talents. He's known for his memorable guest-star appearances. Few can forget the time he was in "The Fall Guy."

Every fall when Charlie's favorite time of year arrives, we head north out of New Orleans to see the color change. No cat should be so lucky as to be able to blend in with a leaf.

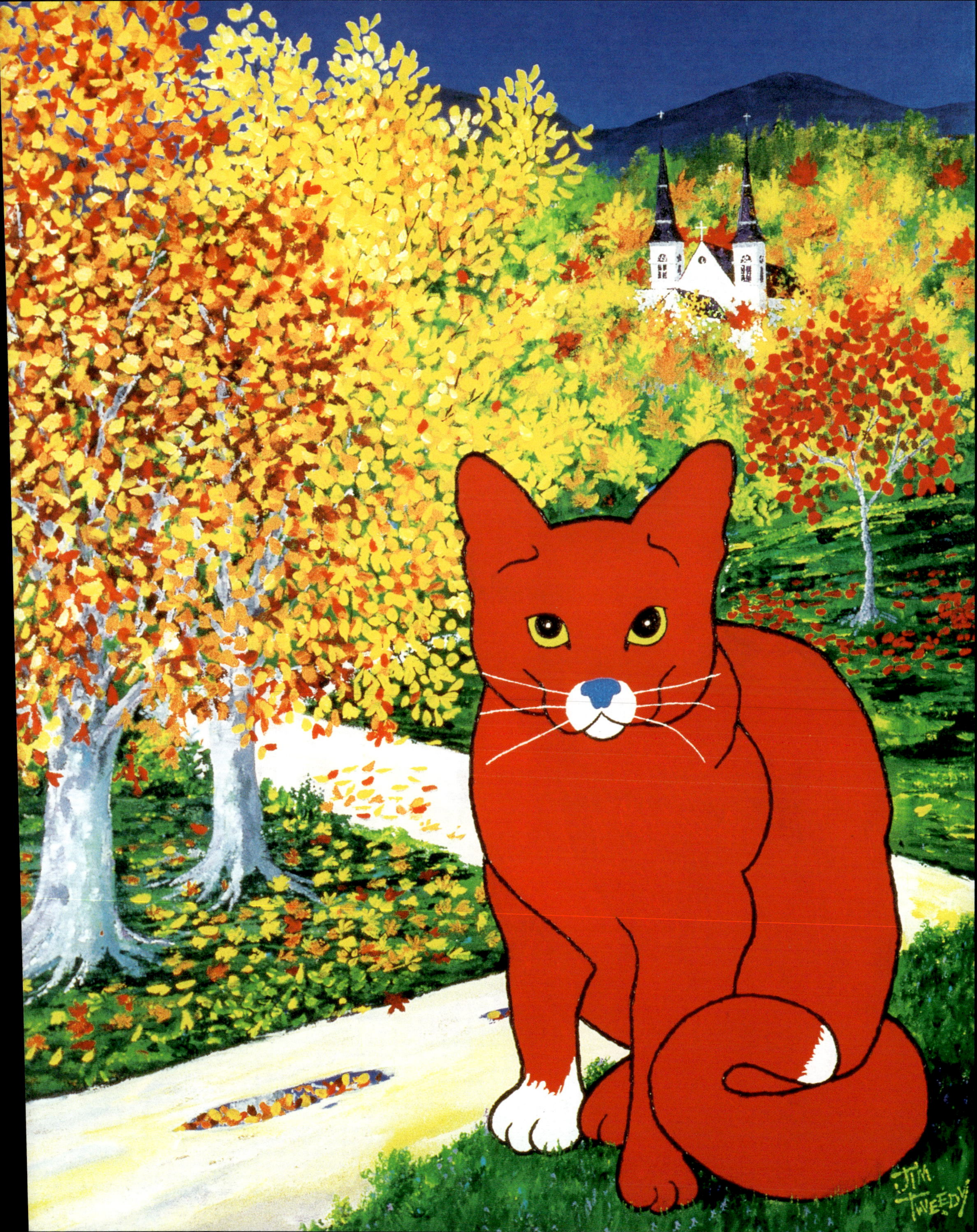

The
Fall Guy

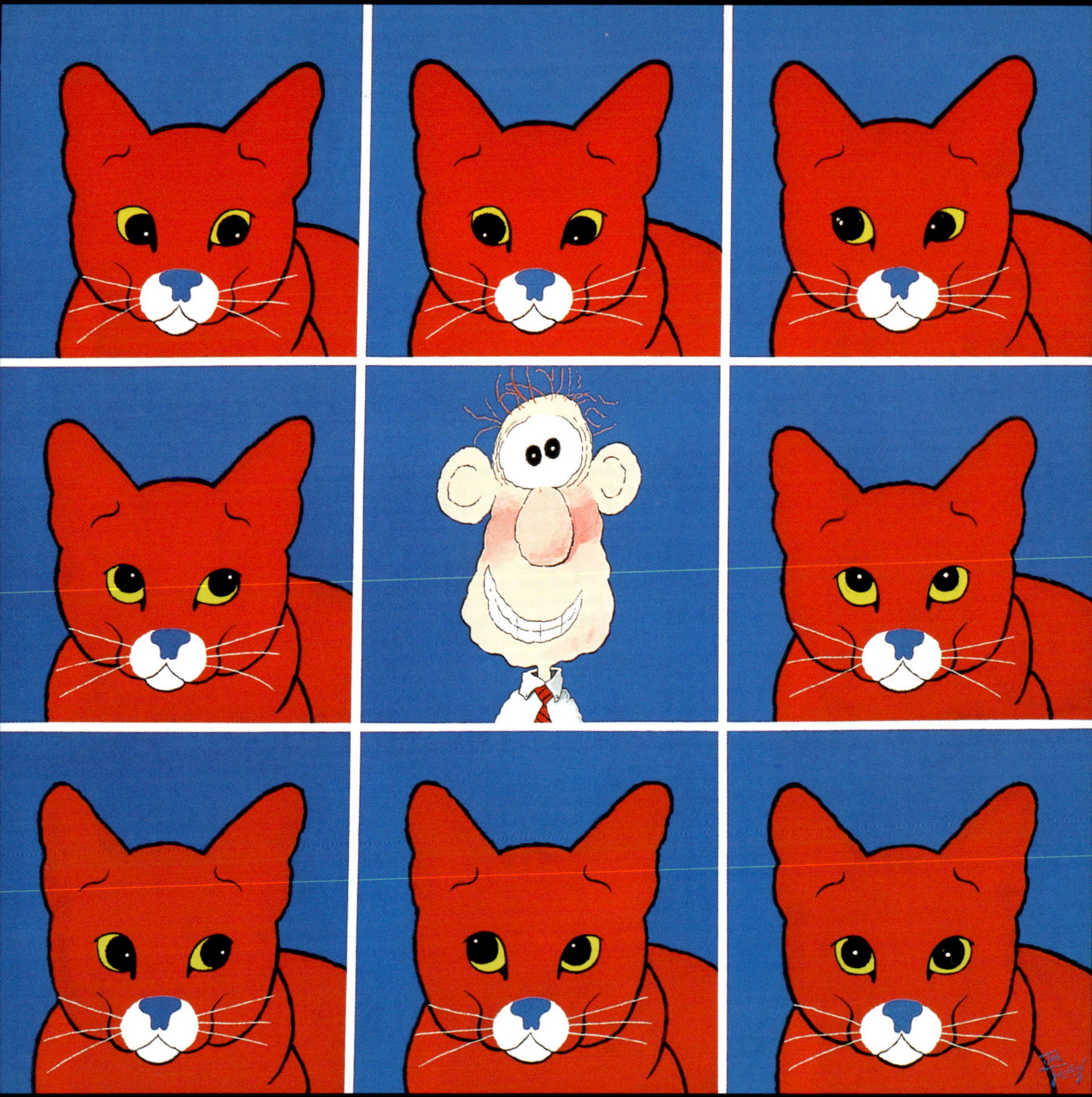

Charlie is most known for his show-stealing role on "The RedCat Bunch" . . .

This scene was to be used during the ending segment for a very promising 1970s television series I wrote. I never heard back from that studio. I'm only glad they were nice enough not to use my idea.

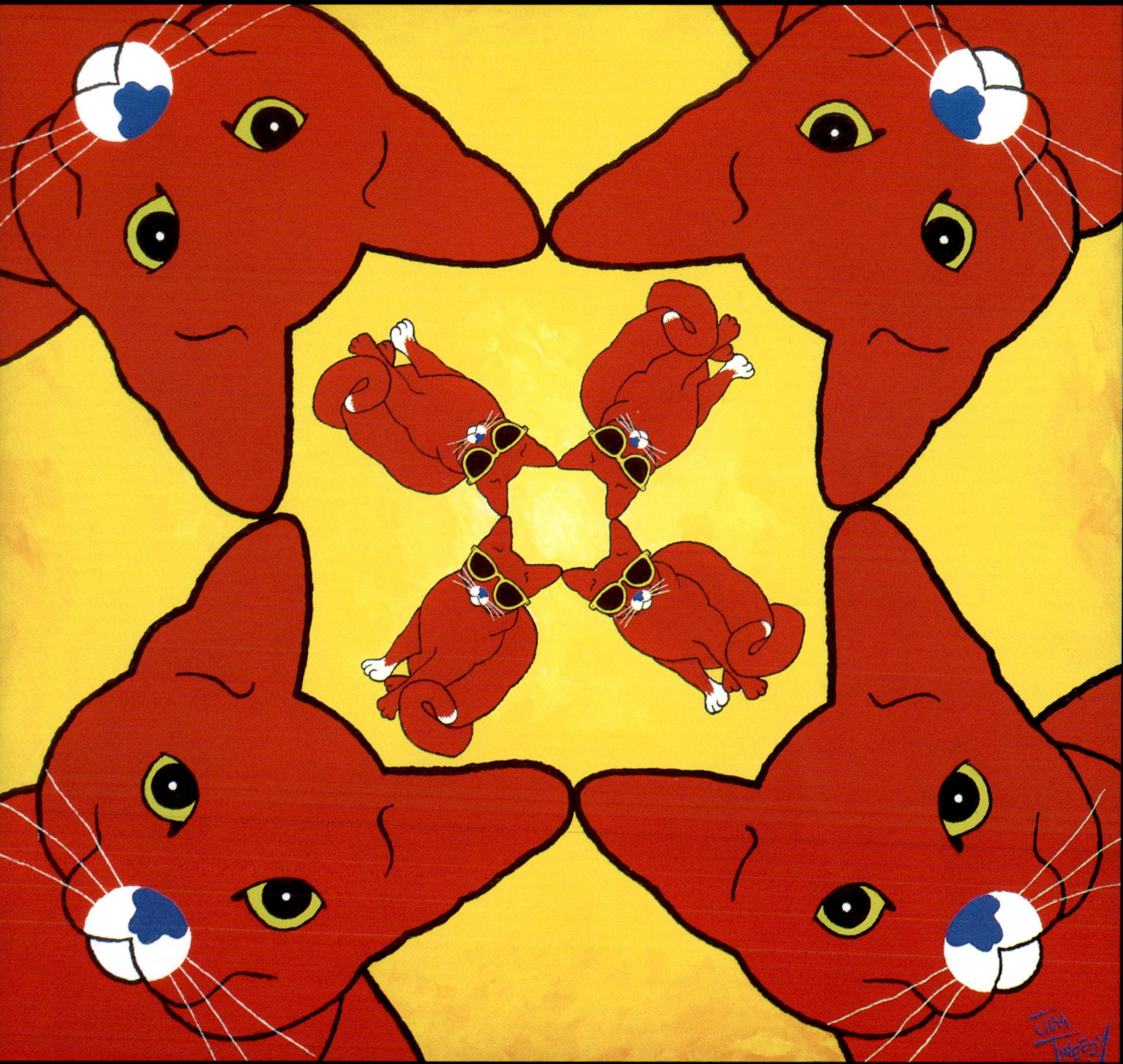

. . . when he performed his tribute to the June Taylor Dancers.

In honor of his favorite dancing group, Charlie the RedCat personally choreographed this dazzling kaleidoscope effect. I think he must've used mirrors.

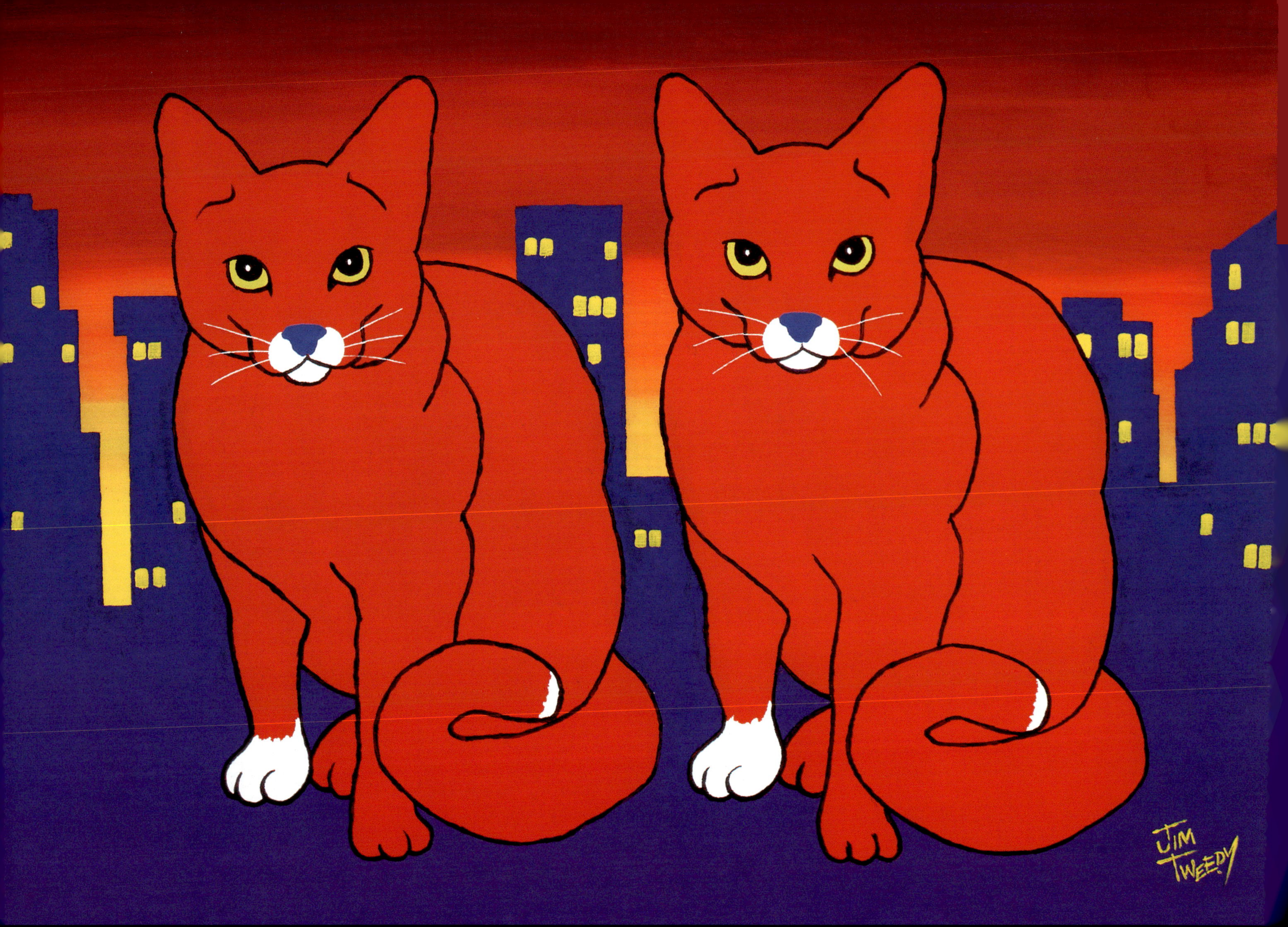

A Tail of Two Kitties

As you can see, this is a story about one cat with two purrsonalities. A tail of two kitties, you might say.

One of the great literary classics went off to press with a typo on the cover that has robbed Charlie of untold riches and fame for decades. A pity indeed.

One of Charlie's personalities likes to spend time on RedCat Pond.

On a trip out west a few years back I visited this peaceful spot known only to a select few Native Americans. After some time I was willing to admit that the rock formation in the background had perhaps a small resemblance to a certain RedCat I know.

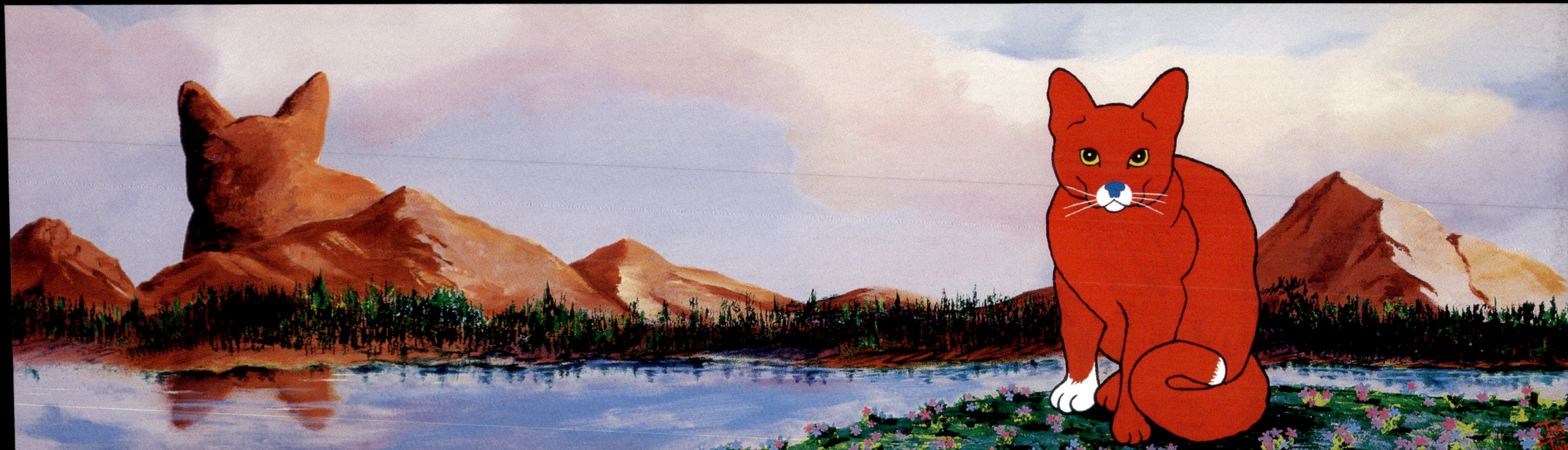

On RedCat Pond

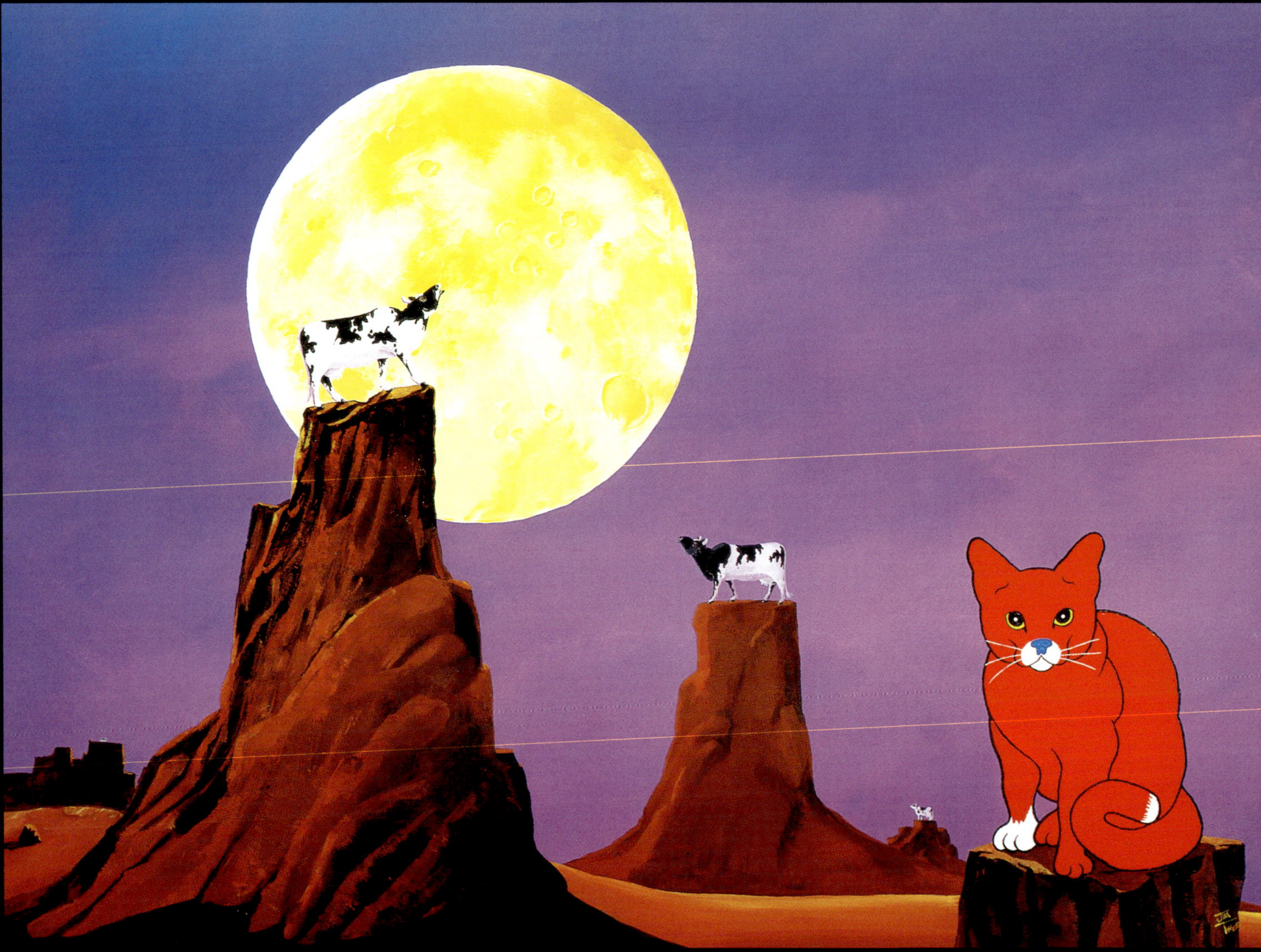

Charlie's other personality answers the call of the weird.

Living in the New Orleans French Quarter, Charlie the RedCat figured he had seen some pretty wild stuff. However, on a recent visit to the great Southwest, even Charlie had to admit that this scene was downright weird. Later that night, he returned to his hotel room and had a nice saucer of warm coyote milk. The whole trip was a mooving experience.

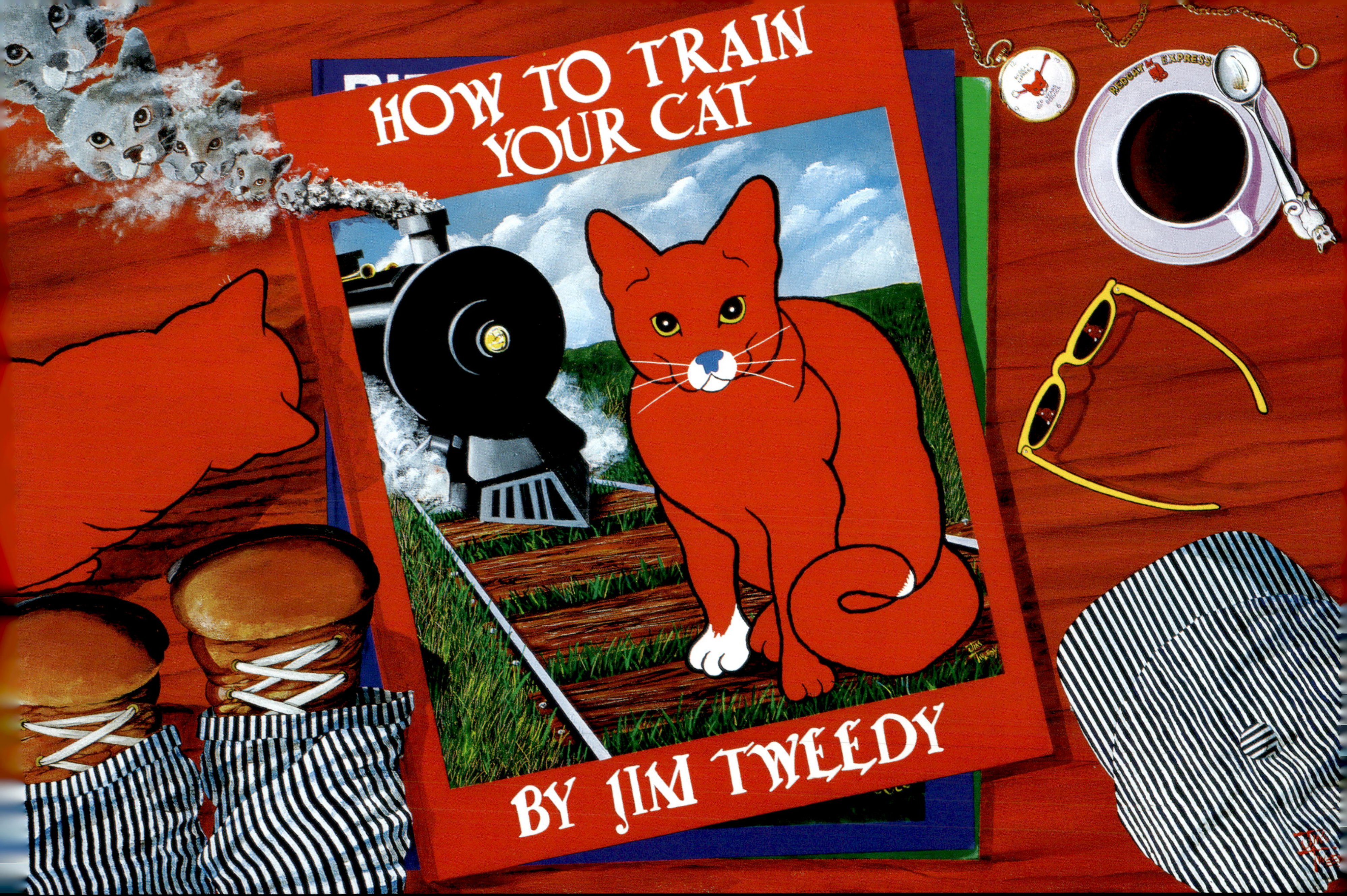

How to Train Your Cat

Learn how to train your cat and avoid this confusion.

The key to all the RedCat paintings is a double meaning in the titles. This one has it all. It is one of the most technically challenging and rewarding paintings I've ever created. A "coffee table" book called How to Train Your Cat rests on top of a coffee table along with related items.

The painting tells the story of an engineer who has just retired from the RedCat Express. Fifty years of service—and he has the gold watch to prove it. Charlie has stopped by, removed his famous yellow shades, and together they're going to read the book. Somebody pass the cream

Charlie is a big-time sports fan, as Evander RedCat will attest.

After the Mike Tyson–Evander Holyfield heavyweight boxing match, Charlie decided to pay a little visit to Mr. Tyson to see firsthand what all the fuss was about.

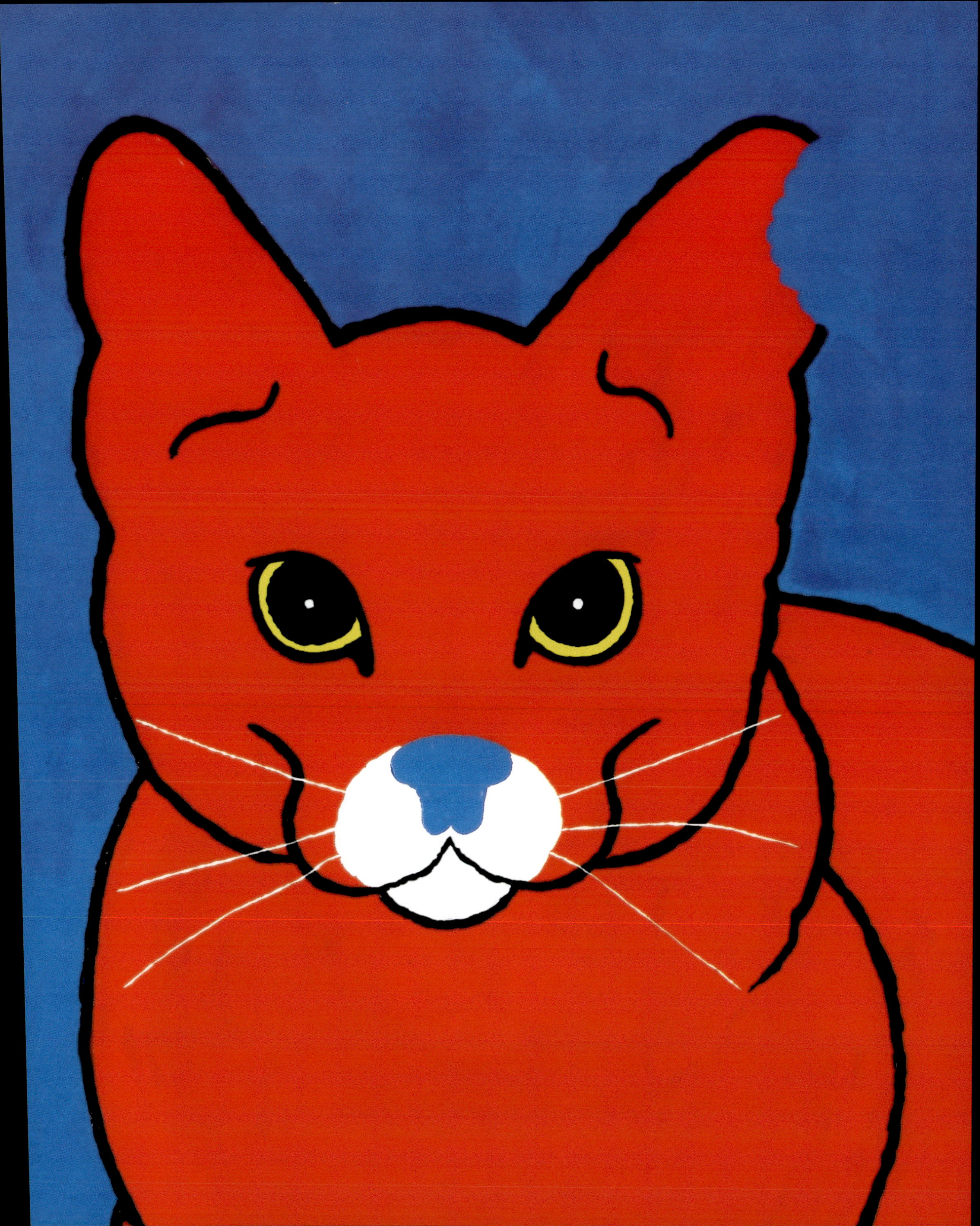

Evander
RedCat

When Don King owned Charlie . . .

They say that guy has some sort of effect on everyone he comes into contact with. Charlie wasn't phased, though.

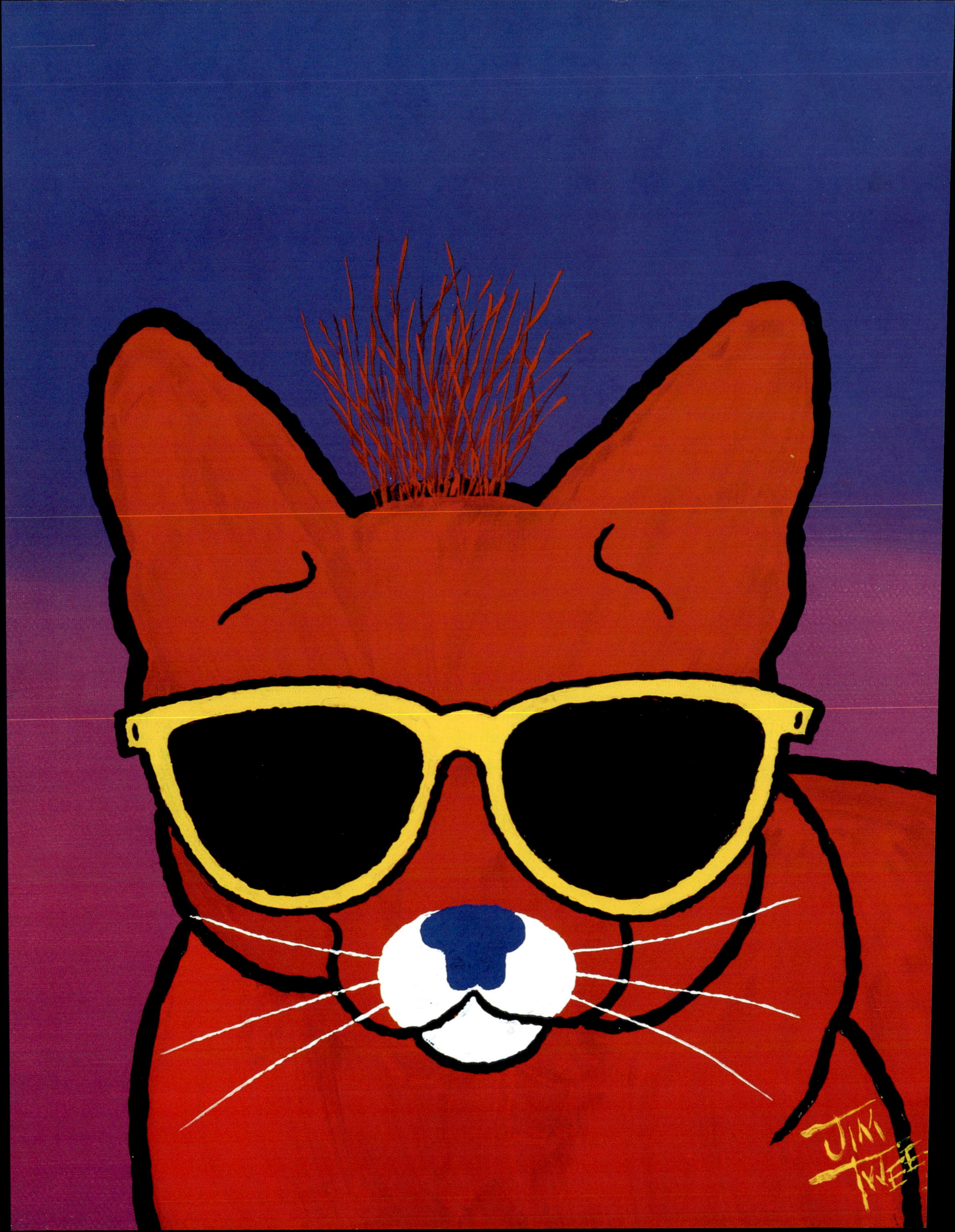

When Don King Owned Charlie

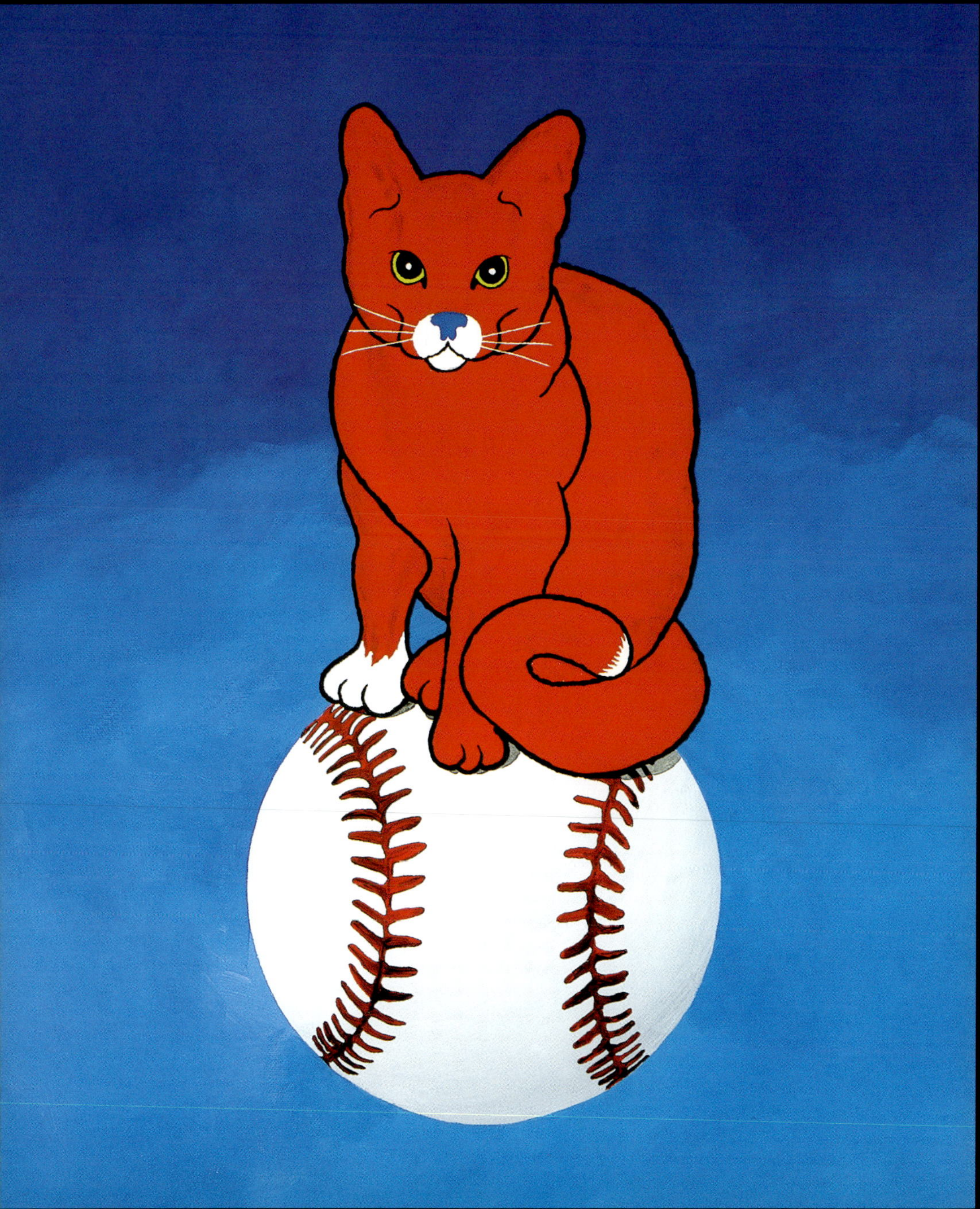

The Designated Critter

… he got into baseball and became the designated critter.

Charlie was hoping this image on a baseball would grab the attention of some of those teams he's heard of. Especially those made up of the likes of cardinals, orioles, and blue jays.

Of course, when Dennis Rodman owned Charlie, his interests became varied.

Dying his hair green was bad enough, but finally his fur grew back and covered up all those tattoos.

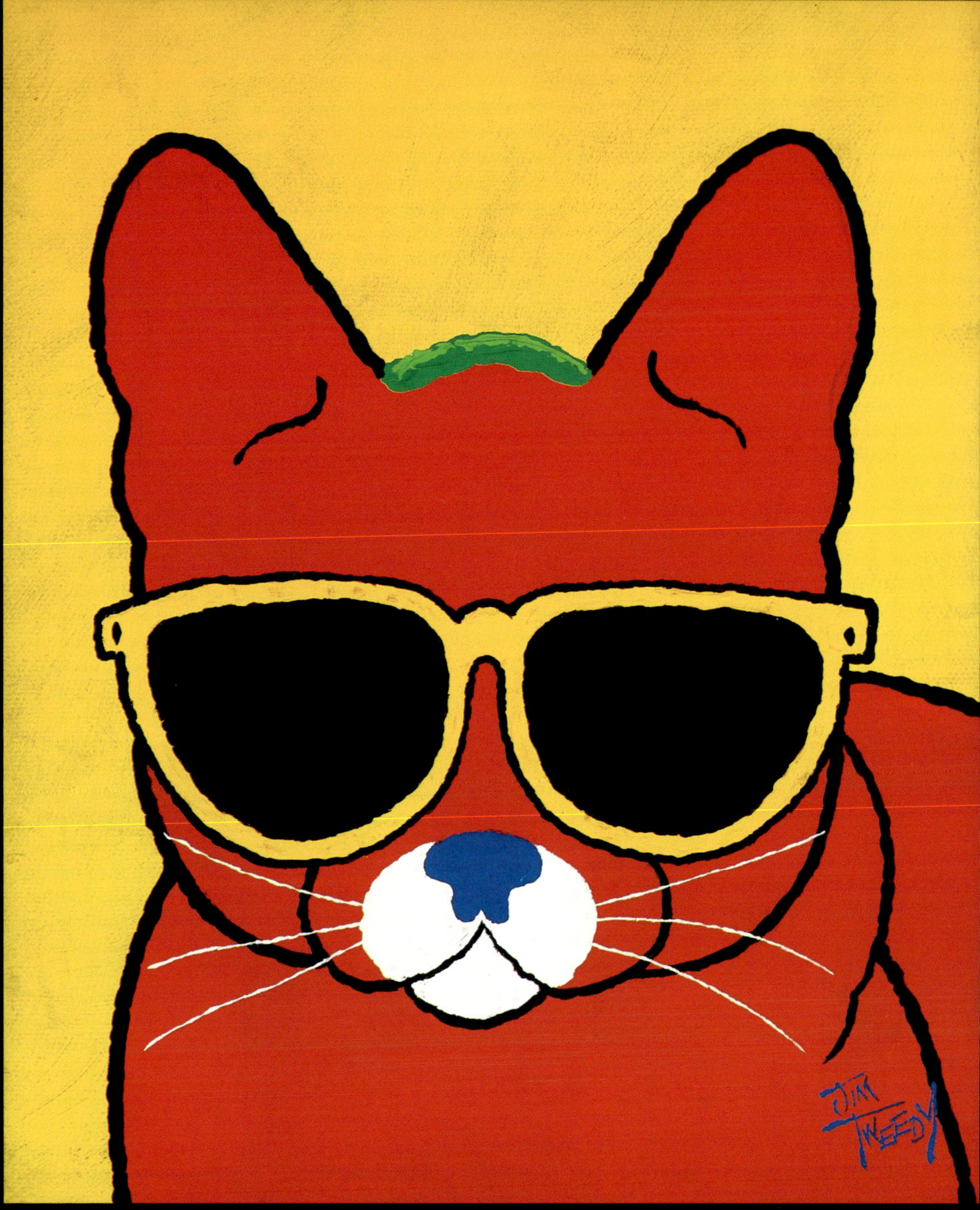

When Dennis Rodman Owned Charlie

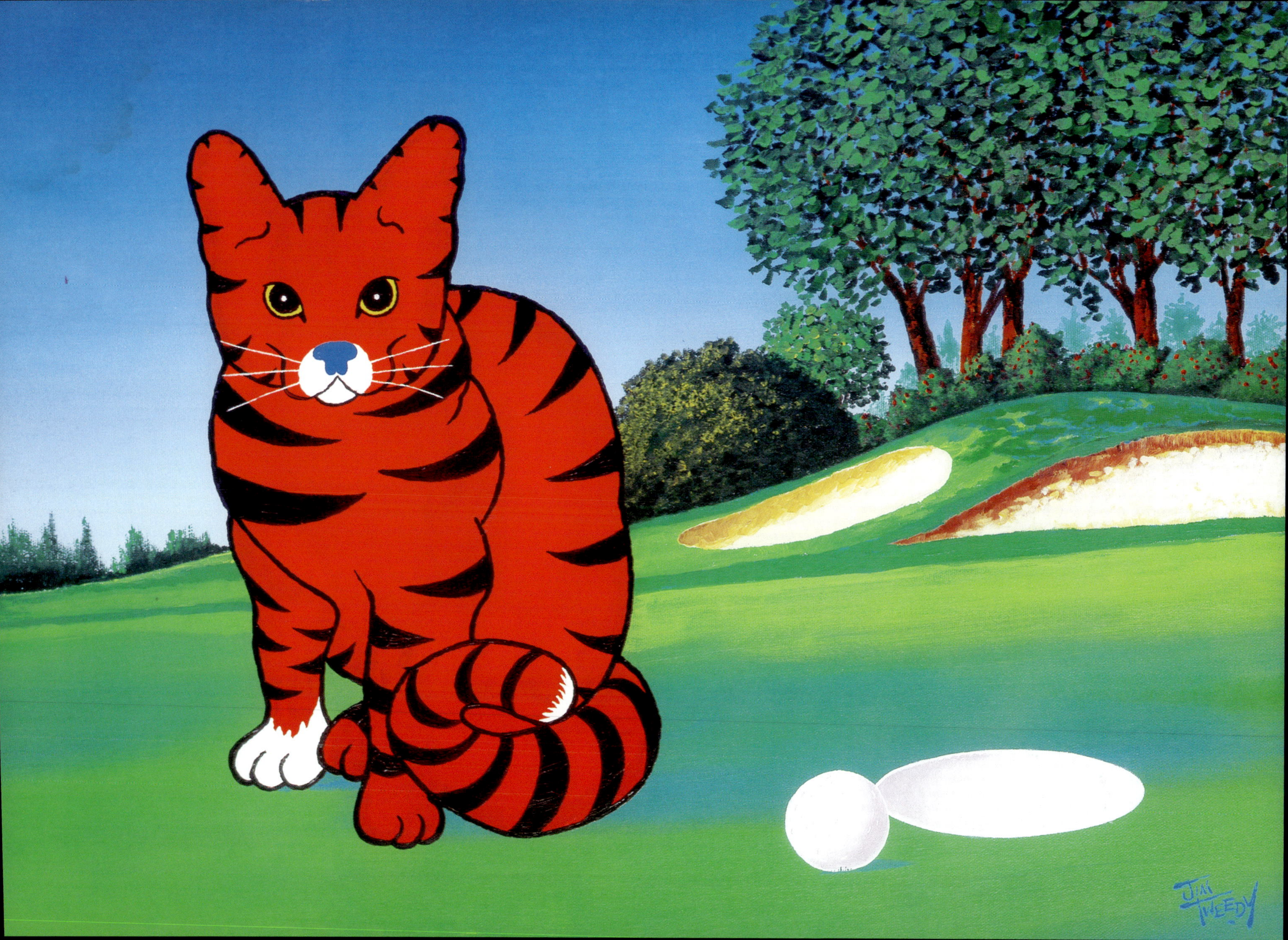

Charlie Woods

Later, Tiger Woods turned Charlie on to golf.

Charlie attempted to psych me out by showing up in this attire for a big match one Saturday morning. He did manage to squeak out a one-stroke victory on the eighteenth hole, but it wasn't the stripes! I promise it wasn't the stripes!

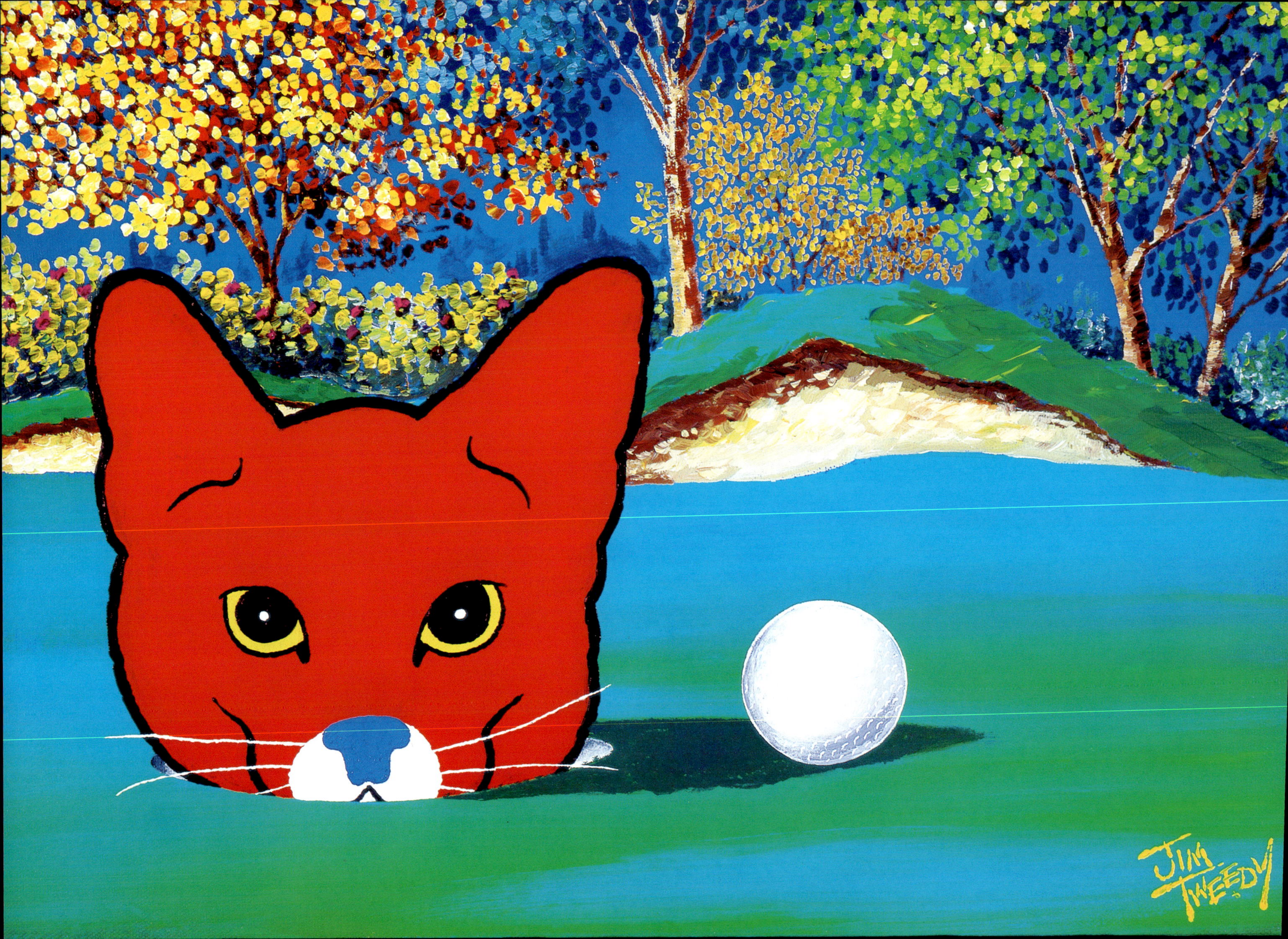

Cat in One

Tiger's been a great teacher. Charlie already has made a "cat-in-one."

Charlie is forever trying to find the birdies that supposedly live in these golf holes. So am I.

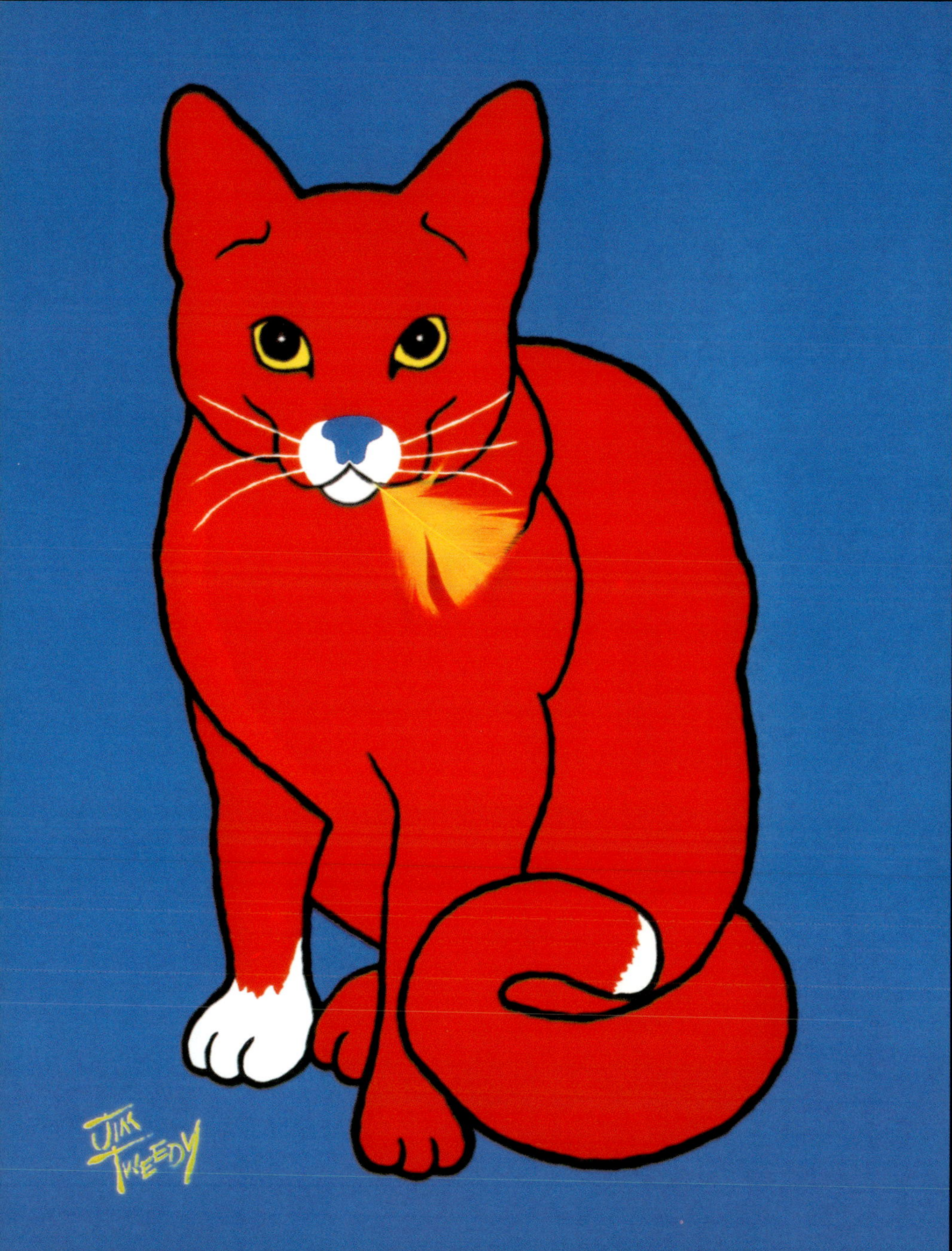

Bye-Bye Birdie

Charlie enjoys golf because it provides a chance to dine outdoors. Bye-bye birdie!

Hey, it's nature. Gimme a break.

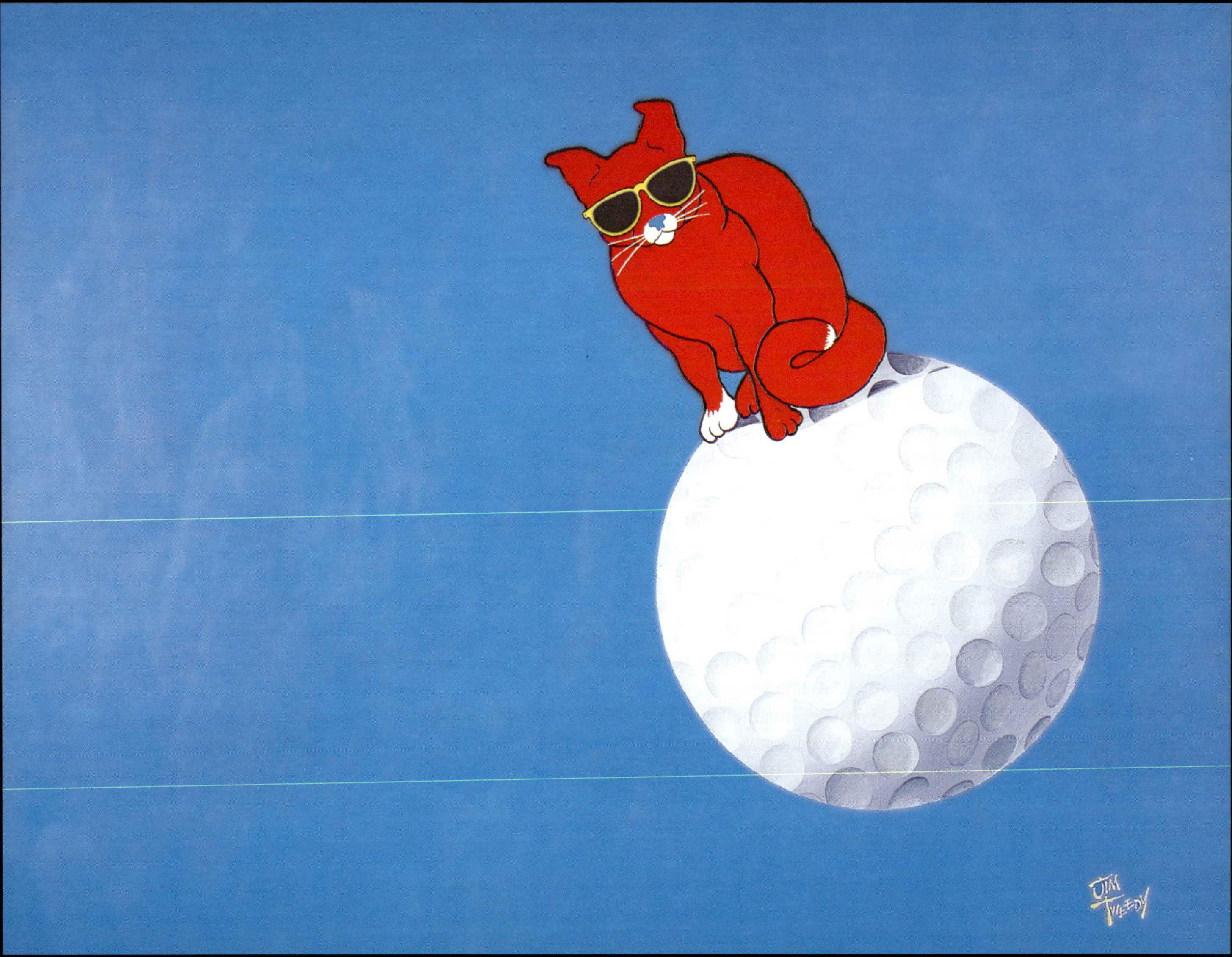

Overall, Charlie finds the game of golf frustrating, but, then again, every time he becomes teed off …

Charlie loves to go to the driving range with me.

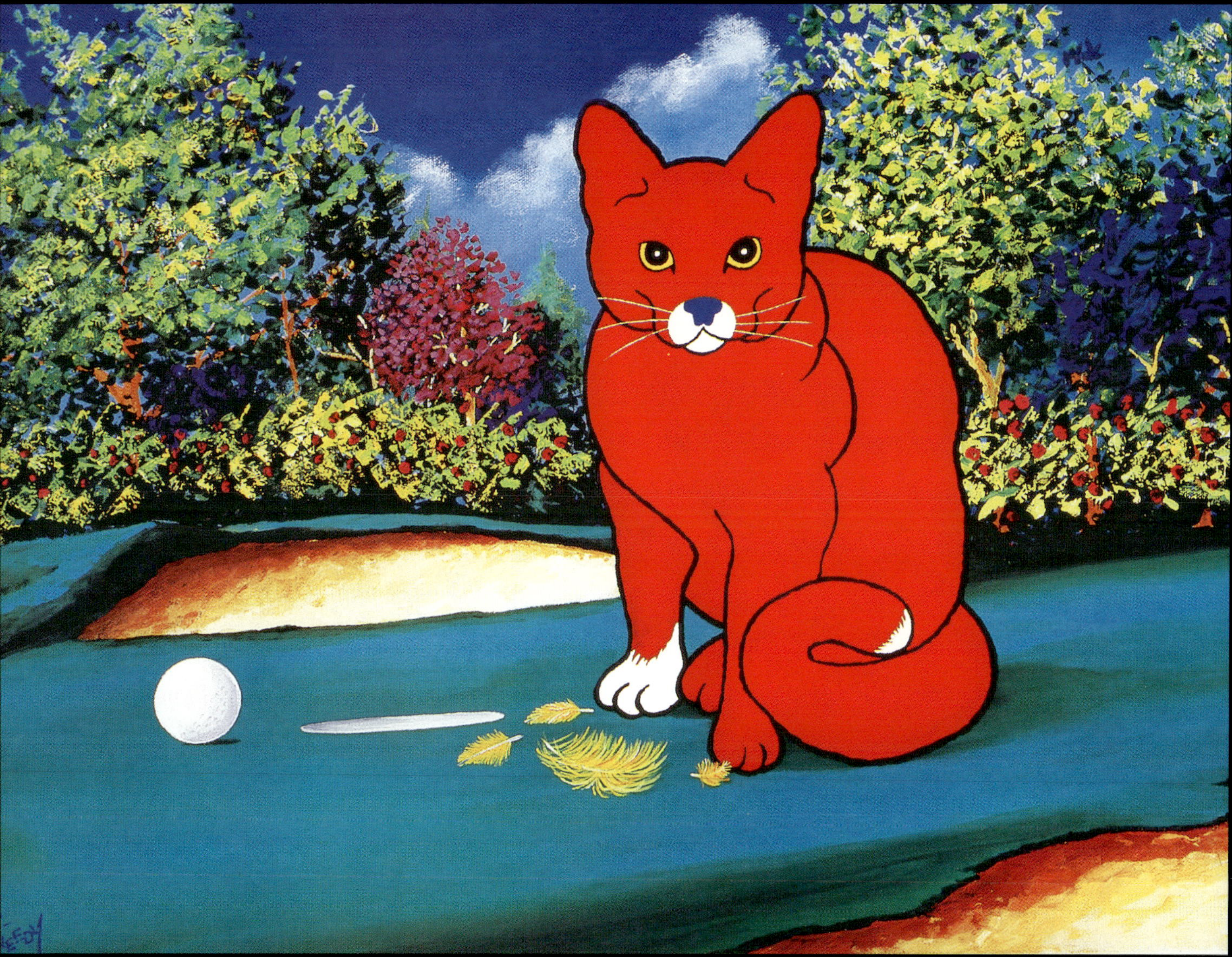

... Charlie scores a birdie.

Charlie wonders why golfers find it so hard to score birdies. Perhaps they'd have better luck if they stopped chasing them with clubs.

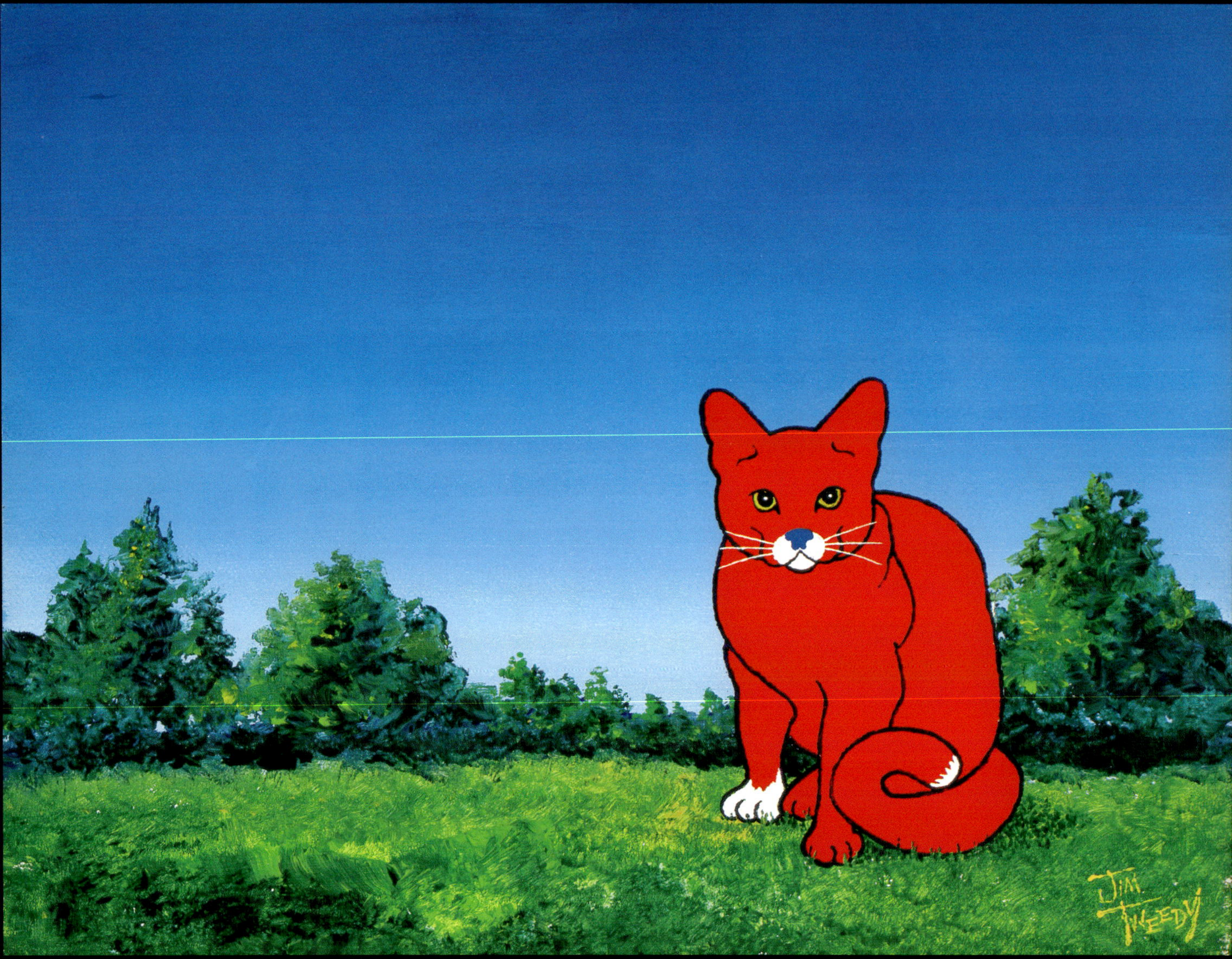

I was outdoors with Charlie after a game of golf …

This pleasing little scene finds Charlie enjoying a cool spring morning as we drove to my art show in Birmingham, Alabama, last year. Charlie always says Alabama has some of the best rest stops because there are complimentary soft drinks and you can feed on the squirrels. I mean feed the squirrels.

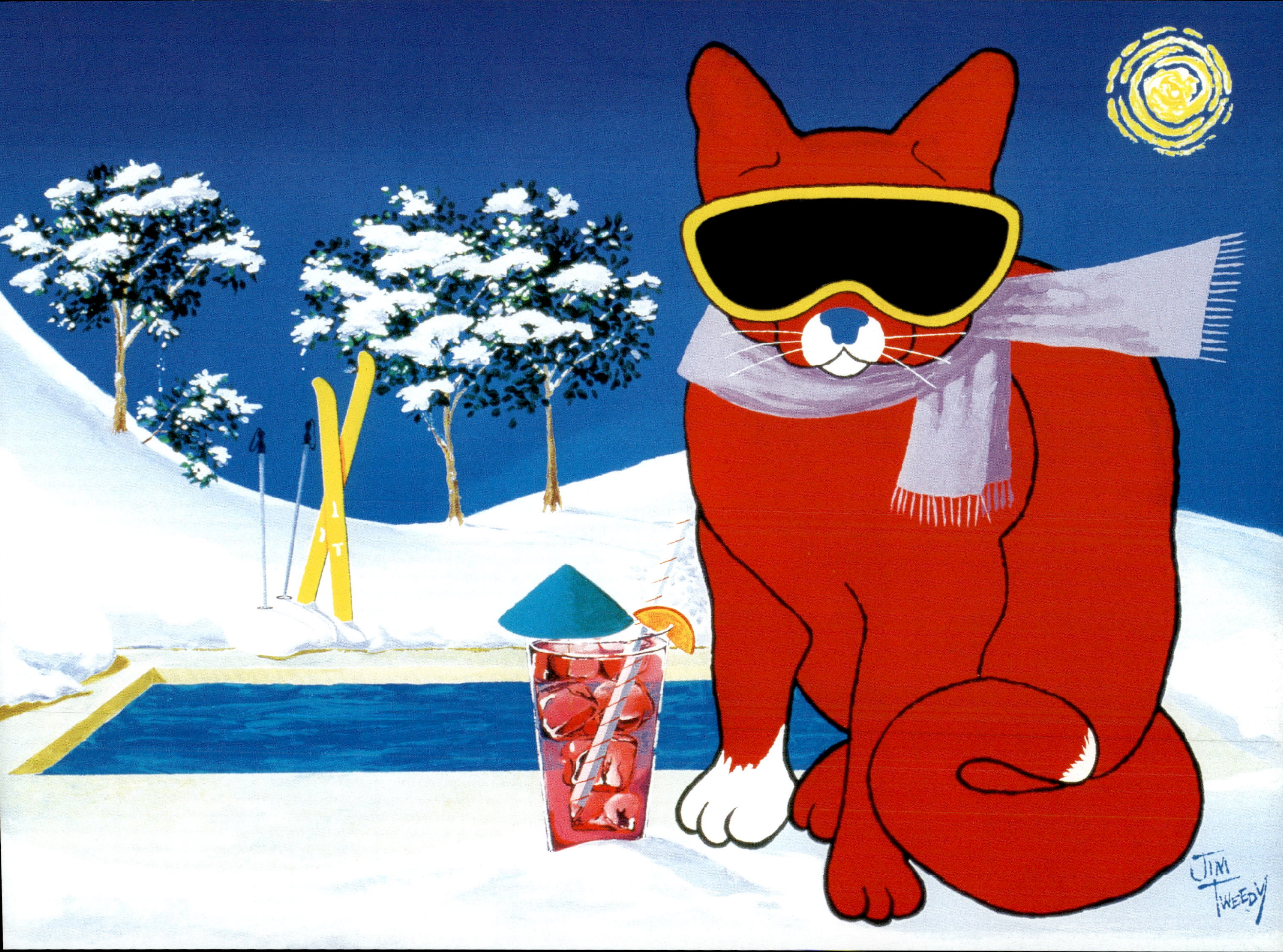

A Cold Day in July

… one cold day in July.

This is a rare occurrence in New Orleans to say the least. Indian Summer this early in the year is highly unlikely.

Charlie just wanted to chill out and watch the sunset.

No one appreciates a pretty sunset more than Charlie does. He spends a lot of time sitting in one spot, sometimes for hours on end, waiting for the sun to set so he can get up and go to sleep.

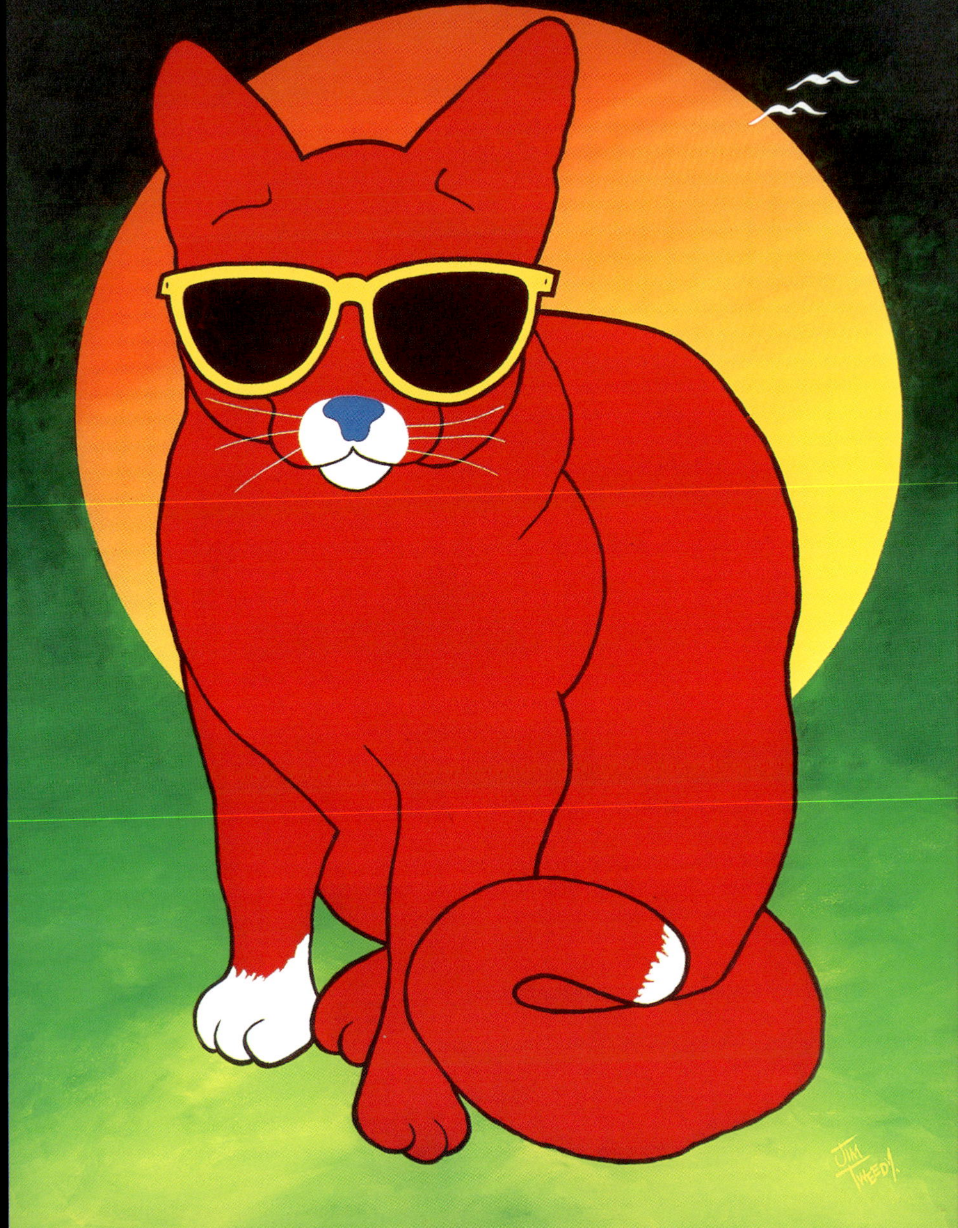

Sunset Charlie

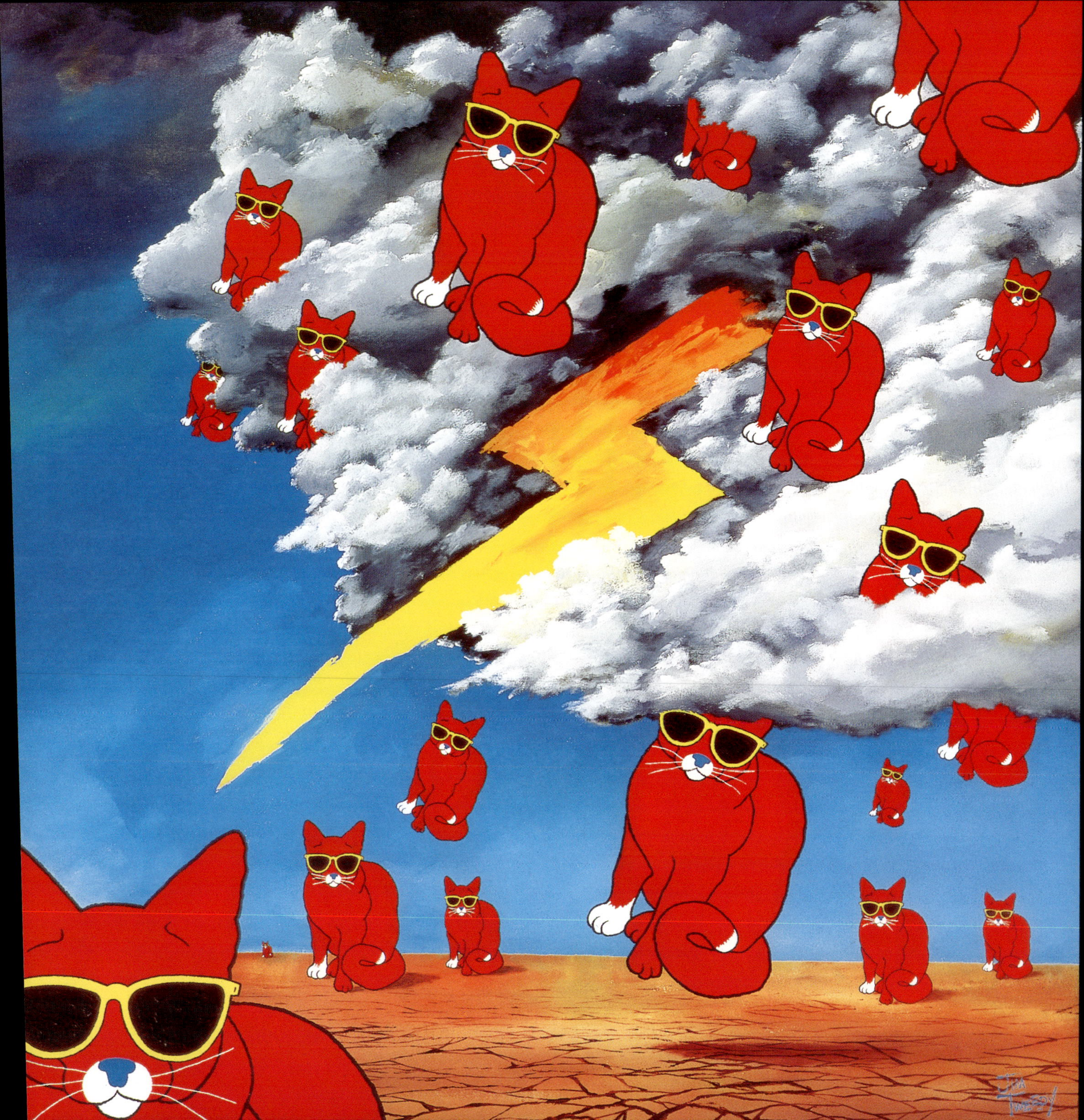

After all, it had been raining RedCats … and that's all.

A rare desert cloudburst is taking place. One might say it's raining cats 'n' dogs. But, as one can easily see, one would be wrong.

It's Raining RedCats … and That's All

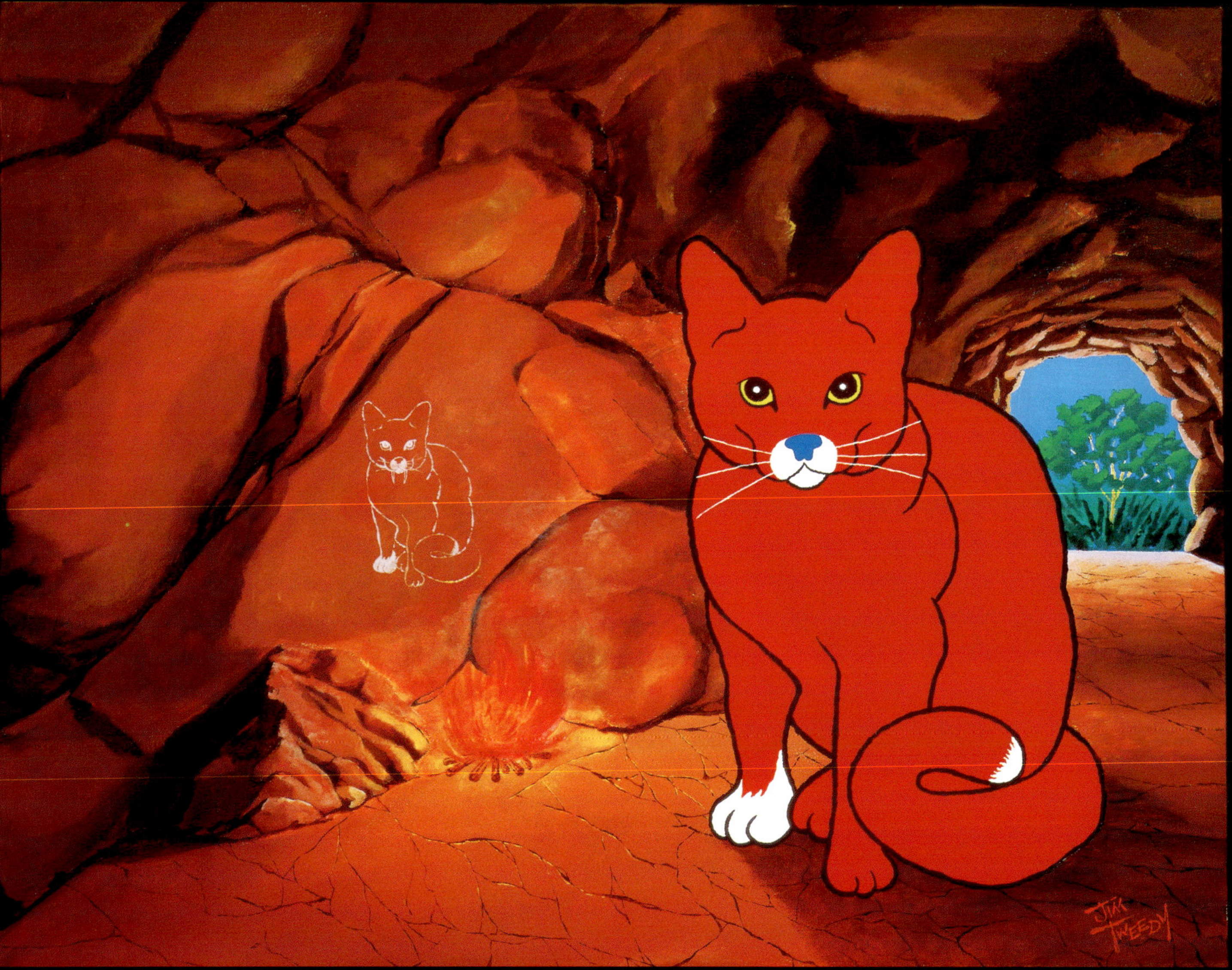

Although he's an active, outdoorsy kind of guy, Charlie's not short on intellect. Recently, as he traveled in search of ancient RedCats …

RedCats supposedly roamed the earth with dinosaurs, so off Charlie and I went for proof. We traveled the earth, exhausting every possibility in every cave known to man. We even learned the difference between a stalactite and a stalagmite. Our search took us to Mammoth Cave, Kentucky. When Charlie wasn't looking, I sketched this saber-toothed RedCat. Charlie proudly posed next to it, beaming with pride. It is a secret I'll carry with me all my life.

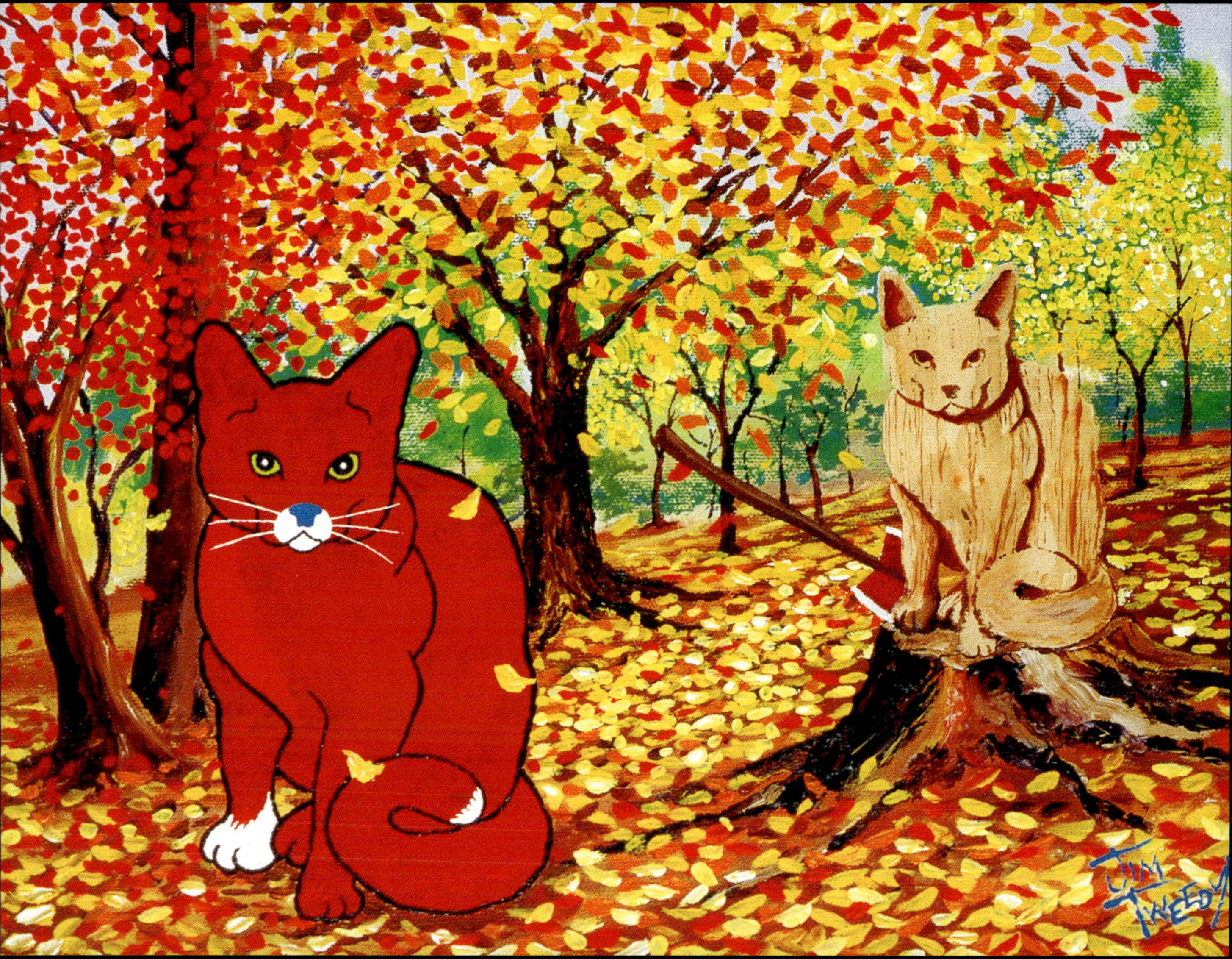

... a mysterious totem appeared.

We are still not sure who whittled this amazing likeness of Charlie or just how long ago it was done. Whoever it was obviously was very good with an ax and must have hated that tree.

Charlie made a startling discovery.

Before Neil Armstrong took that one small step Charlie the RedCat had already been there and done that. But here's what no scientist or mapmaker wants the world to know. Charlie is not of the land. The land is of Charlie.

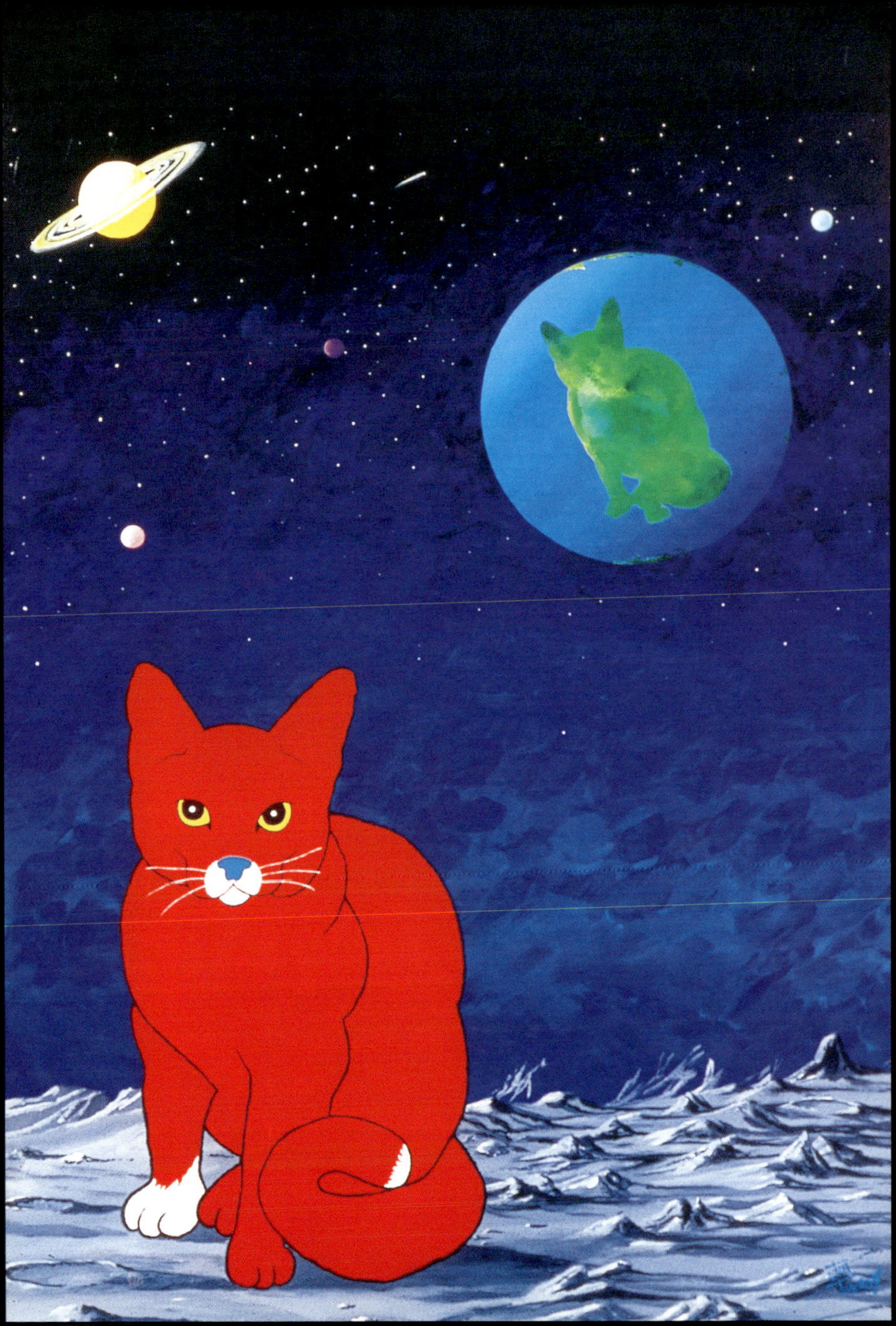

A Startling Discovery

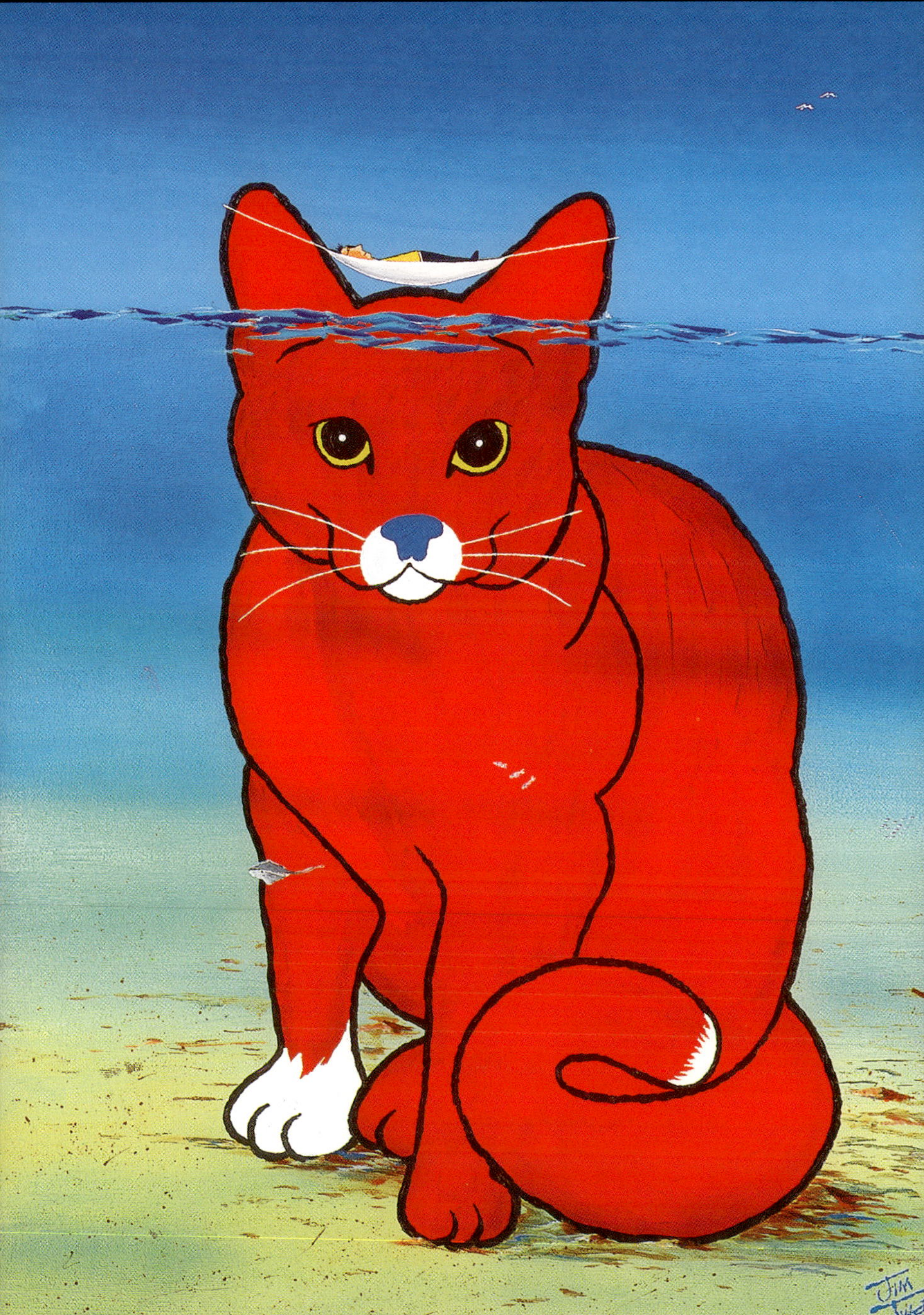

He concluded that no cat is an island.

Not true! This small island with its one very relaxed inhabitant exists in a remote area of the South Pacific. There is not a whole lot to do, but on the other hand, it's not stressful either.

No Cat is an Island

“Guess who’s coming to dinner?” Charlie asked me one day.

No, it’s not what you think. Charlie is an invited guest. The little guys just bought some new art for the walls and wanted to show it off, break some cheese, and share a little after-dinner catnip with their neighbor.

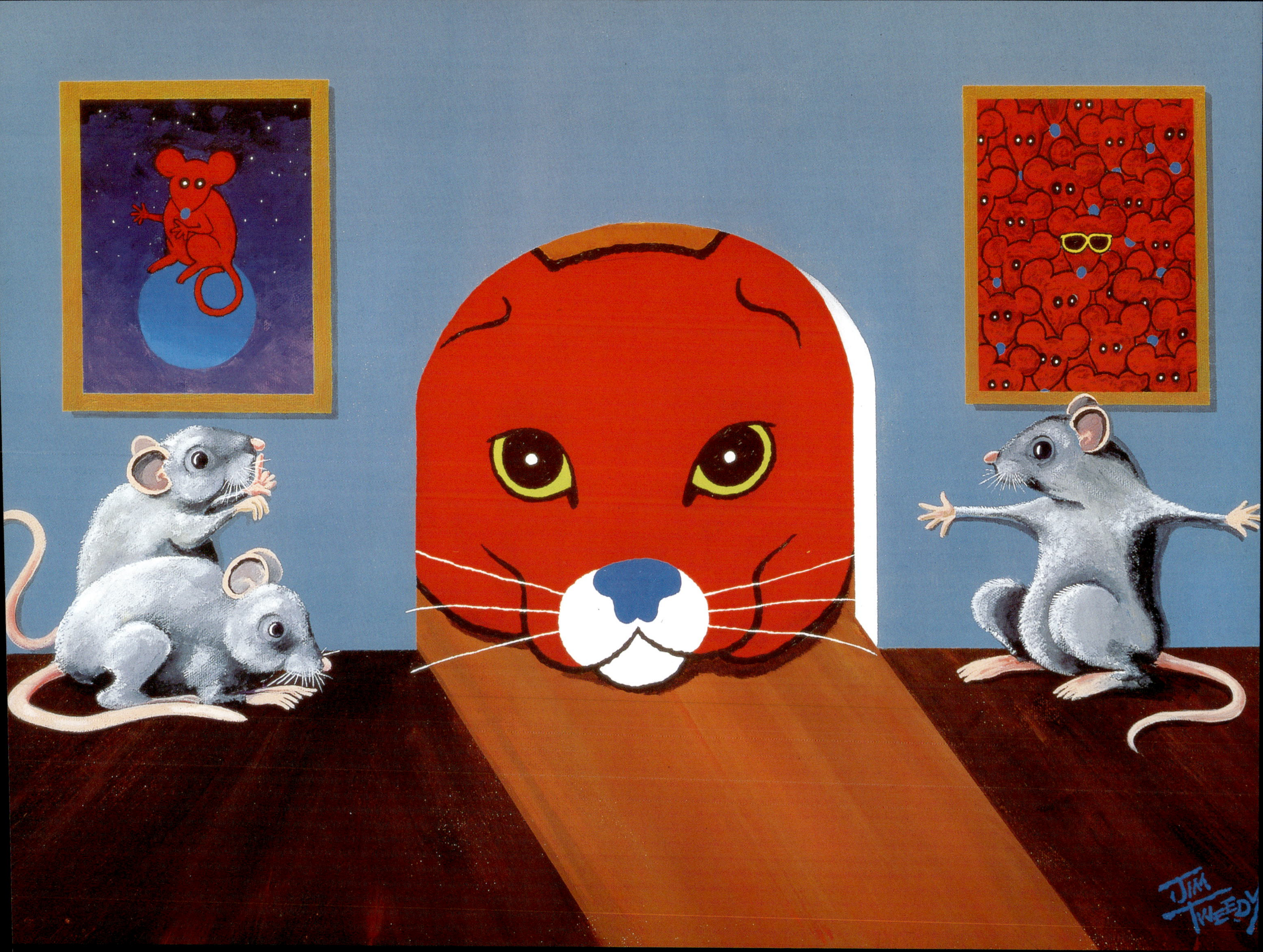

Guess Who's Coming to Dinner?

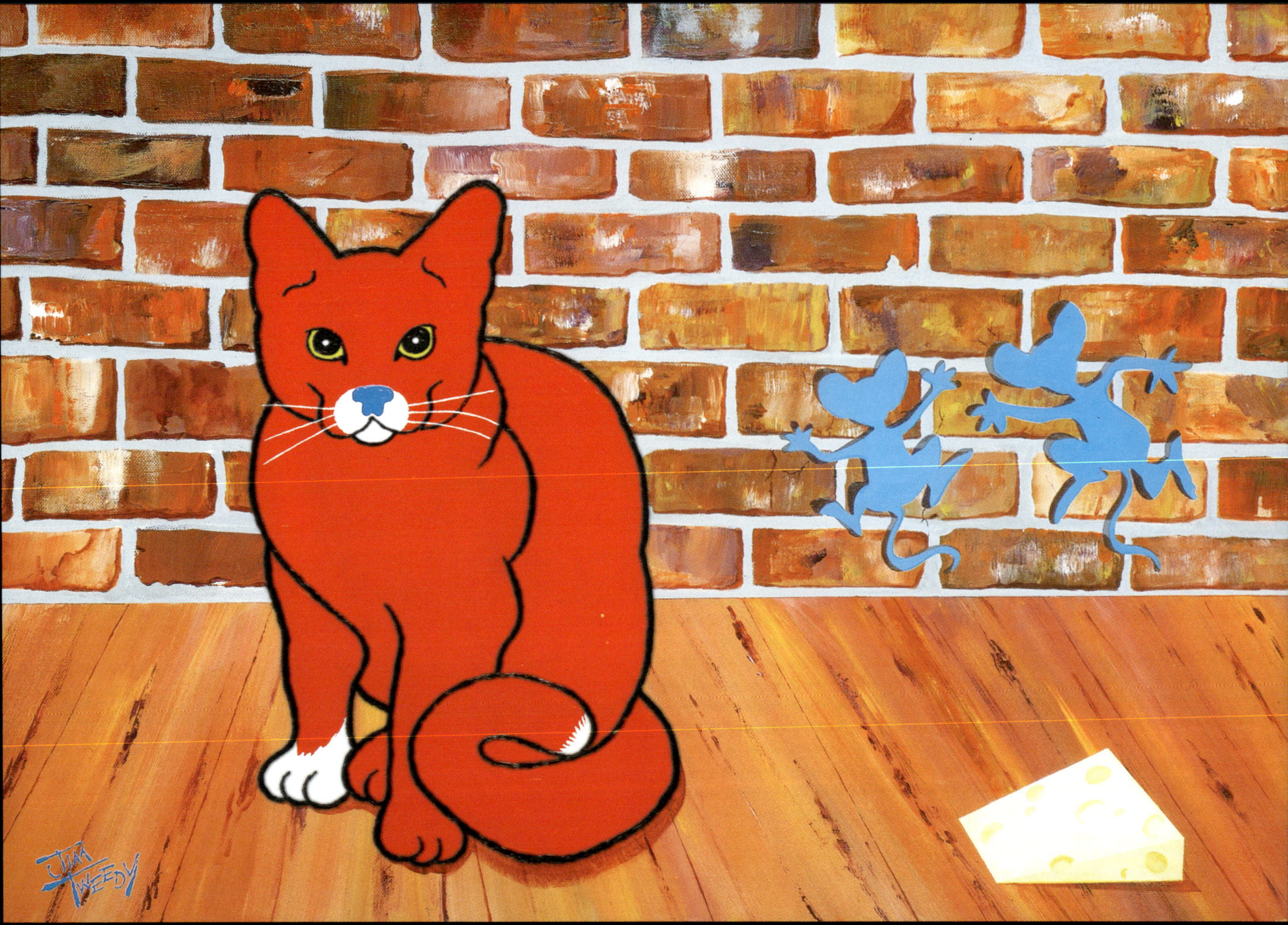

Charlie asked me about dinner guests as he raced through my dining room chasing some scaredy rats.

In moments of sheer panic a rat is capable of performing unimaginable feats of strength. Maybe it's best they got away.

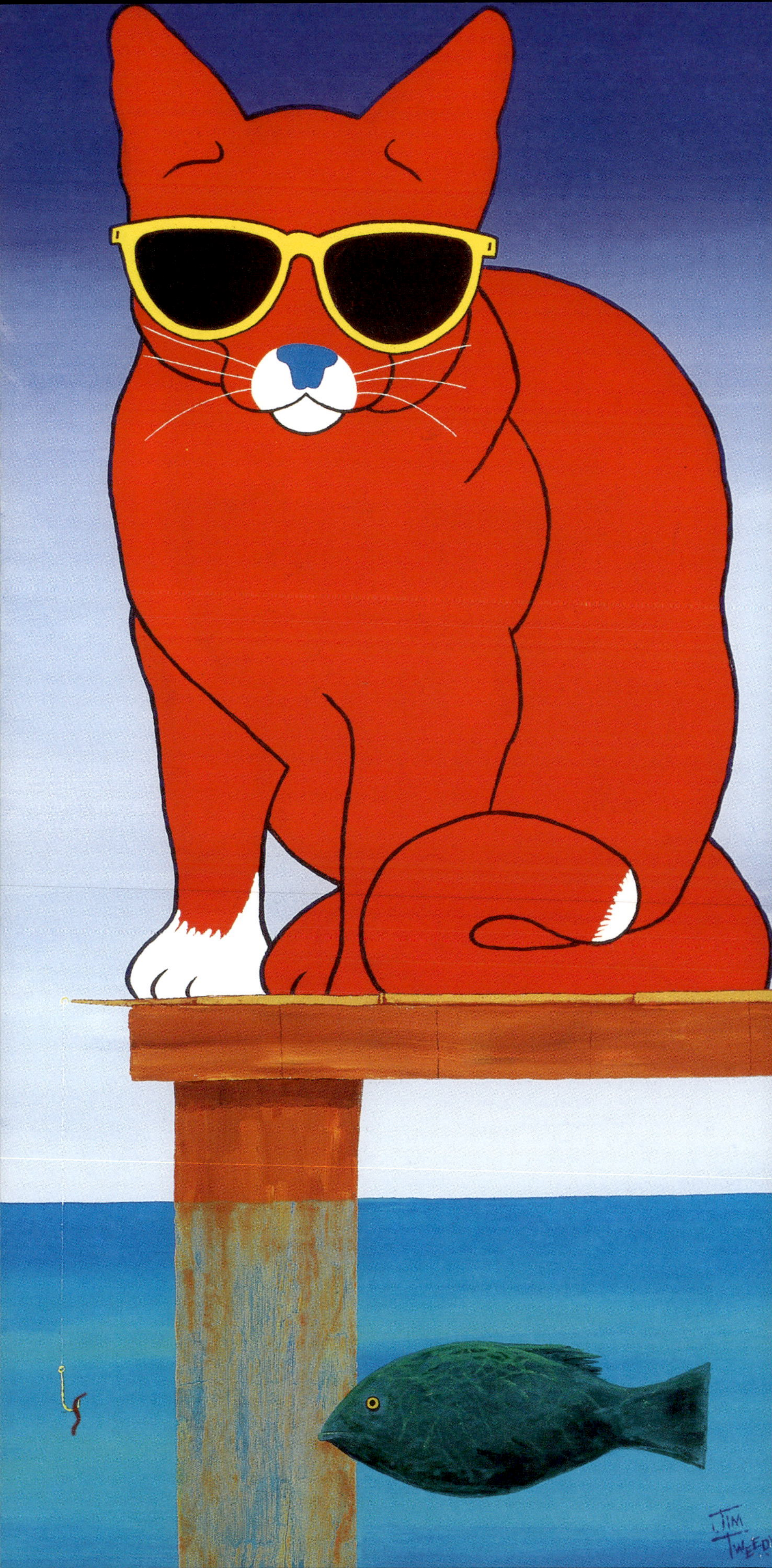

Up until that point I had considered serving catfish.

Charlie finally learned what it takes to put food on the table. It was a proud moment for both of us. The best part about Charlie's new knowledge is that now I don't have to run down to the pet shop quite as often.

Cat, Fish

Did you ever get the feeling …

Did you ever get the feeling you were being watched? Not Charlie—he's too relaxed. I've got a sneaky feeling it's about to get him into trouble.

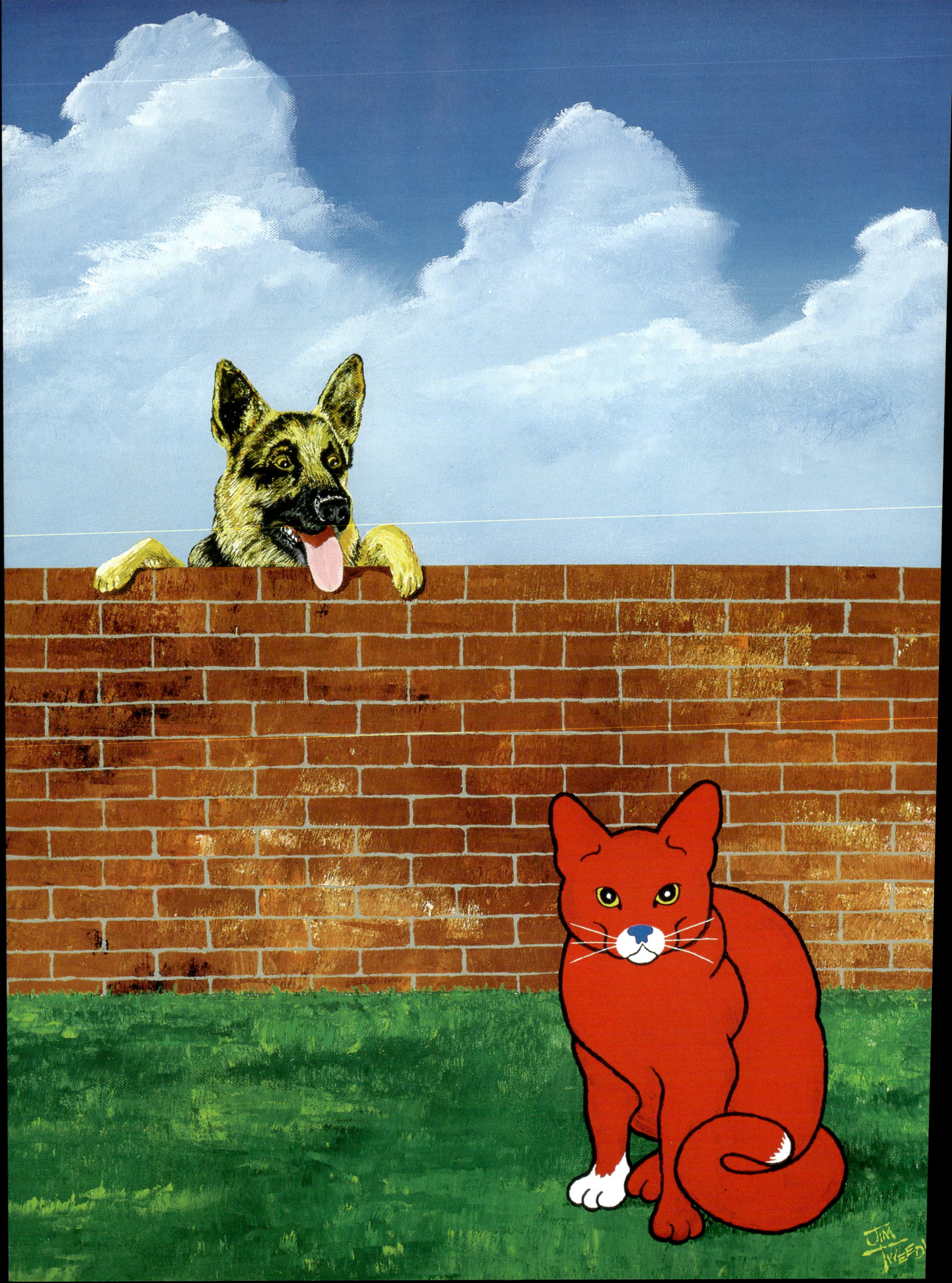

Did You Ever Get the Feeling …?

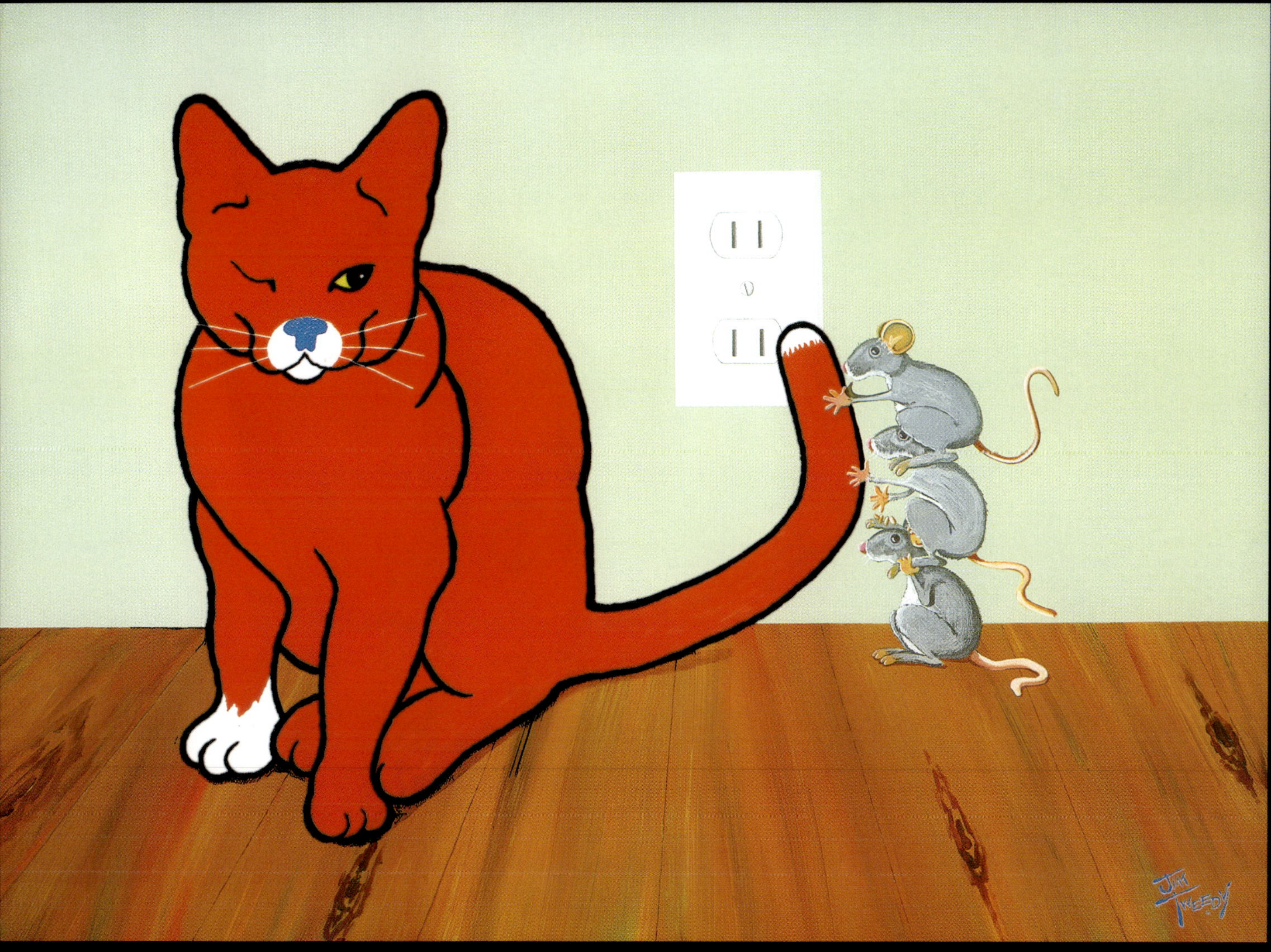

… you were in for a rude awakening?

Charlie's in for quite a shock if these rascals get their way. But the smart money is on the red guy.

Charlie went off for a cat nap ...

Charlie proves once nd for all that he's got a soft spot in his heart as well as between his ears.

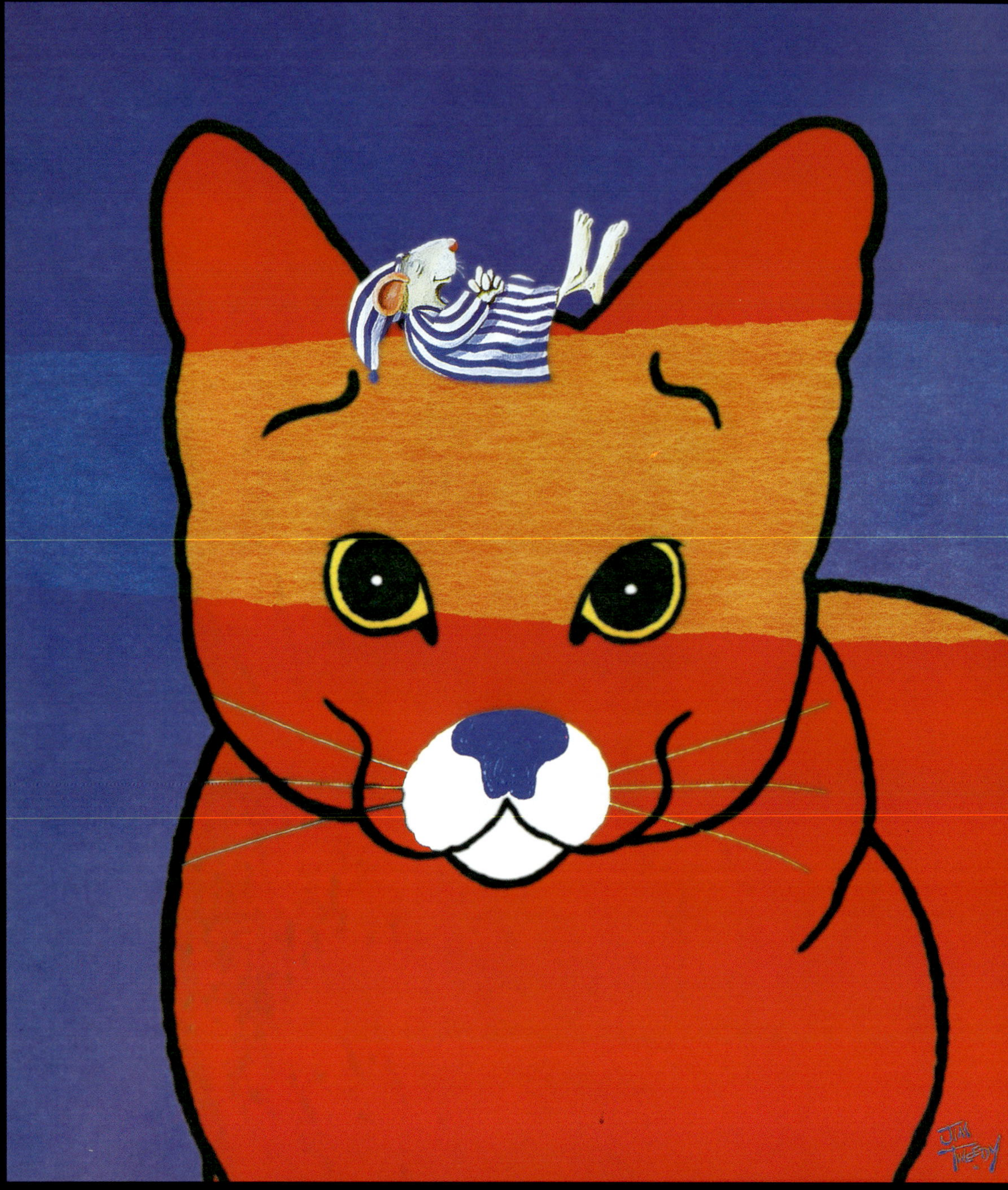

Cat Nap

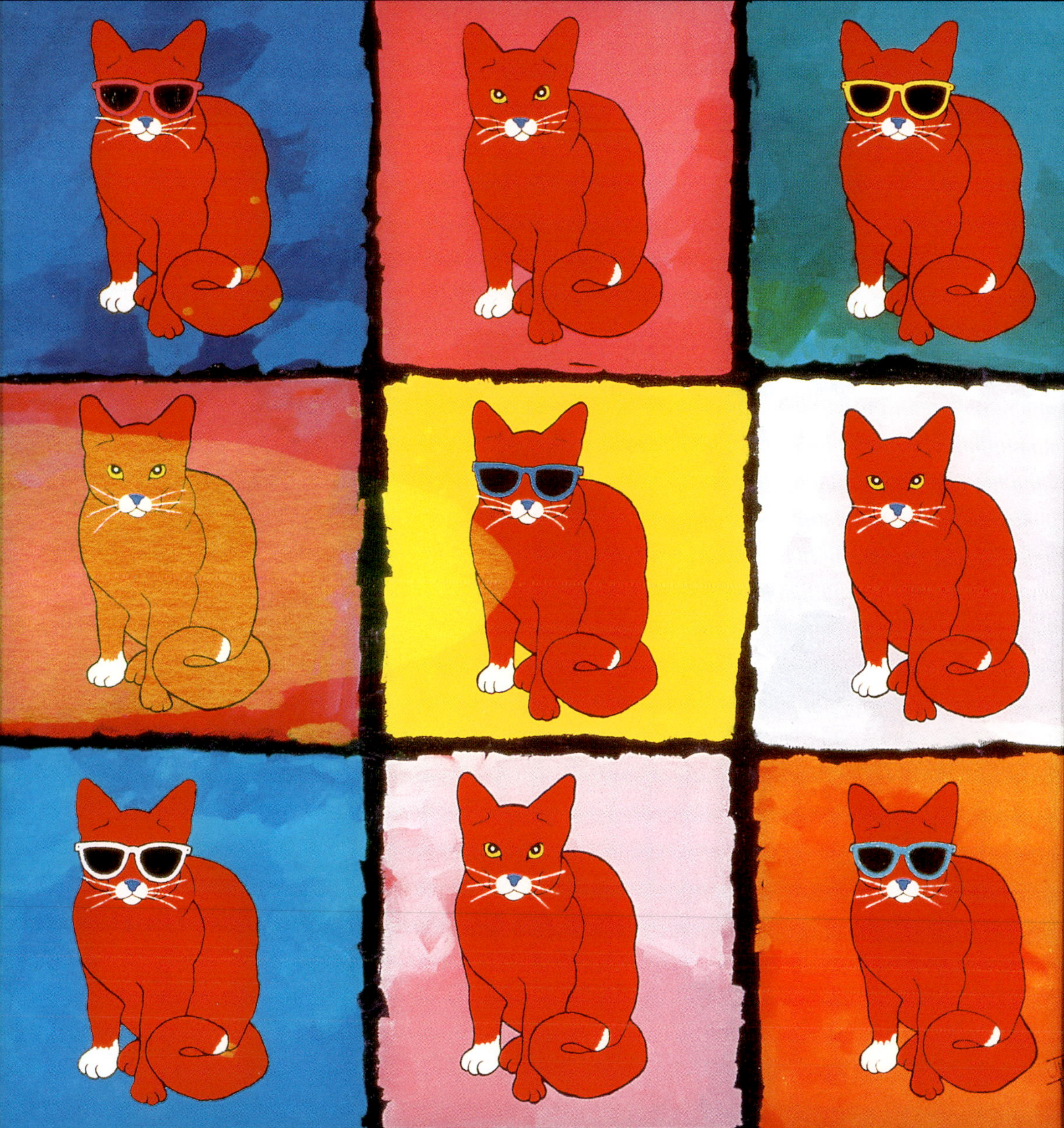

Nine Lives

... before gulping down his 9-Lives cat food.

This was the first large RedCat painting ever sold, and the first to contain multiple RedCats. I finished this piece thirty minutes before it was scheduled to appear in an art show near my studio. I was painting it on a flat table rather than on my easel, and I left it there to dry. Then I ran into the next room to get ready for the show. When I returned several minutes later I found Charlie footprints from one end to the other. "Nine Lives" didn't make the opening that night. I did manage to fix it in time for the next morning. Somebody bought it that afternoon.

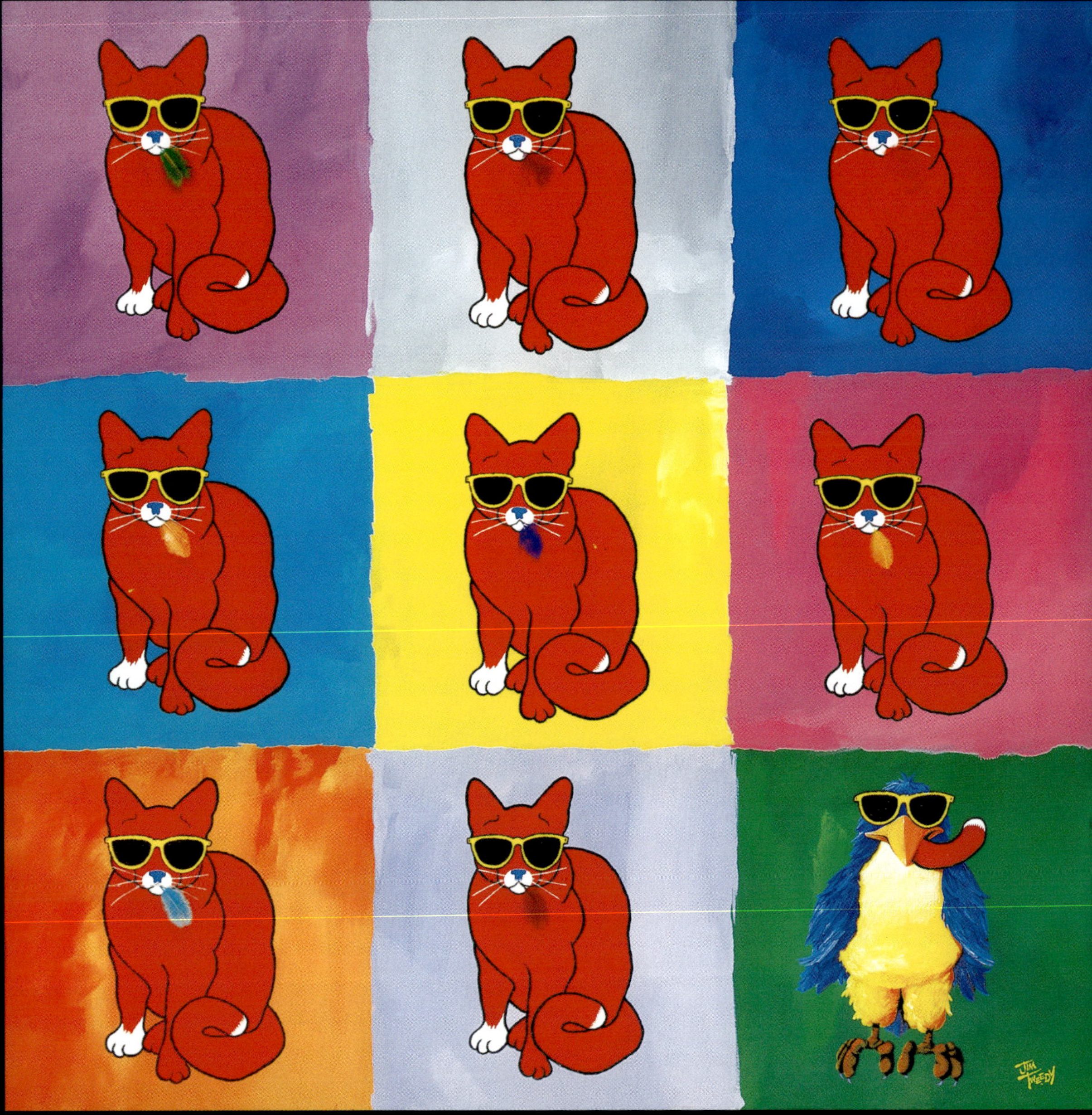

Well, after he ate lives . . .

Eight lives got ate. And then Charlie got ate. It's a good thing he's got nine lives. Well, now of course he's got eight.

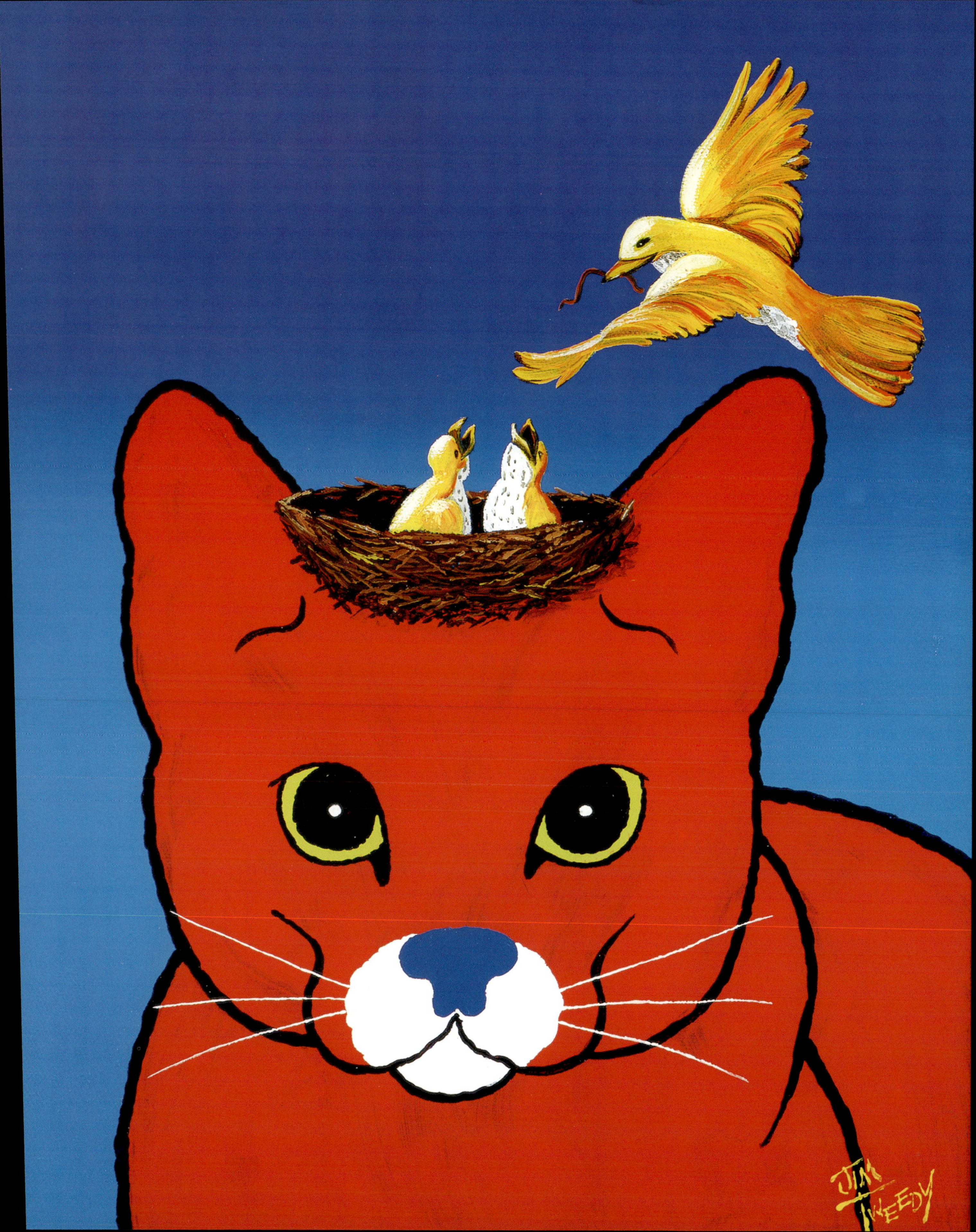

. . . a humiliating scene took place.

The real embarrassing thing about this is that until the eggs hatched Charlie thought it was just a really cool hat somebody had given him.

A Humiliating Scene

“Me-Ow!” Charlie hollered as he awoke.

Charlie the RedCat has had a slight mishap, which causes him to utter the only word he knows: “ME-OW!”

Me-Ow!

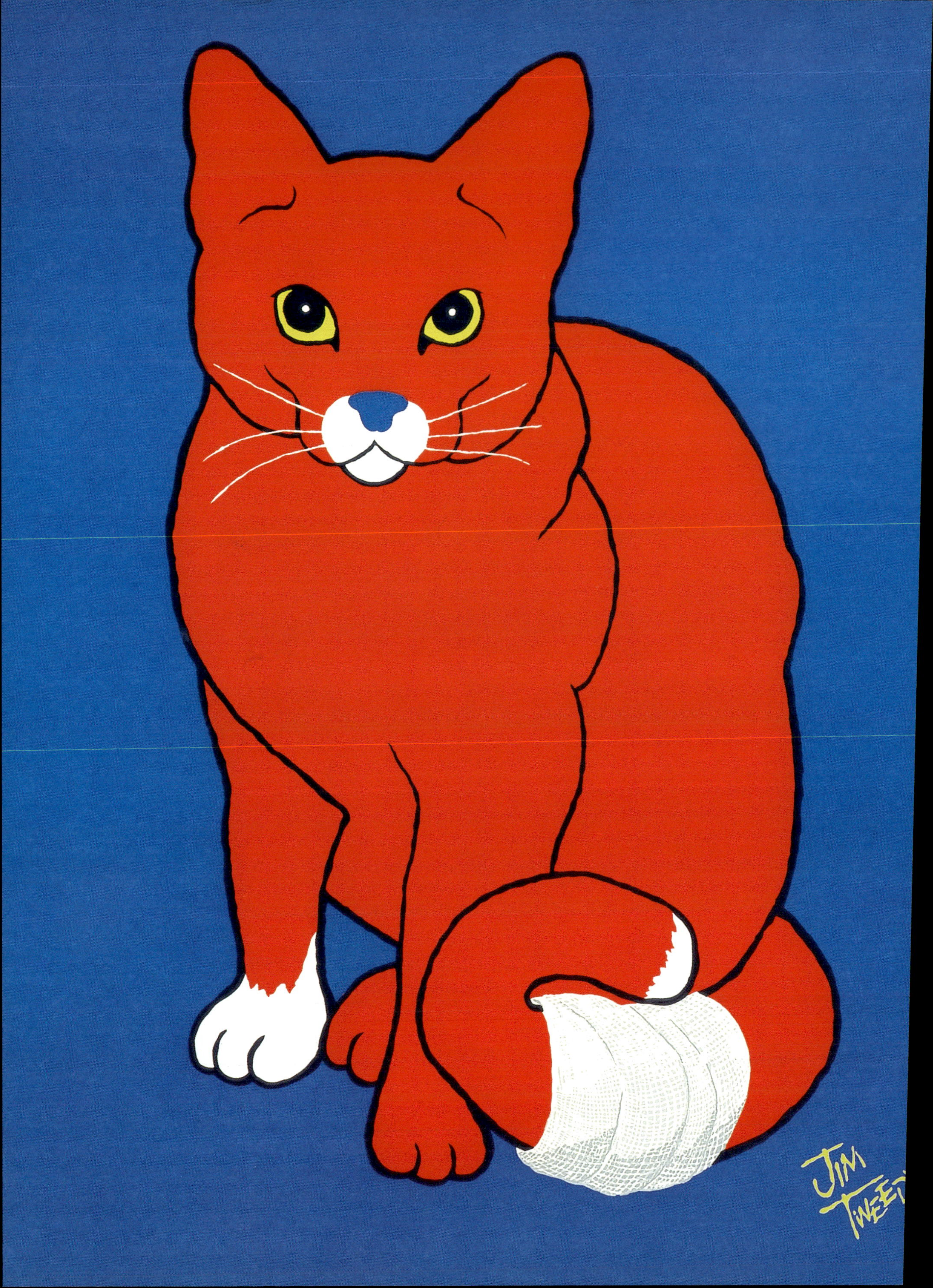

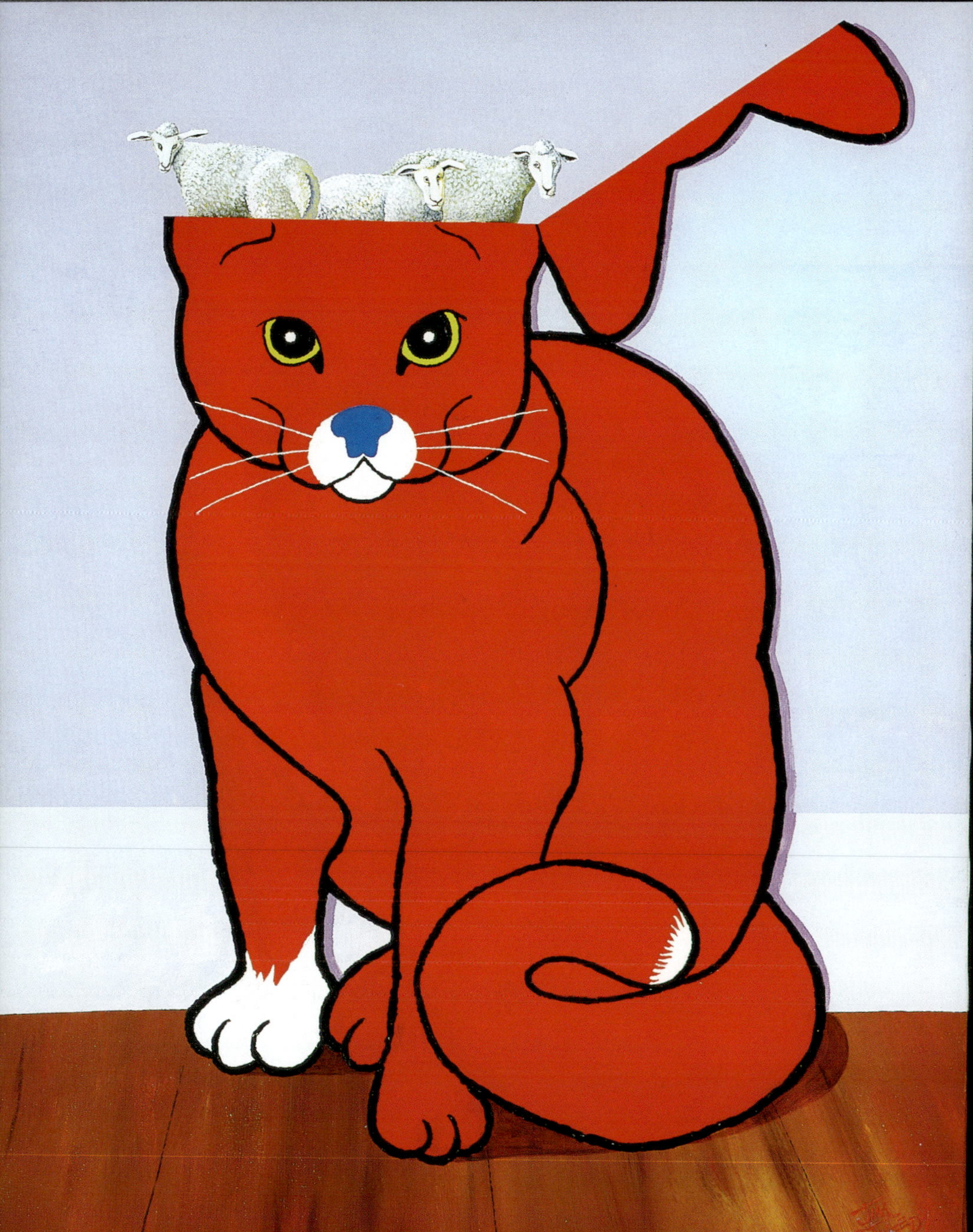

Charlie suddenly realized he had nothing but sheep for brains.

This is what's inside a cat's head. This is why they sleep so much.

Sheep for Brains

The Hareball

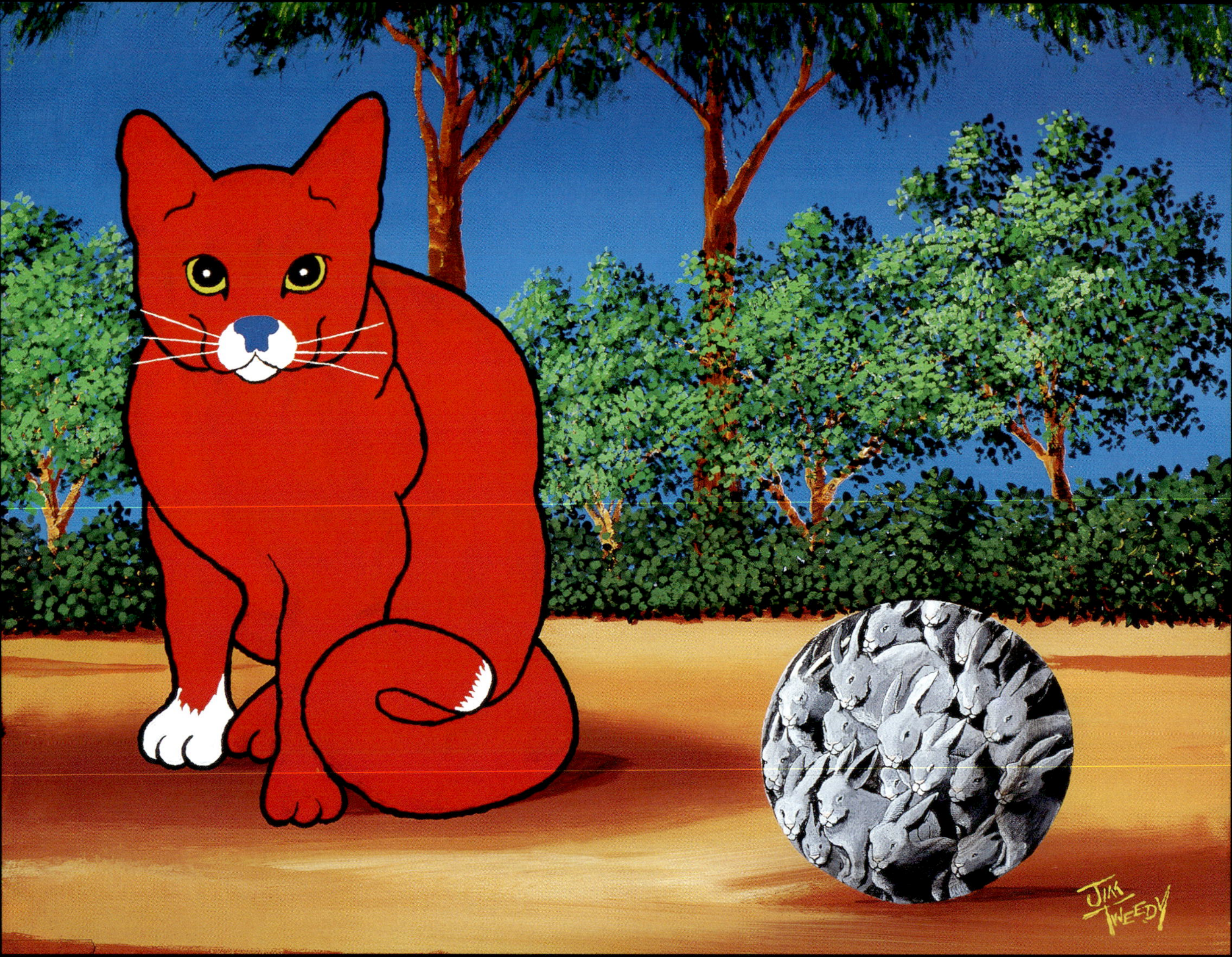

The hairball that ensued caused everyone to flee the scene.

This strange phenomenon occurs when rabbits feel threatened. The presence of a RedCat can trigger this effect. This time the attacking bunnies missed their mark, and Charlie countered with a hairball of his own.

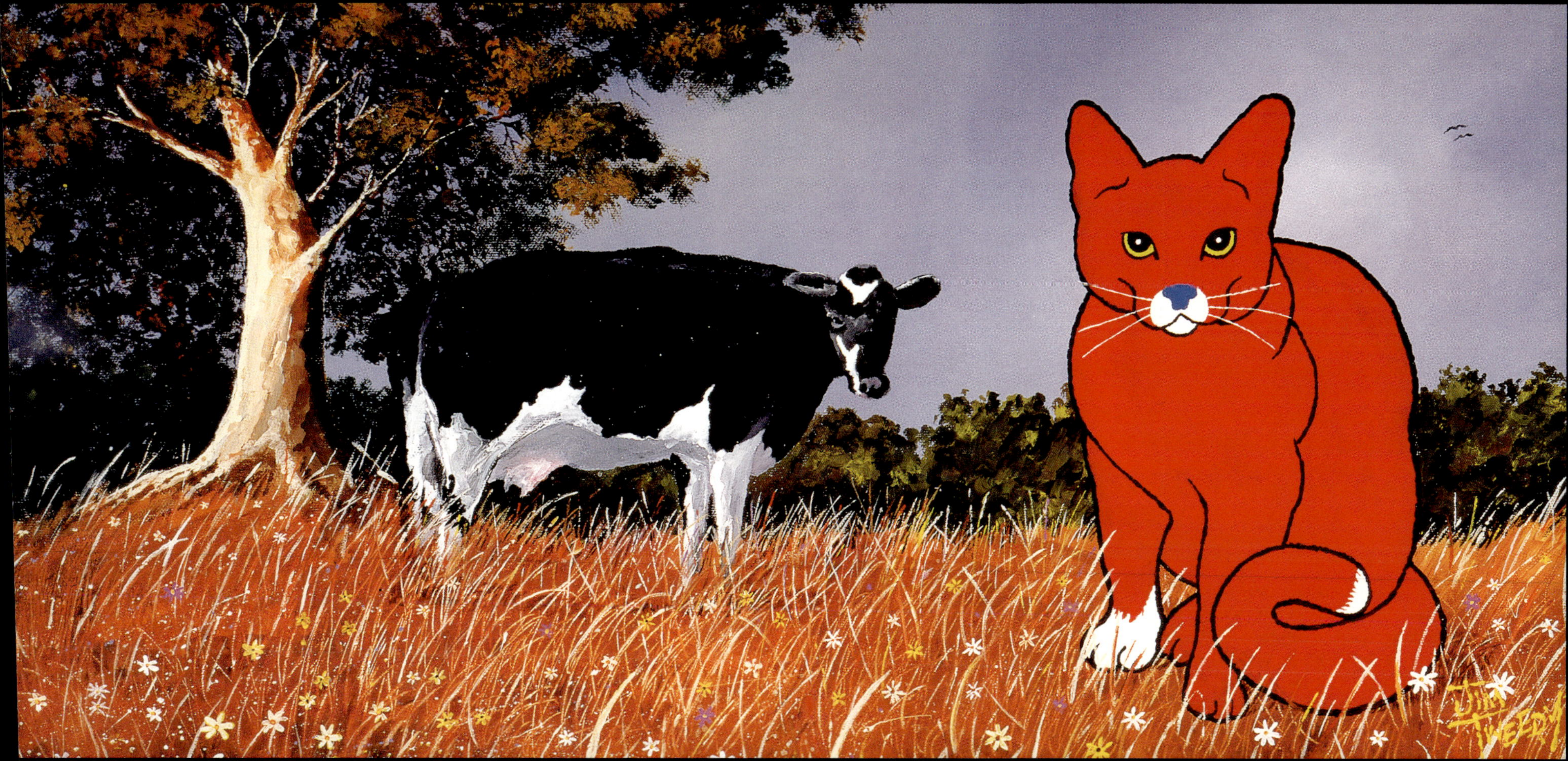

It's a good thing I love milk because it's all Charlie has touched for months now.

Charlie can spend hours on end admiring the milk cow. The shape of her ears. The sound of her moo. And four stomachs! Wow! Most important of all, of course, is the milk. He can't seem to live without it. Milk drives him udderly wild.

With Charlie it's always a one-of-a-kind day.

"Gather two of every animal," Noah was told. But Charlie the RedCat is definitely one of a kind. Our feline friend has a firm grip on the olive branch and his place in history as Mr. Dove beats a hasty retreat. Never send a bird to do a cat's job.

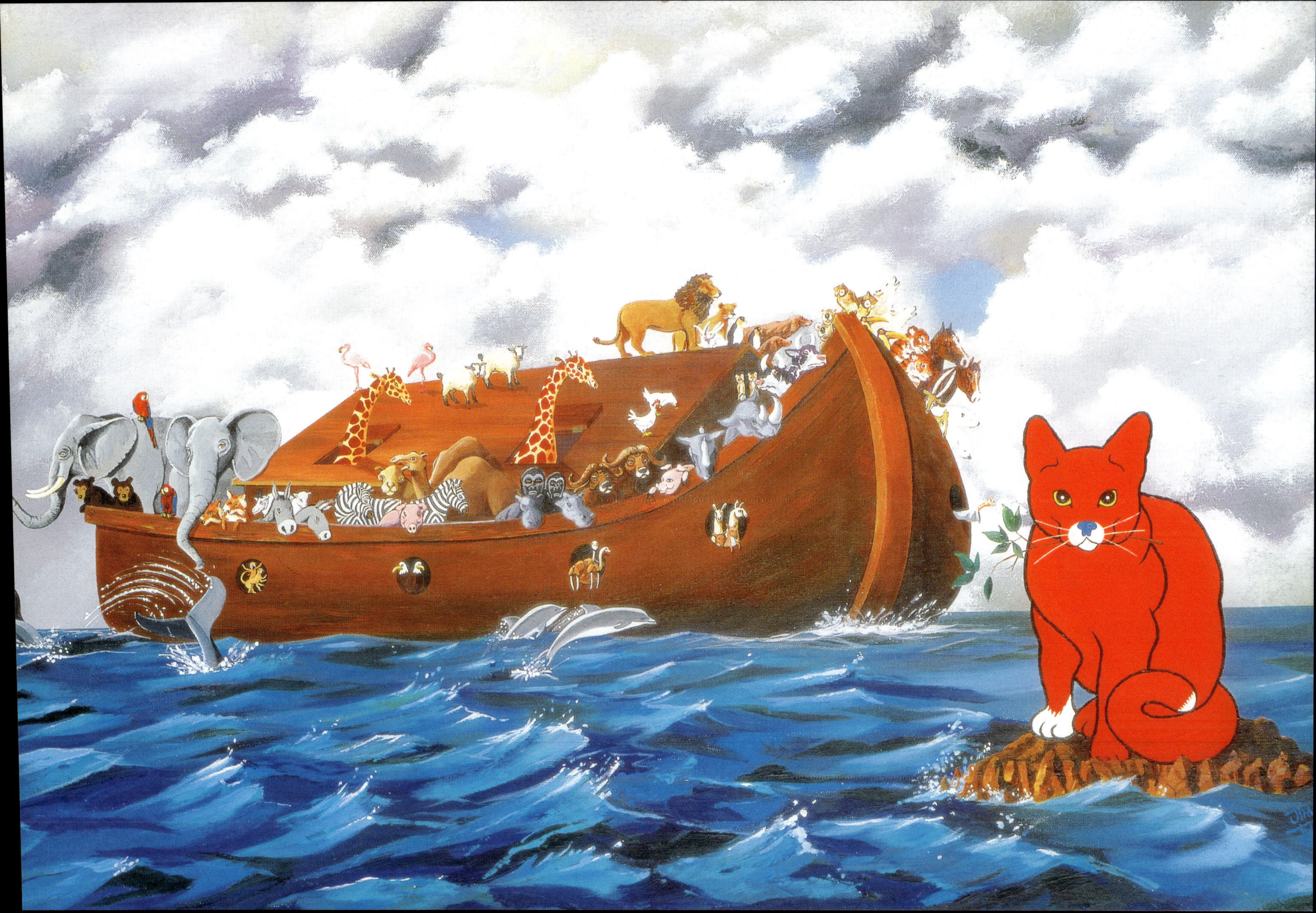

One of a Kind

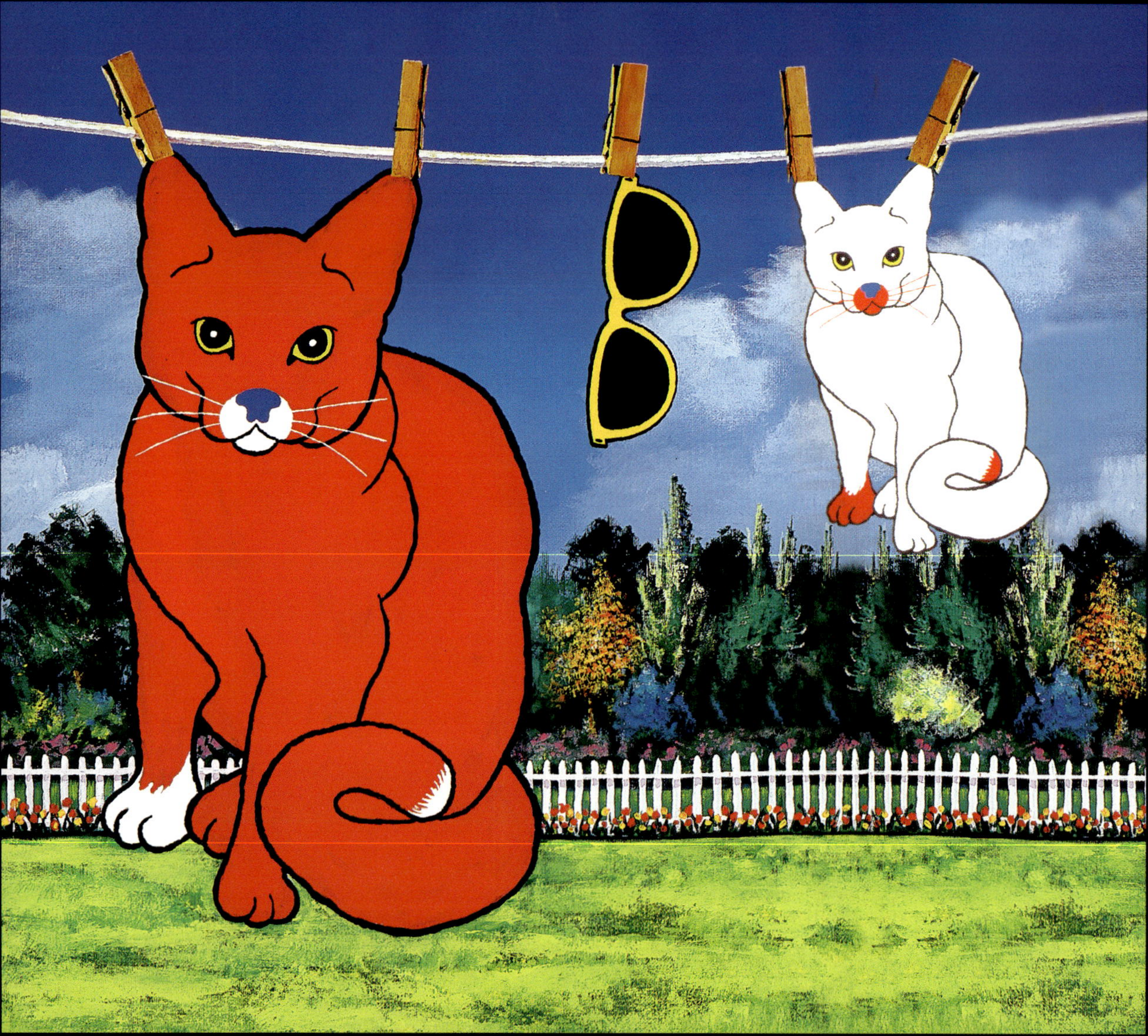

Charlie's son, Chip, was hanging out with Charlie.

Cats hate baths. They hate it worse when it's over.

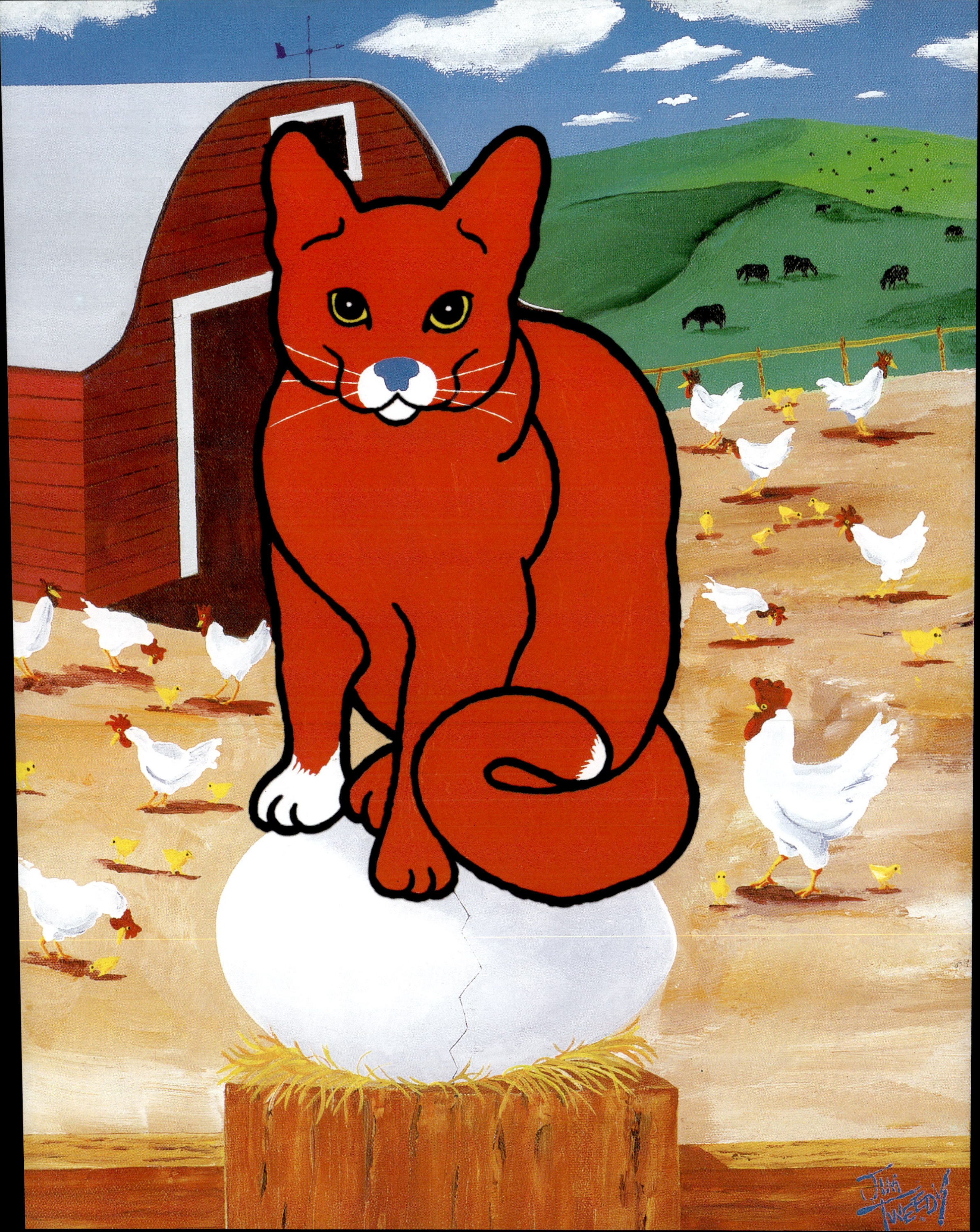

Together they were pondering the question of which came first, the Charlie or the egg.

This is a question scholars have debated for centuries. I'd have to say the egg showed up first because Charlie follows food and just loves omelets.

Which Came First, the Charlie or the Egg?

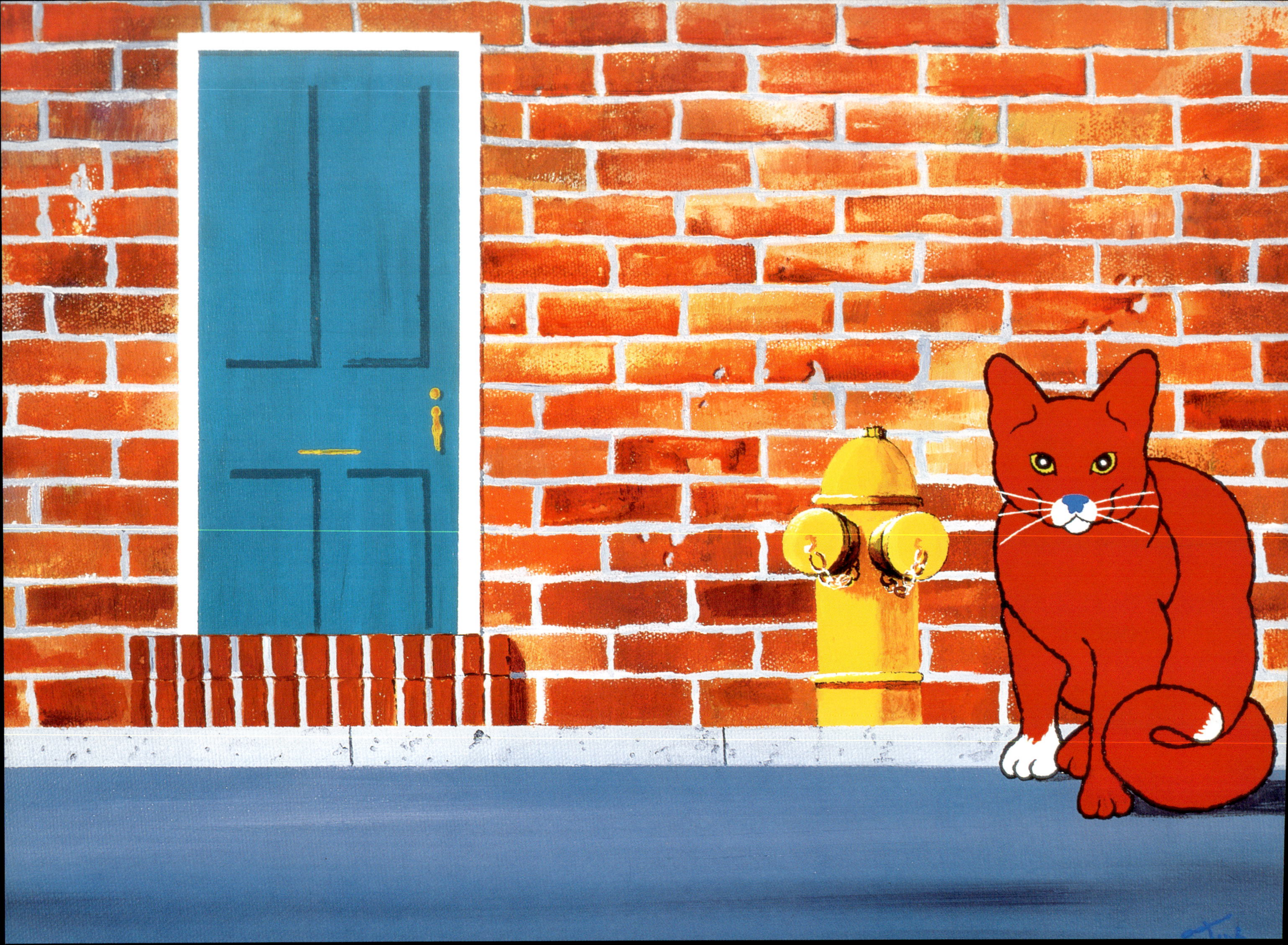

A Moment of Confusion

There was a moment of confusion ...

Charlie's wondering what you do with these things. Supposedly they have another use besides squirting water, and cats don't like being squirted with water anyway. After pondering the situation for some time, Charlie had to leave to go find a bathroom.

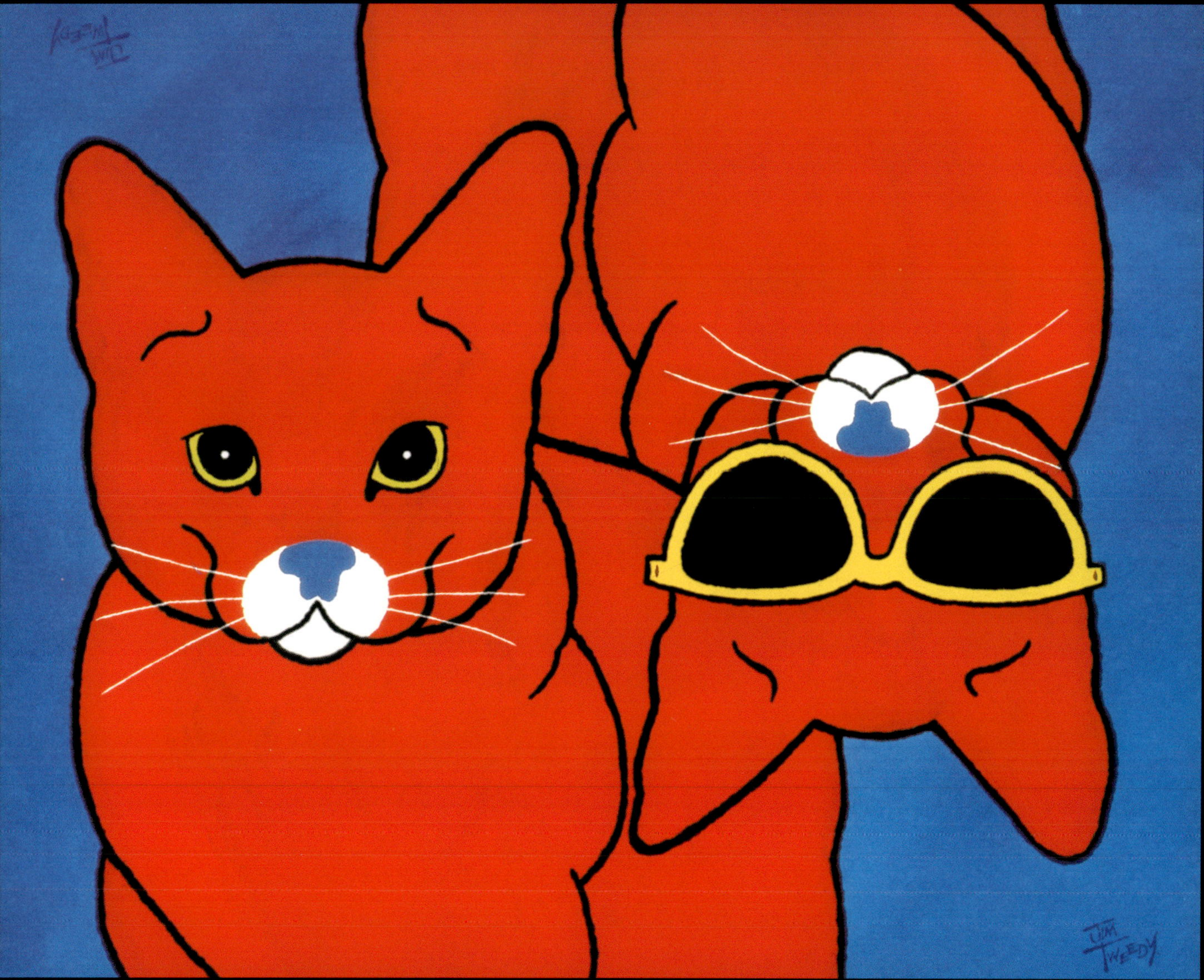

... when everything seemed to be wrong-side down.

This painting was designed to hang correctly in a home in Australia as well as it does in the United States.

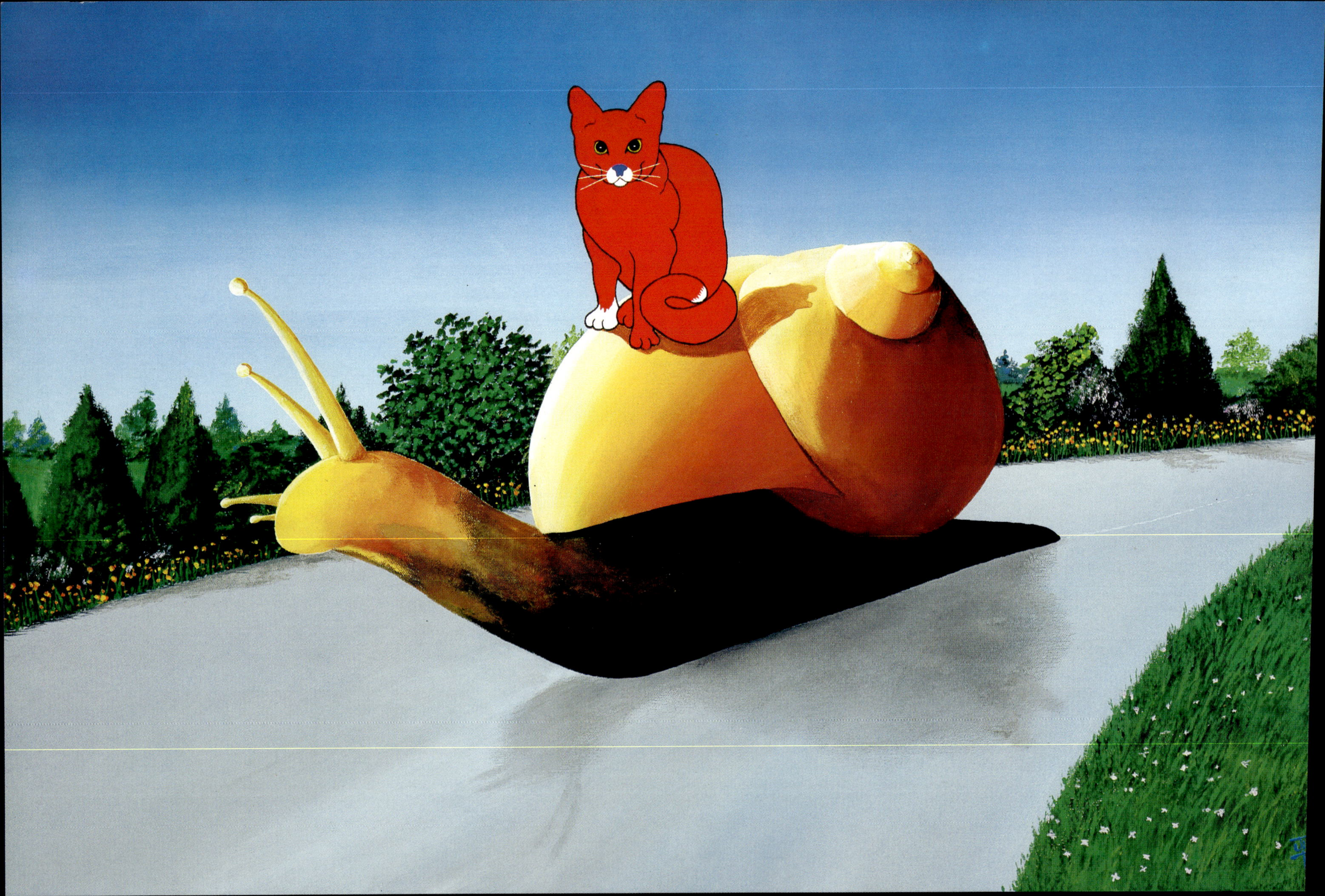

The Traveling Snailsman

Along came a traveling snailsman ...

You should see the size of the garden that this guy lives in.

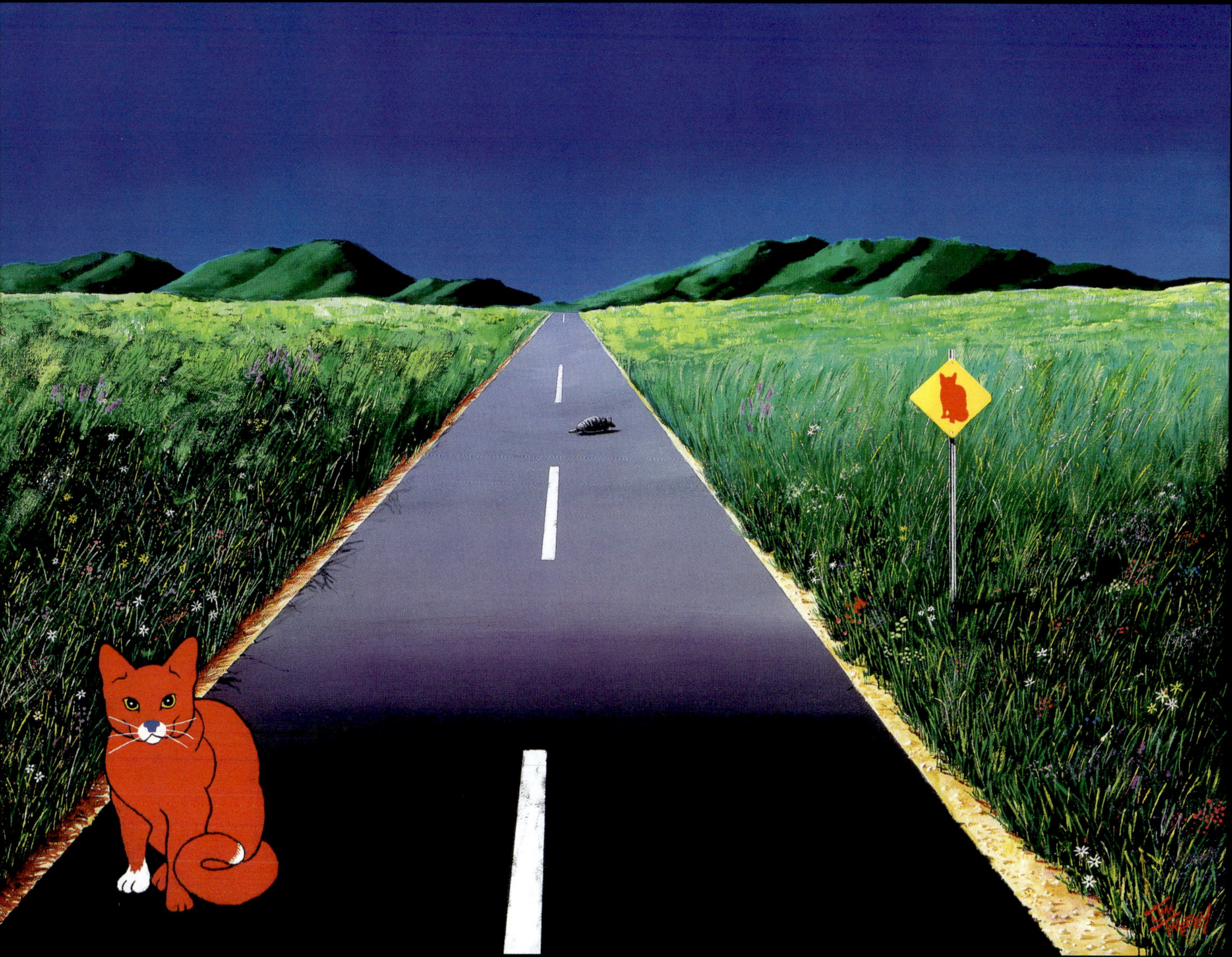

… who said he was looking for a RedCat crossing.

I spotted this sign on an old Texas back road. It was placed there by a psychic.

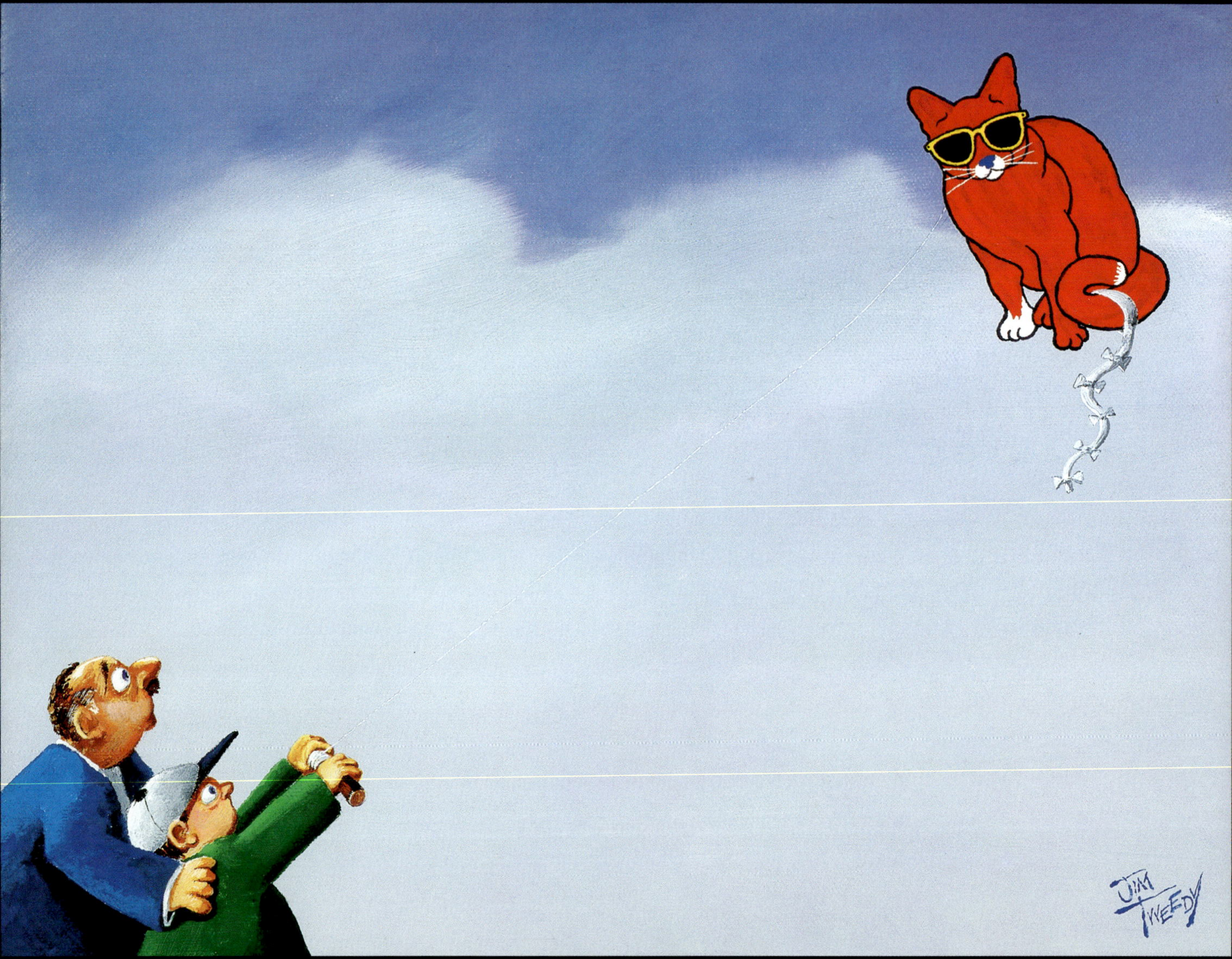

It's no doubt that two tails are better than one.

Although I silhouetted some musicians in the 1992 Baton Rouge Blues Festival poster, this was really the first time I used people in a RedCat painting. It only took me six years to do it. There just never did seem to be a situation that called for them.

However, I'll never forget this nice man who was with his son after work one day. The boy's kite became stuck in a tree. It was a good thing Charlie and I happened along.

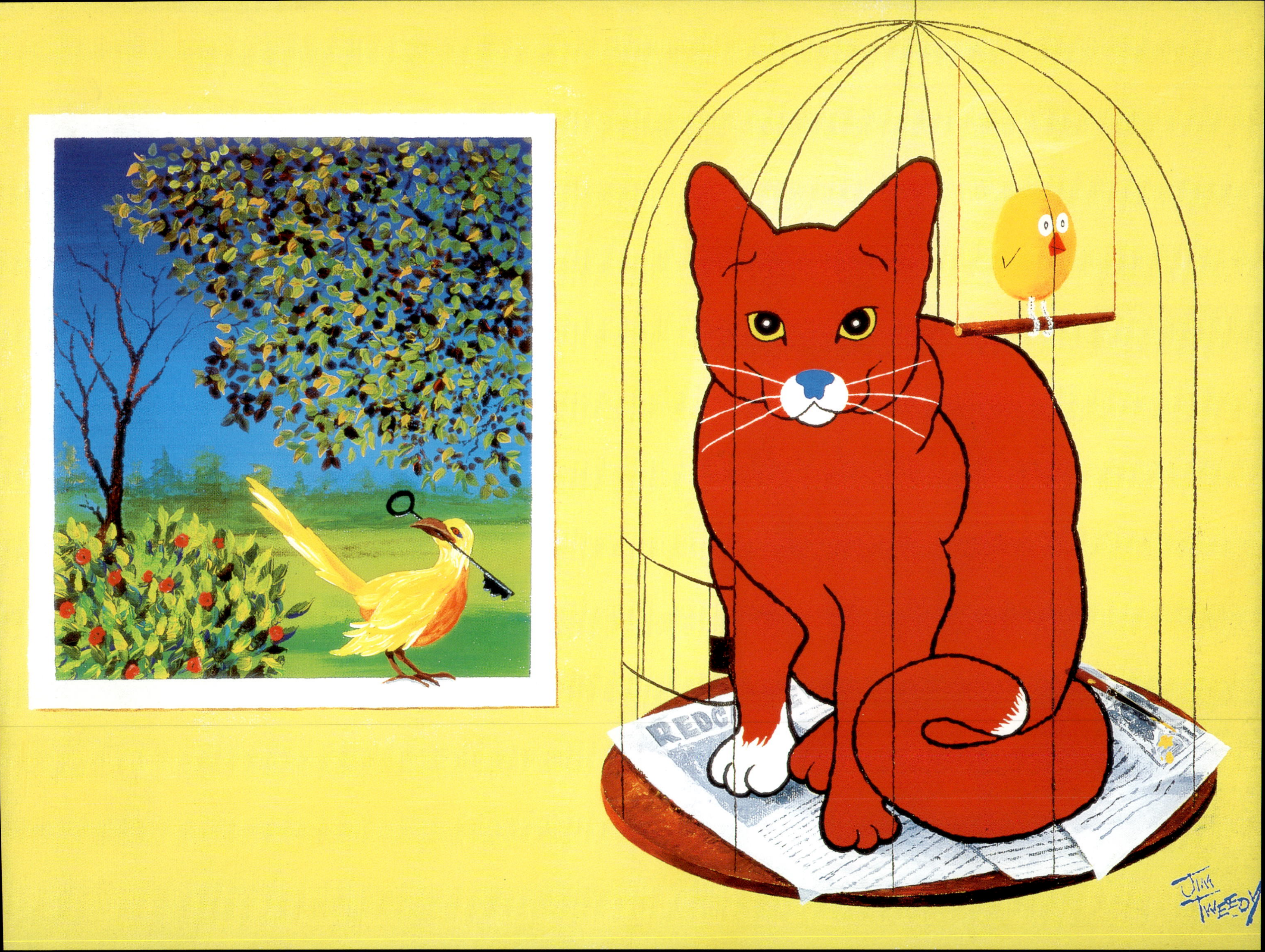

The Ole Bait 'n' Switch

But, one tail became a tale of woe when a bird pulled the ole bait 'n' switch on Charlie.

The neighborhood's bird lived in terror until he devised a brilliant plan. Being nimble with pipe cleaners didn't hurt either.

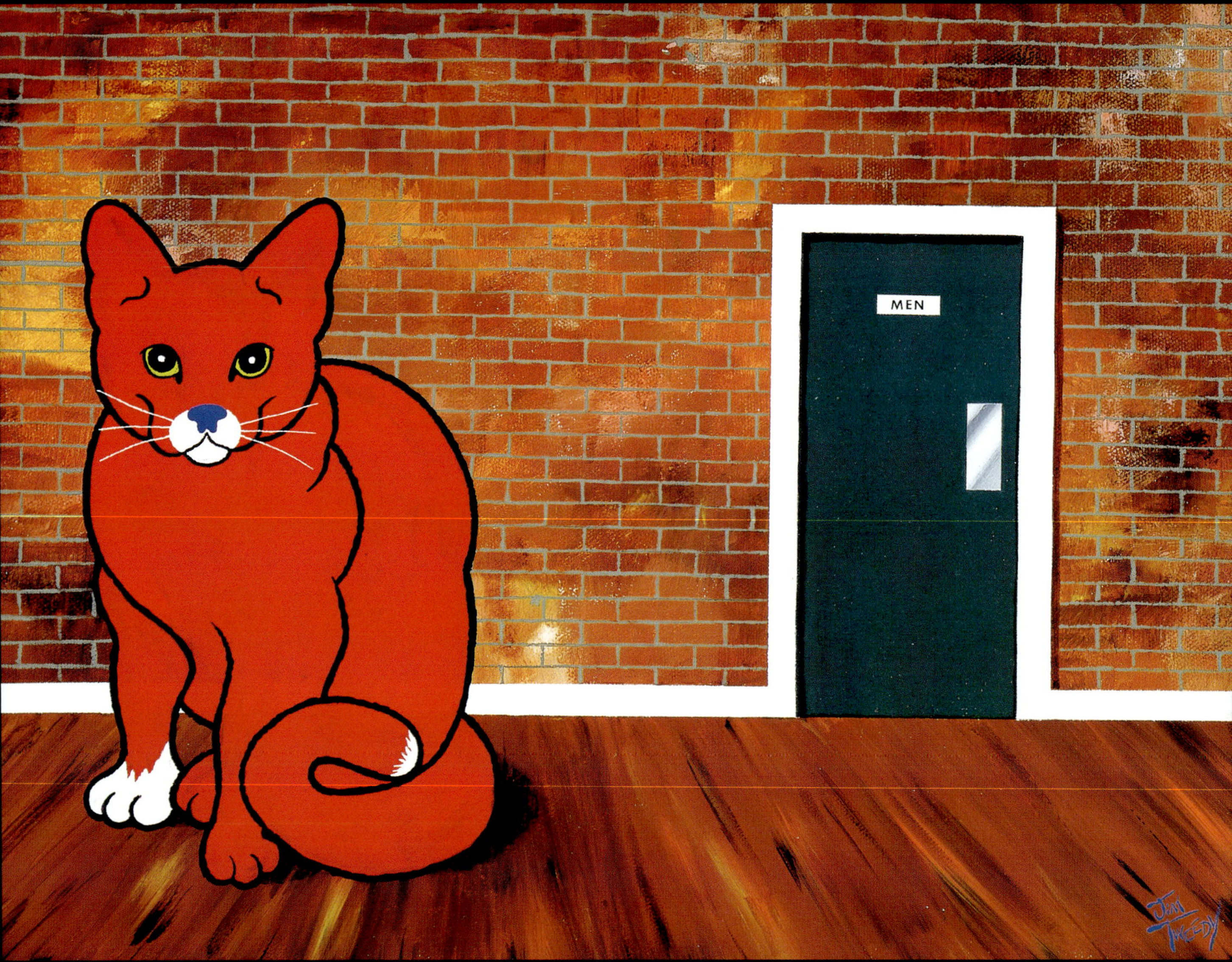

"Take me to your litter," Charlie demanded.

Human bathrooms are intimidating because cats are afraid of water.

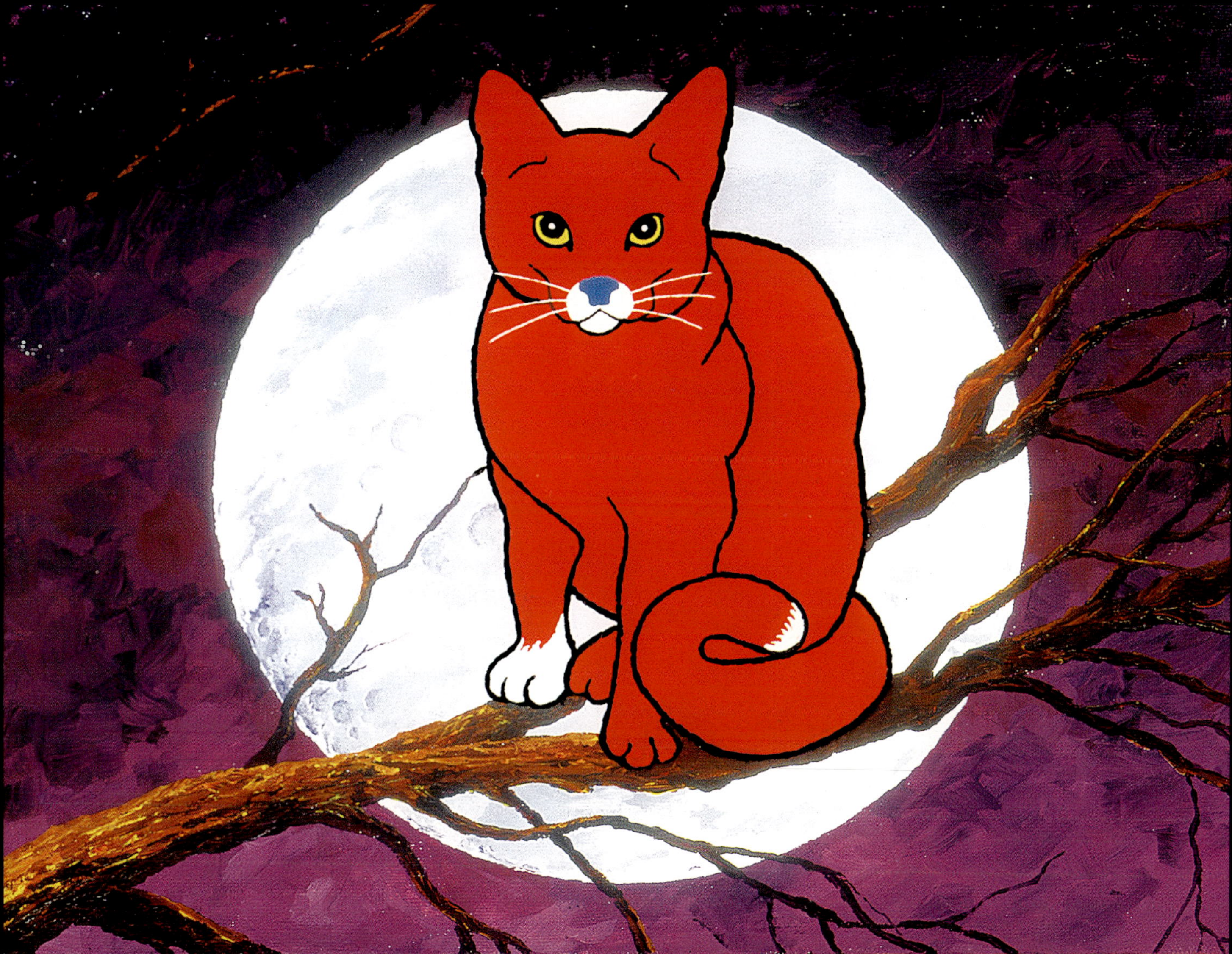

From that moment on, Charlie went out on a limb when searching for his midnight snack.

Like a lot of cats, Charlie loves climbing trees. Like a lot of cats, he gets stuck. But, with the full moon out on this night, I told him to hold still for just a few hours. By dawn, "out on a limb" was a reality.

"When RedCats fly those birds won't stand a chance," cried Charlie.

Oh, sure it's rare for a pig to fly, but just imagine how rare it is for something like this to occur.

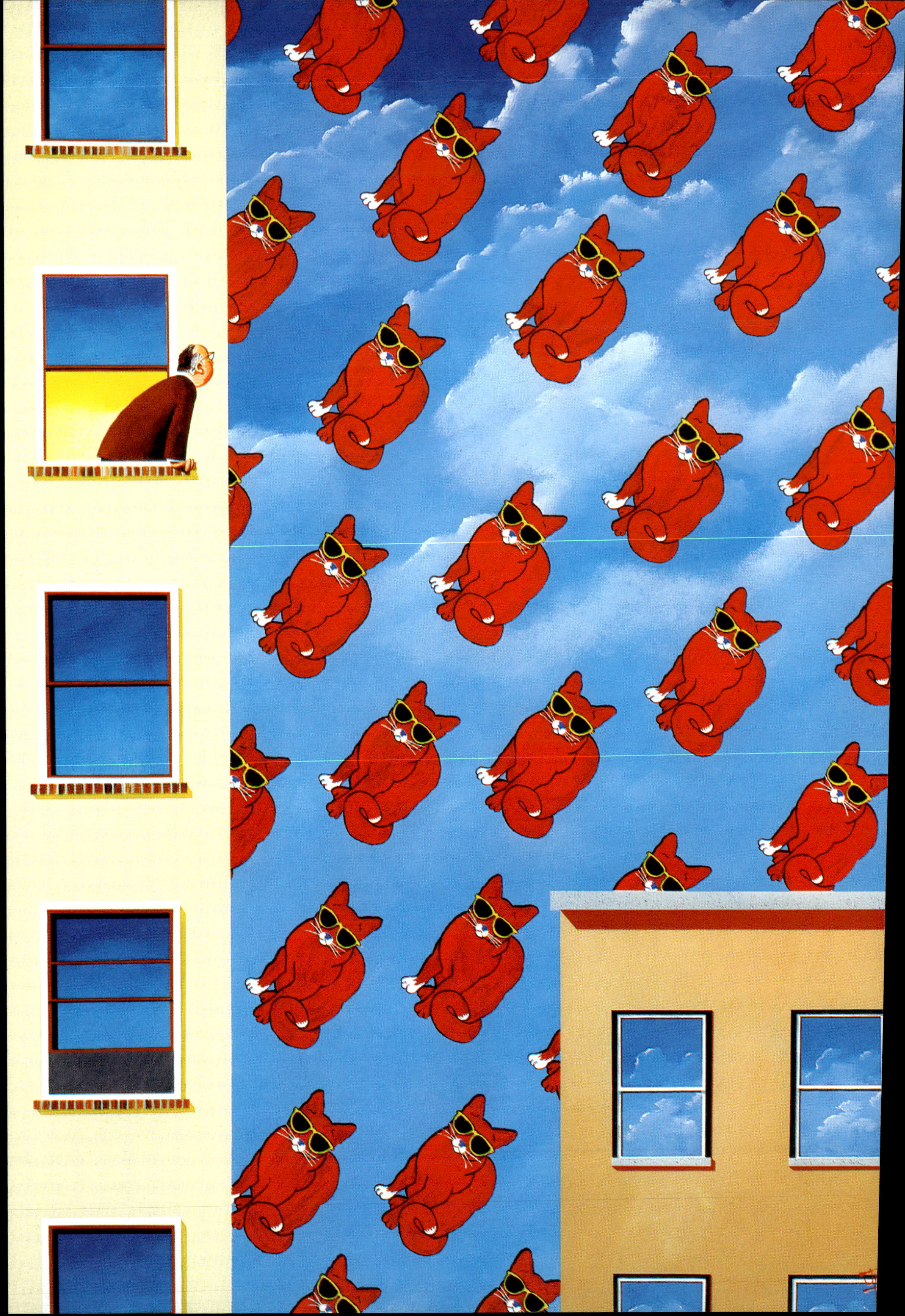

When RedCats Fly

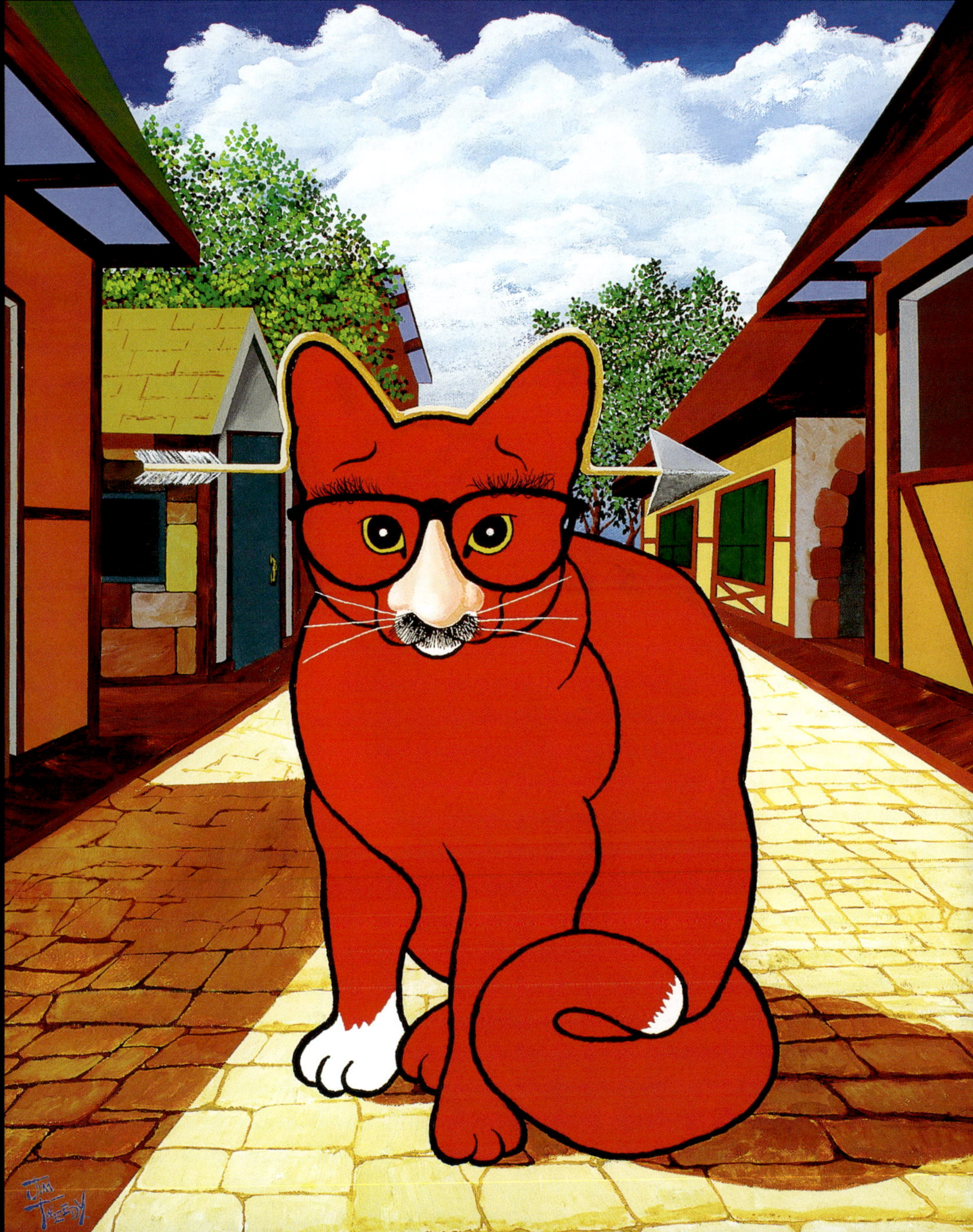

It Takes a Village Idiot

But it takes a village idiot to put one over on Charlie the RedCat.

Charlie's found a job for which he's highly qualified. On a recent European tour Charlie and I decided to stay over and sample a bit of the local culture. Turns out all Bavarian villages employ a local village idiot to scare away giant rodents. It is the most important position one can hold. Charlie begged me to let him audition for the post. I agreed, and this get-up landed him the job. Unfortunately Charlie is petrified of giant rodents, and as soon as one showed up he fled the scene and left me to face a village full of angry citizens and giant rodents.

“The tables are turned,” Charlie meowed as he treed an offending doggie.

Charlie is a defender of the underdog. In this case it is the undercat. After a number of sleepless nights spent in this tree, this little fellow did the only sensible thing he could do. He called Charlie the RedCat. Now the little guy can sleep at night in the comfort of his own box.

As for the pooch, well, he's learned his lesson and soon he'll be branching out into other, safer dog activities such as chasing cars.

The Tables Are Turned

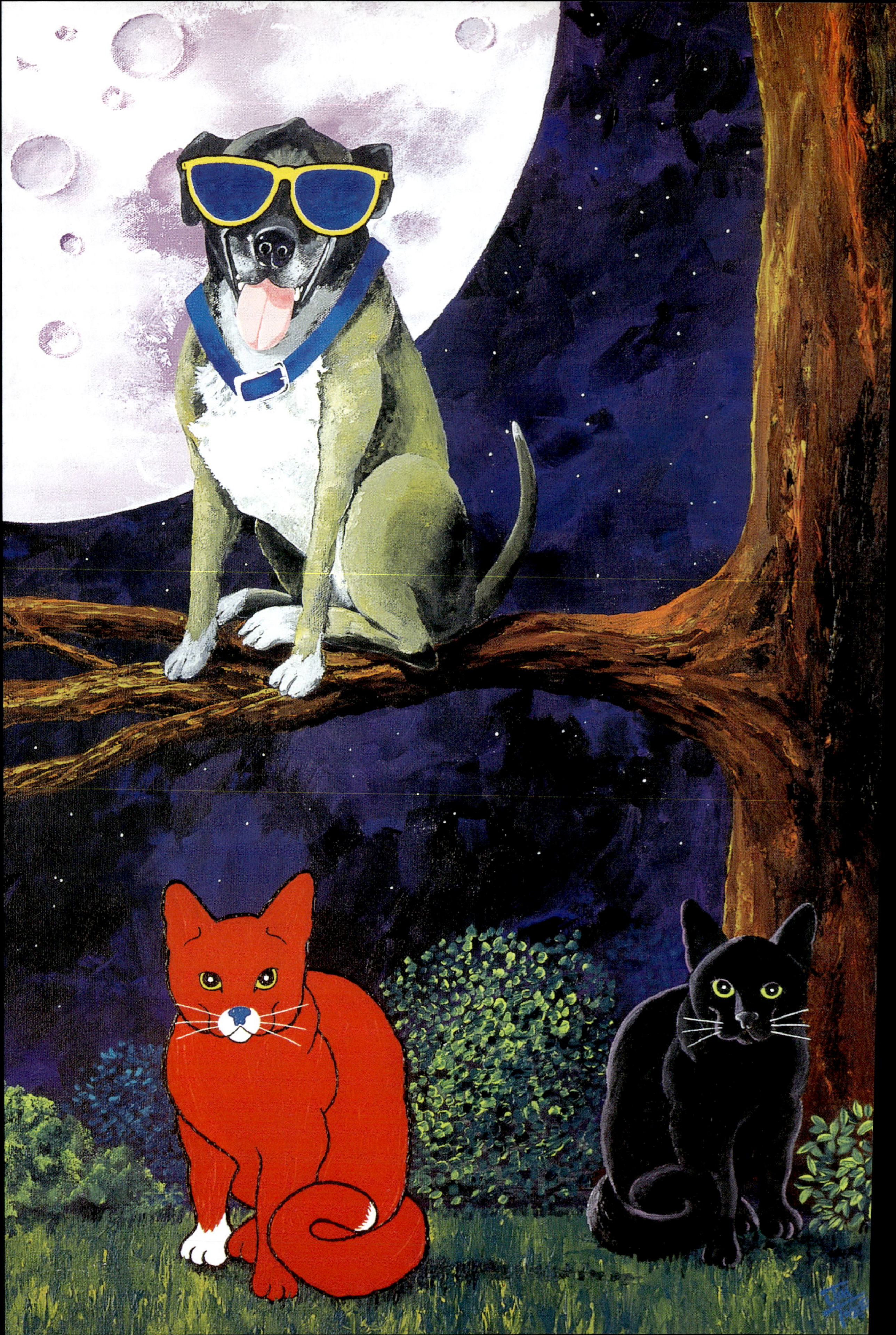

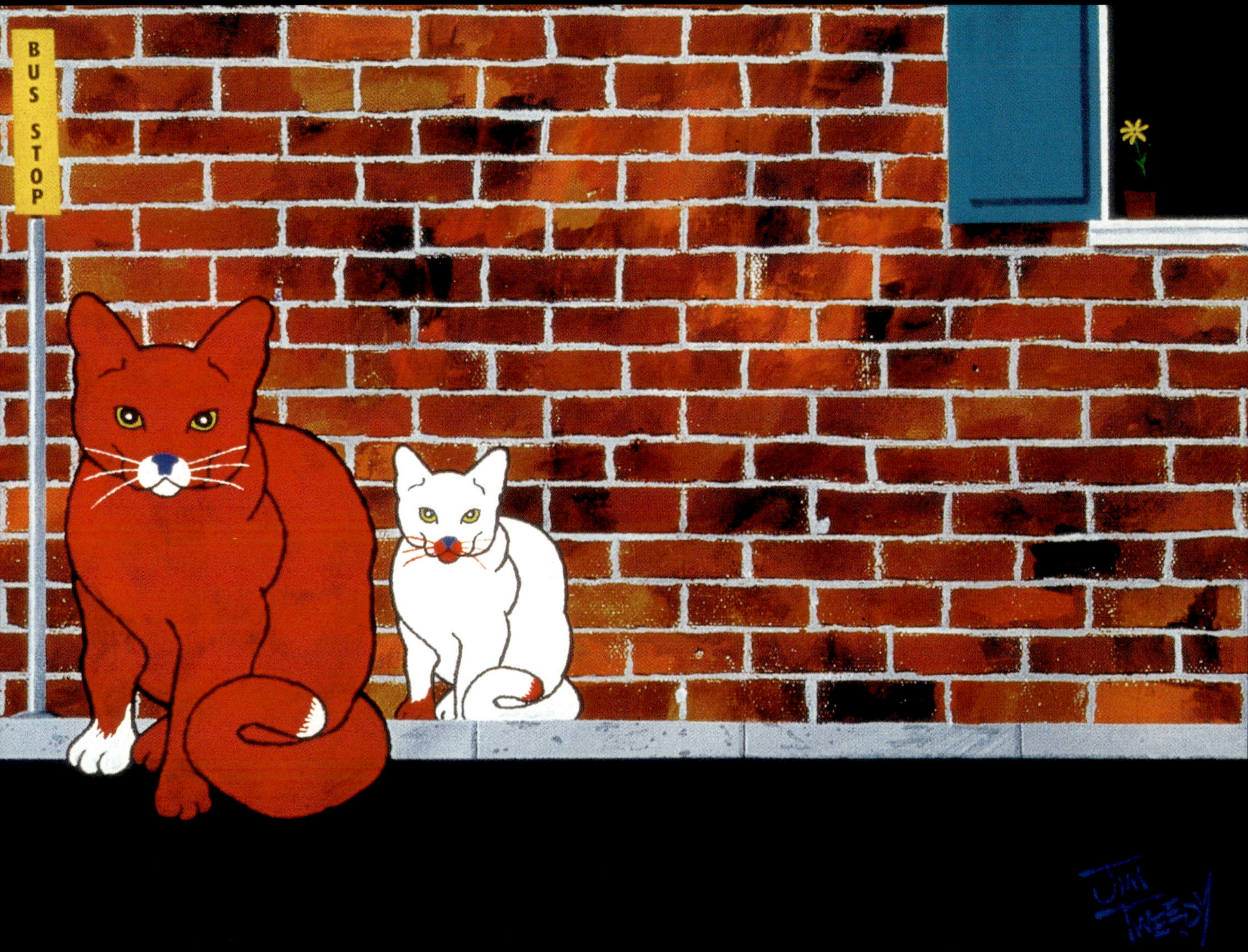

"And the bus stops here!"

Charlie's son, Chip, is making a rare appearance. He and the old man are off to do a little shopping. First, a visit to the docks to greet the fishing boats. Next it's on to a discount catnip store, and on the way home the Dumpster in the alley behind the butcher shop always has much to offer.

Through it all public transportation offers the most efficient way around town. Besides, I won't let him eat in my car.

"It's a beautiful day," said a passing eagle. "Let's go fly a cat."

Well, apparently all those birds Charlie has been messing around with couldn't take a joke, so they called in the heavy artillery. Charlie is not amused.

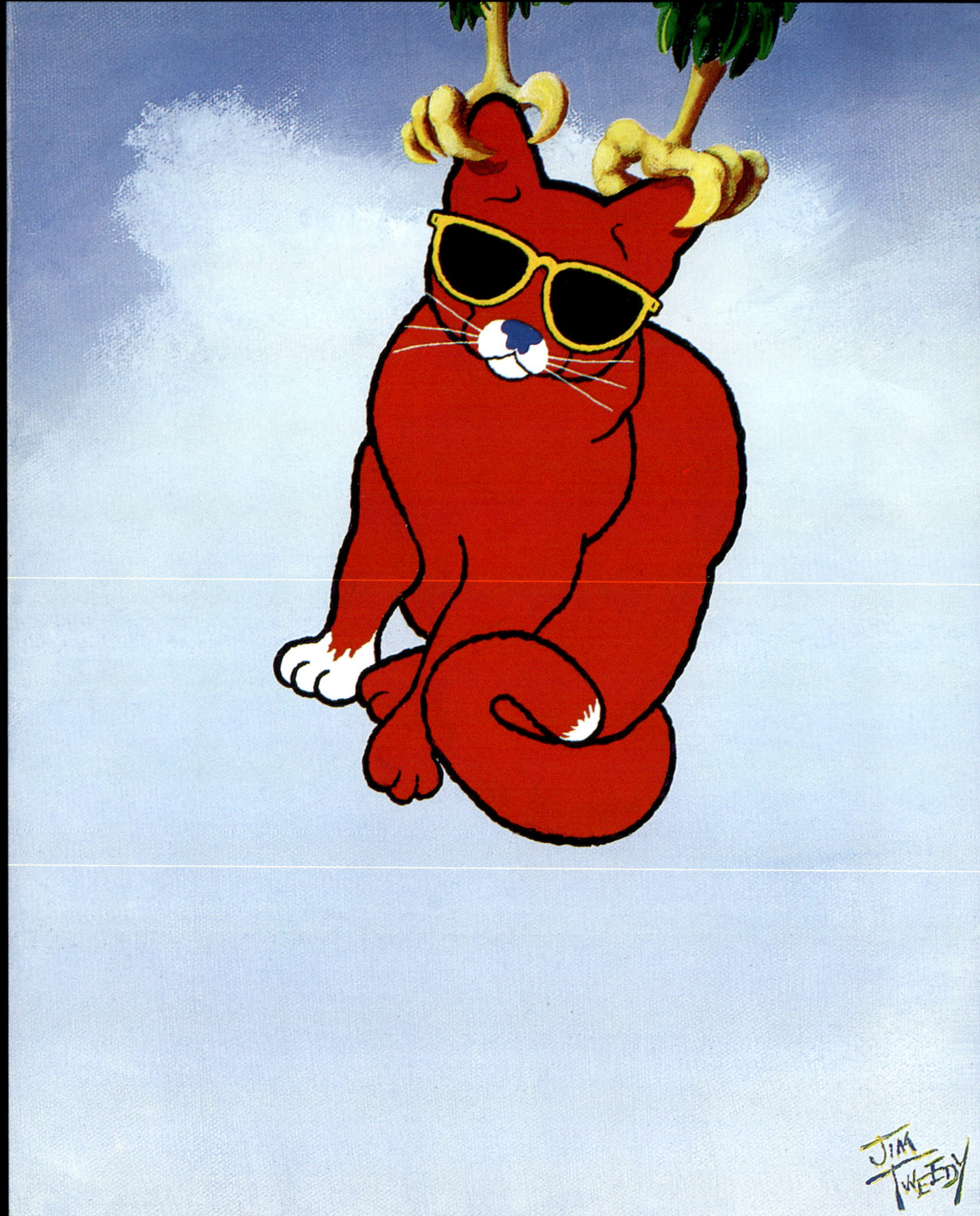

Let's Go Fly a Cat

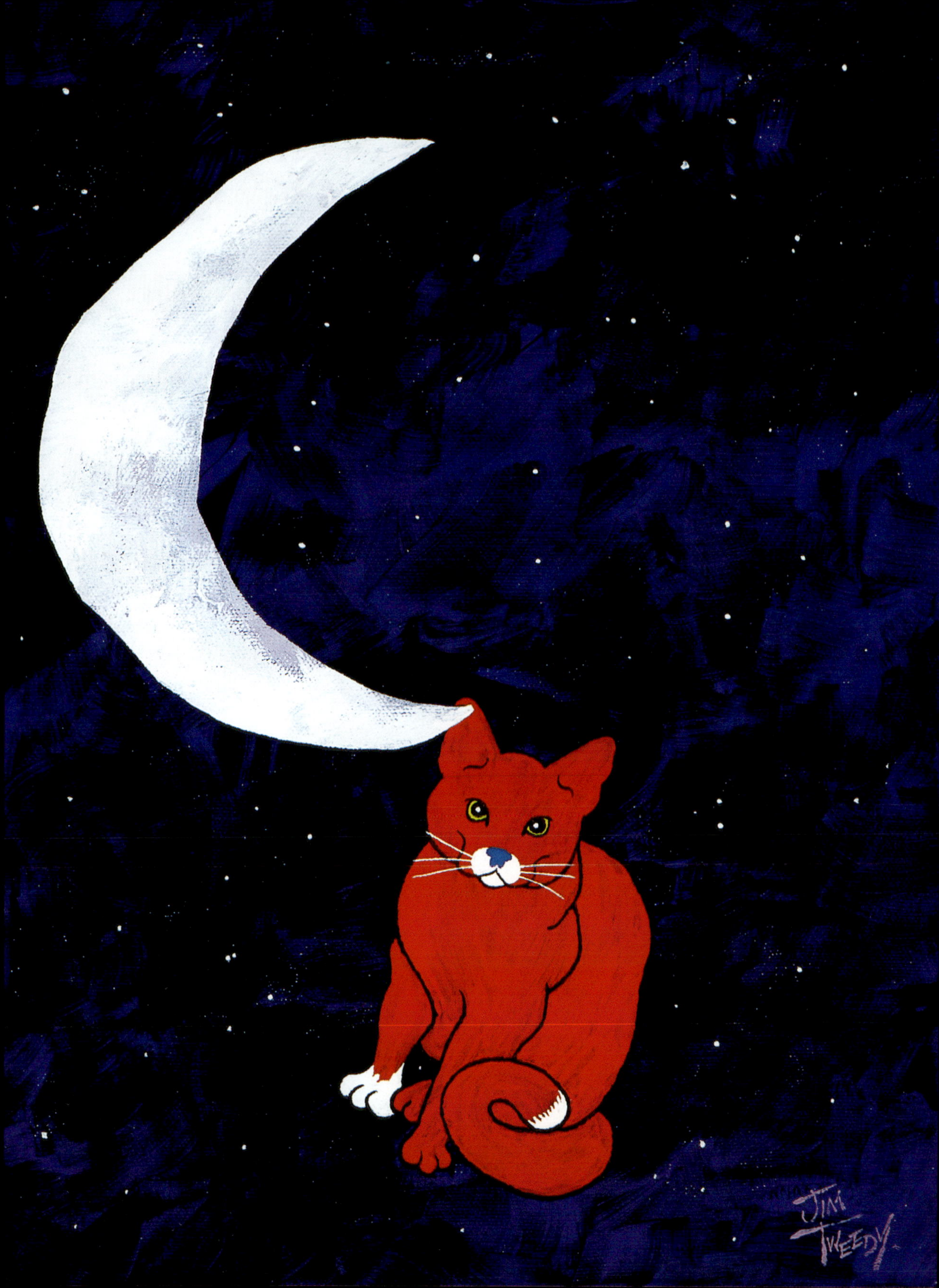

And they traveled so high Charlie became "moonstuck."

The Blues Cruise came to a screeching halt today, thanks to this crescent moon. I'm sure that when the full moon comes along Charlie will be back on Earth in no time.

Moonstuck

Not many people have seen a close-up of Gorbechev's birthmark.

While in New York City for an opening some years back, I hailed a taxi. I was running behind and just had to get to the gallery. I couldn't be late for my own show. As I opened the door of the cab, a little stocky man tried to force his way into the back seat ahead of me. We jostled back and forth for position—elbows flying, legs flailing. Together we landed in a heap on the back floor of the taxi.

As the cab sped away, the glow of a street light showed me what no Soviet TV camera dared to get close enough for the rest of the world to see. I had come face to face, nose to forehead, eyeball to birthmark, with my very own Charlie the RedCat.

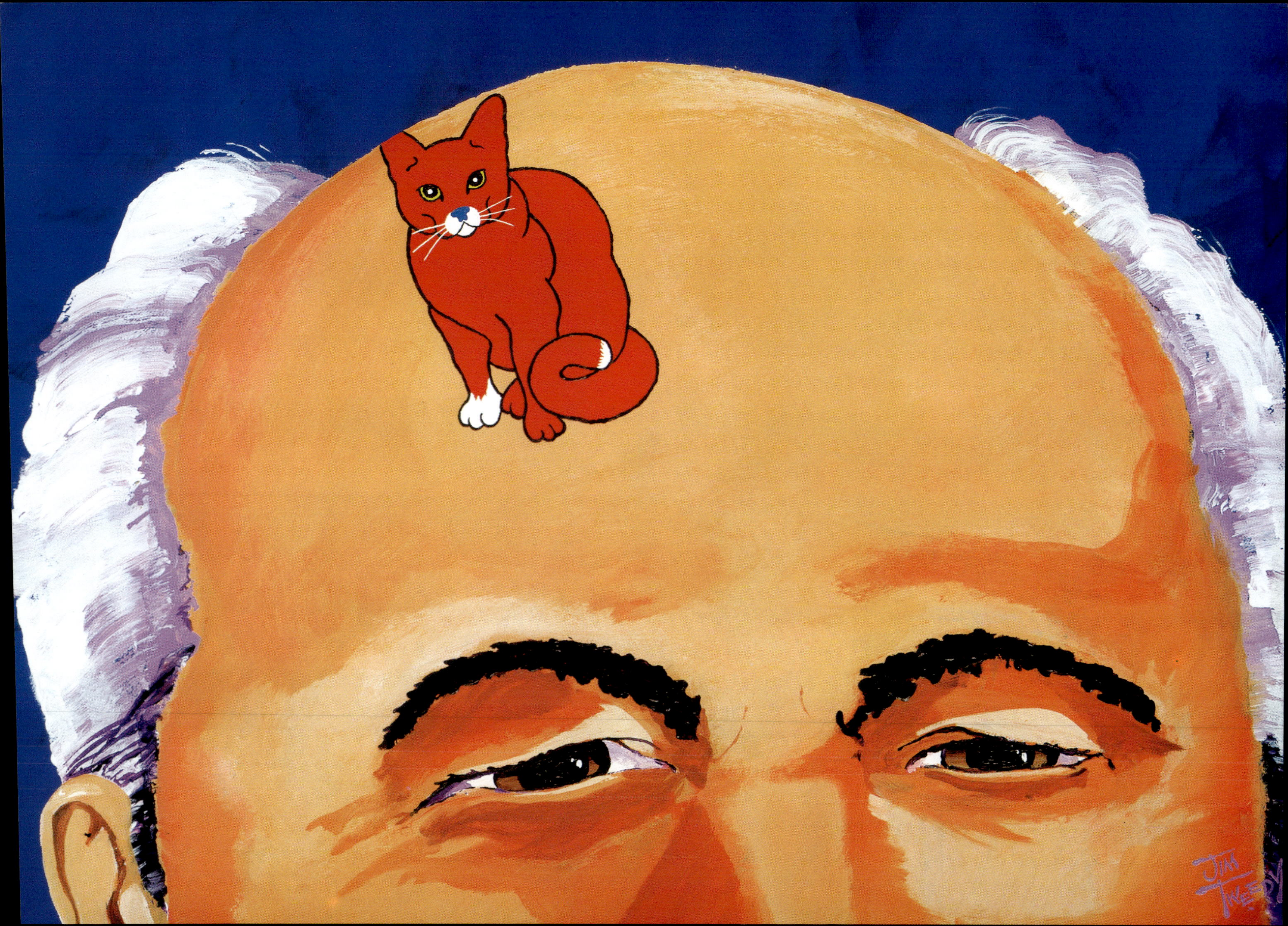

A Close-up of Gorbechev's Birthmark

During Desert Storm it was the picture of Charlie that kept American troops on Red alert.

Charlie the RedCat is having one of those days. Nothing seems to be going right. Even this trip to the desert to enjoy its beauty has resulted in a downpour. It's a gloomy day for now, but you can't keep a RedCat down. Charlie will find a way to turn this little setback into something positive. Perhaps a sand castle! After all, a cat's sand is his castle.

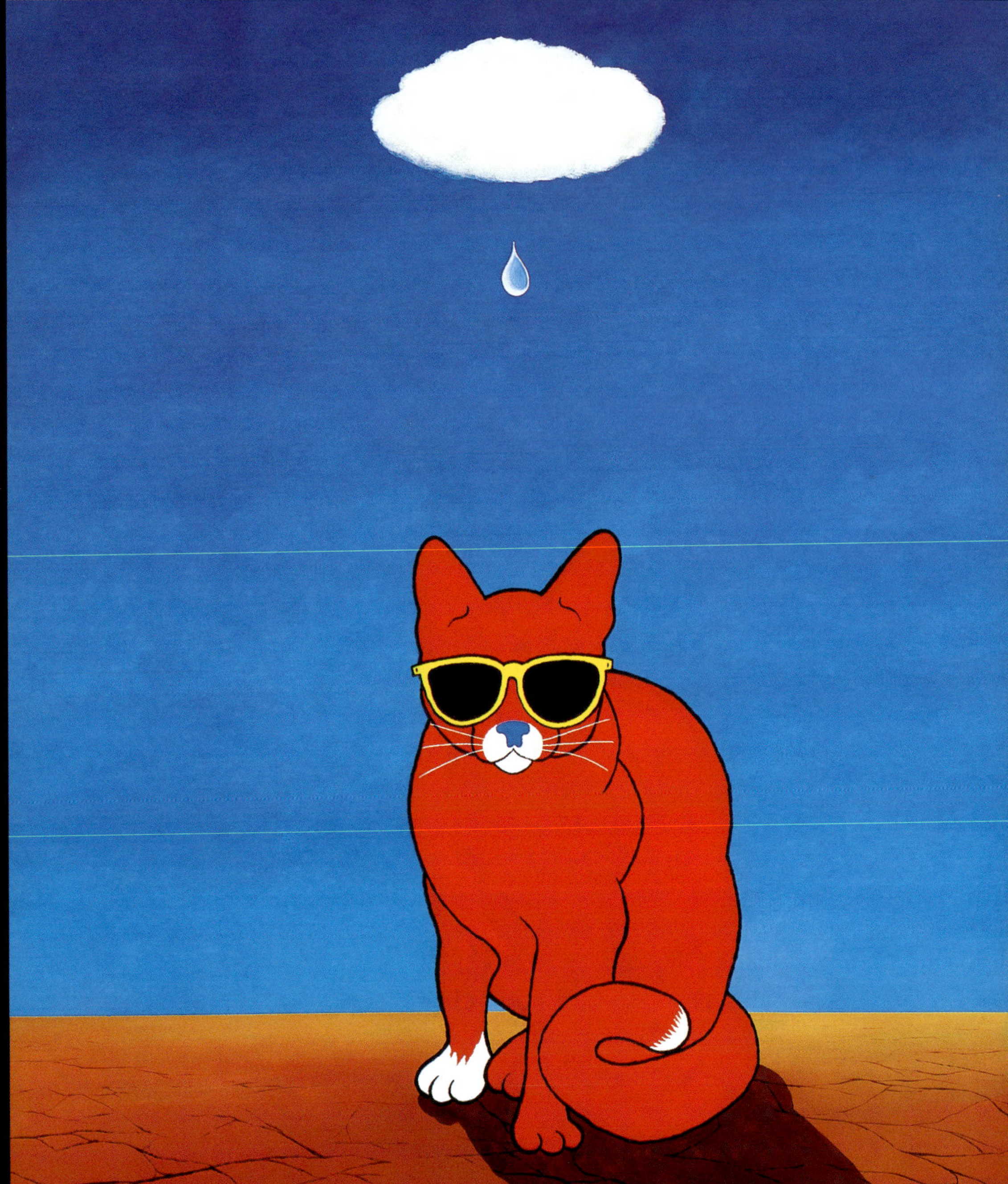

Desert Storm

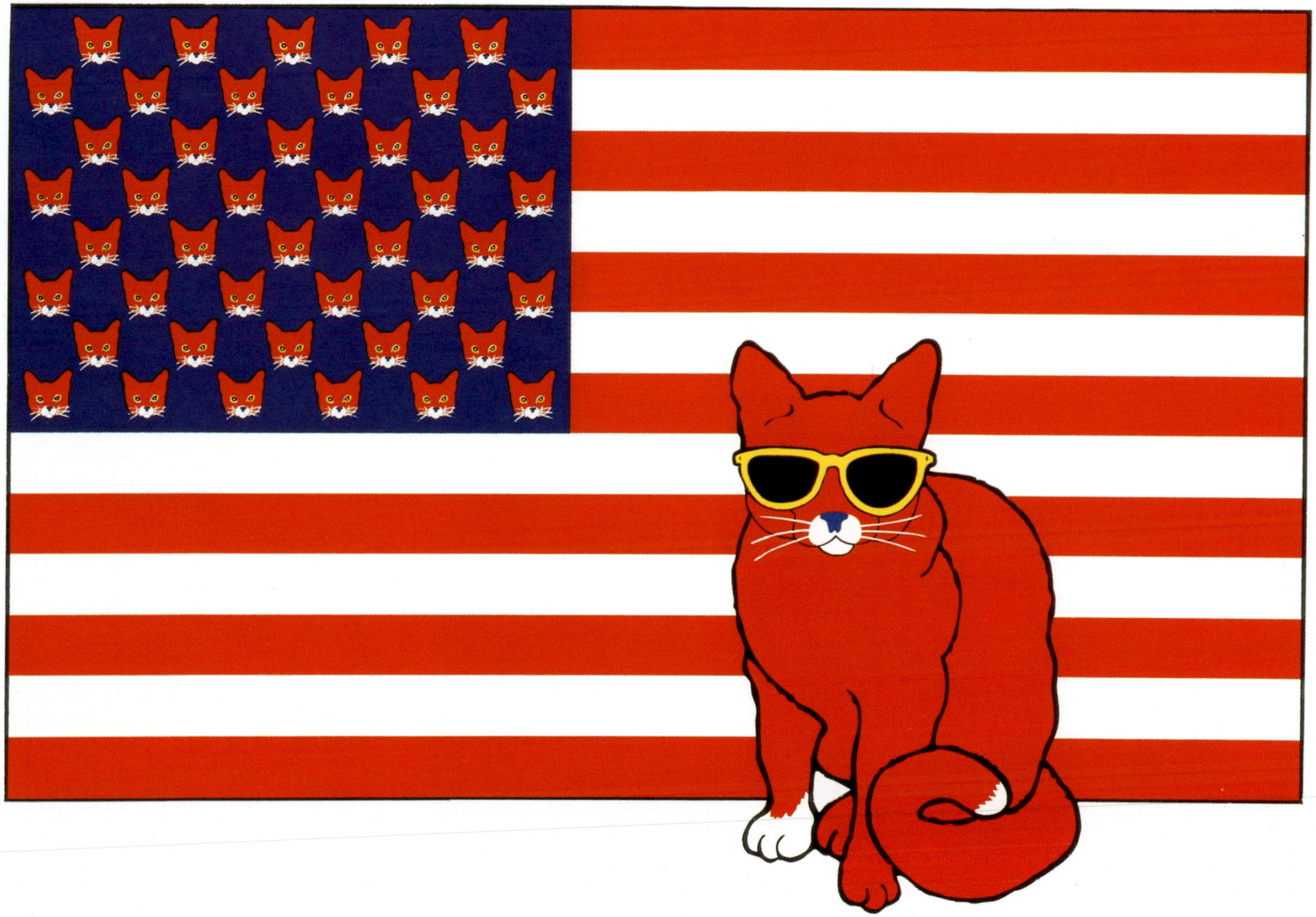

RedCat, White 'n' Blue Flag

There's a movement in the American military to adopt the RedCat, white, and blue flag as their own.

The RedCat, white, and blue flag depicts Charlie in a proud and patriotic moment. He truly loves his country.

As a famous patriot and celebrity, Charlie is surrounded by adoring young kittens wherever he goes. On a recent visit to Dodge City, Charlie allowed his true love to be known. But in an attempt to meet his idol, Miss Kitty, Charlie was thwarted again.

Years of watching "Gunsmoke" reruns drove Charlie west, only to have his heart broken by a dumb sign. To this day he still

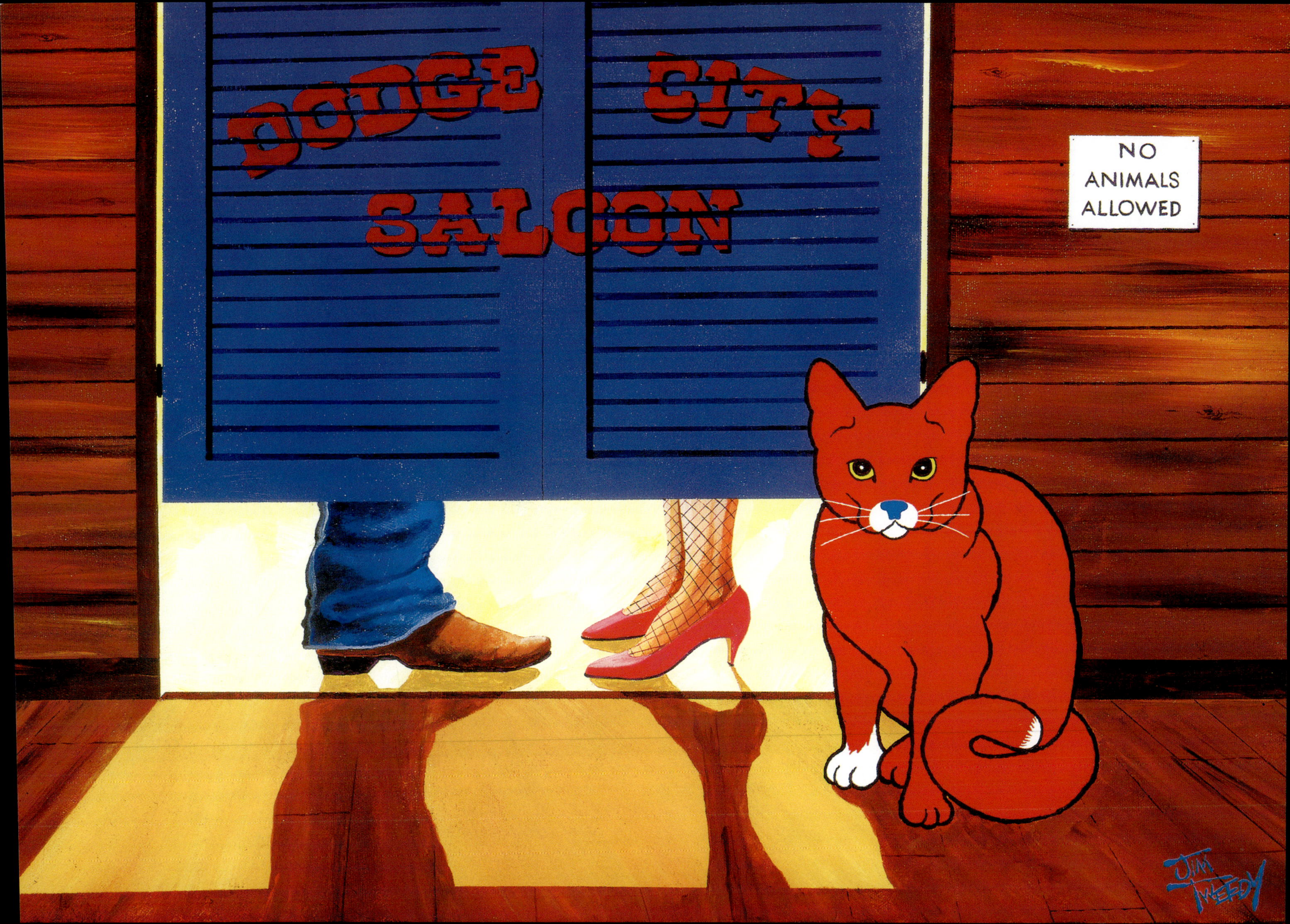

In an Attempt to Meet His Idol, Miss Kitty, Charlie is Thwarted

Due to an Unfortunate Shift in the Wind, Charlie Smells the Dairy Air

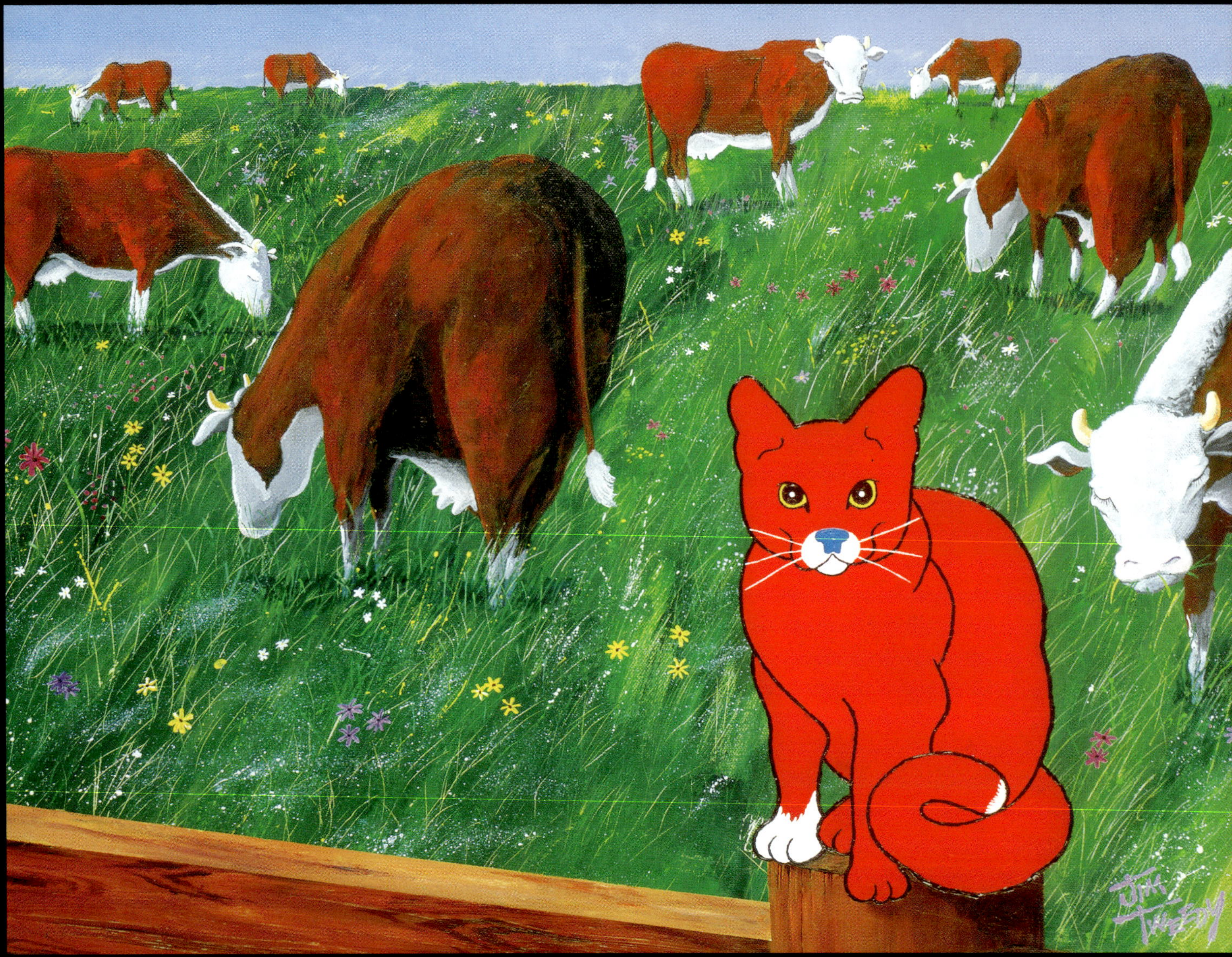

Charlie can't stand rejection. Just then, due to an unfortunate shift in the wind Charlie smelled the dairy air.

This was a devastating occurrence. We were out west when we spotted these cows. I stayed in the car and sketched furiously against time. Suddenly, Charlie was face-up in the tall grass. I knew in an instant what had happened. Mouth-to-muzzle had to be applied, but nobody there liked kissing cats. So I yelled at him: "CHARLIE, WAKE UP!" He snapped to. "Are you okay," I asked.

"Yes," he meowed. "It was a mooving experience."

Despite Repeated Denials It Became Painfully Obvious: Belle Was Charlie's Little Girl

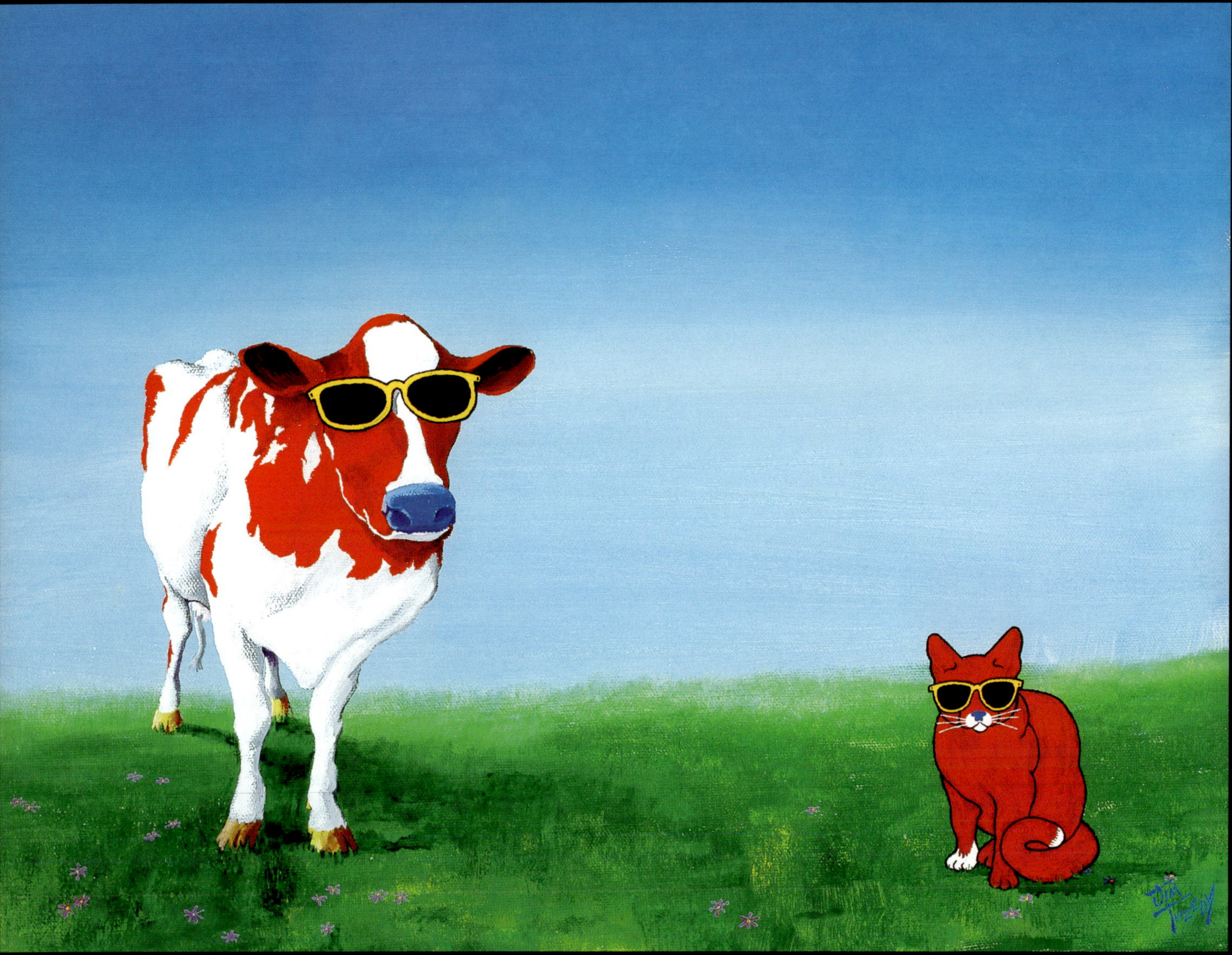

After being shunned by Miss Kitty, Charlie turned his affections toward another. And sadly, despite repeated denials, it became painfully obvious that Belle was Charlie's little girl.

Time and again I cautioned Charlie about those lonely milk cows. "Oh, I'm just fond of fresh milk," he'd reply.

Now he'll have to get a real job—and we'll have to get a bigger litter box.

Charlie's world tour is underway.

This is the triumphant pose Charlie struck after our first art show. The show was called "Charlie's World Tour," and this was made into my first ever serigraph. Charlie's considered himself a supermodel ever since.

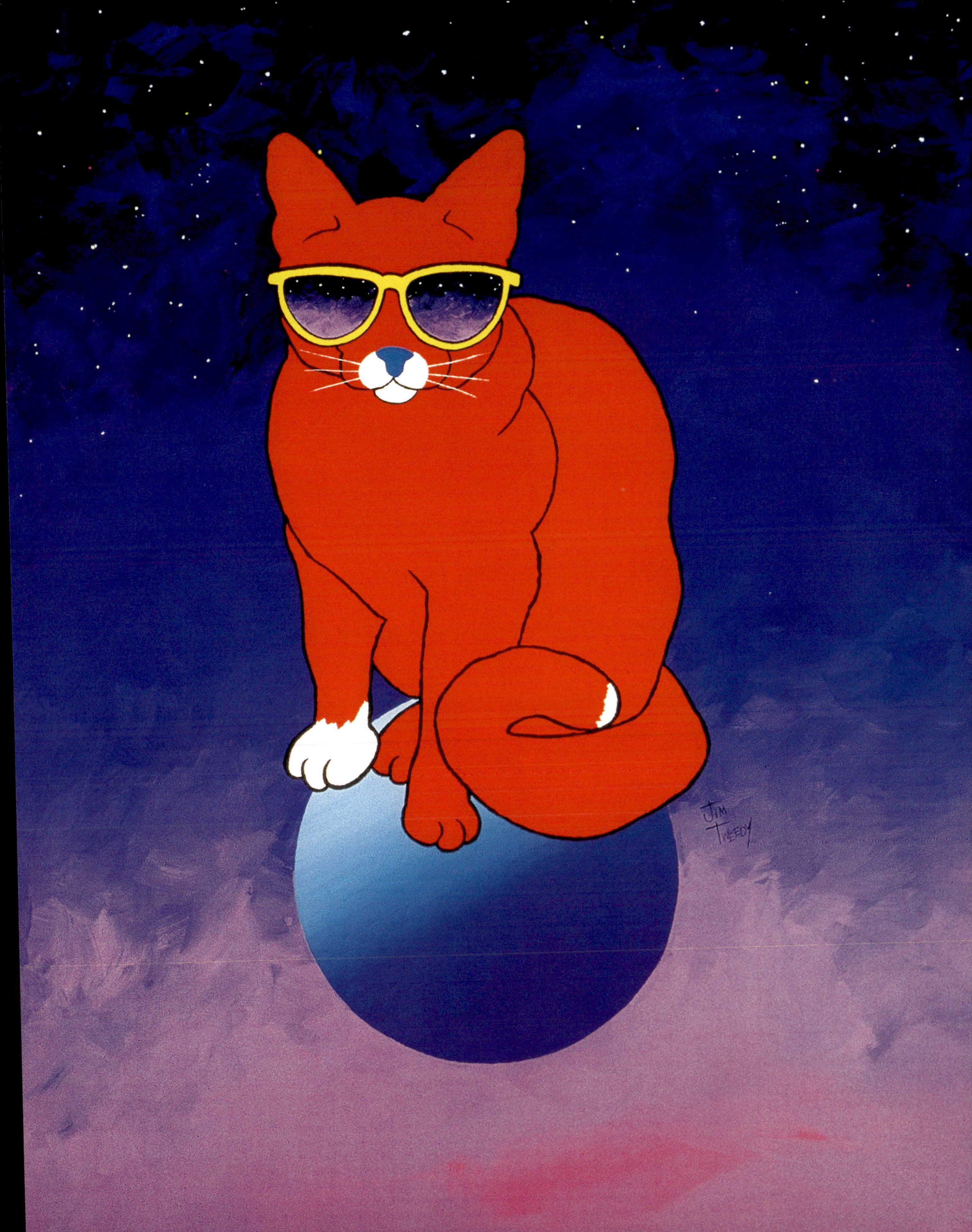

Charlie's World Tour

On Monday, Charlie takes New York …

While most people want to take a bite out of the Big Apple, Charlie had other ideas.

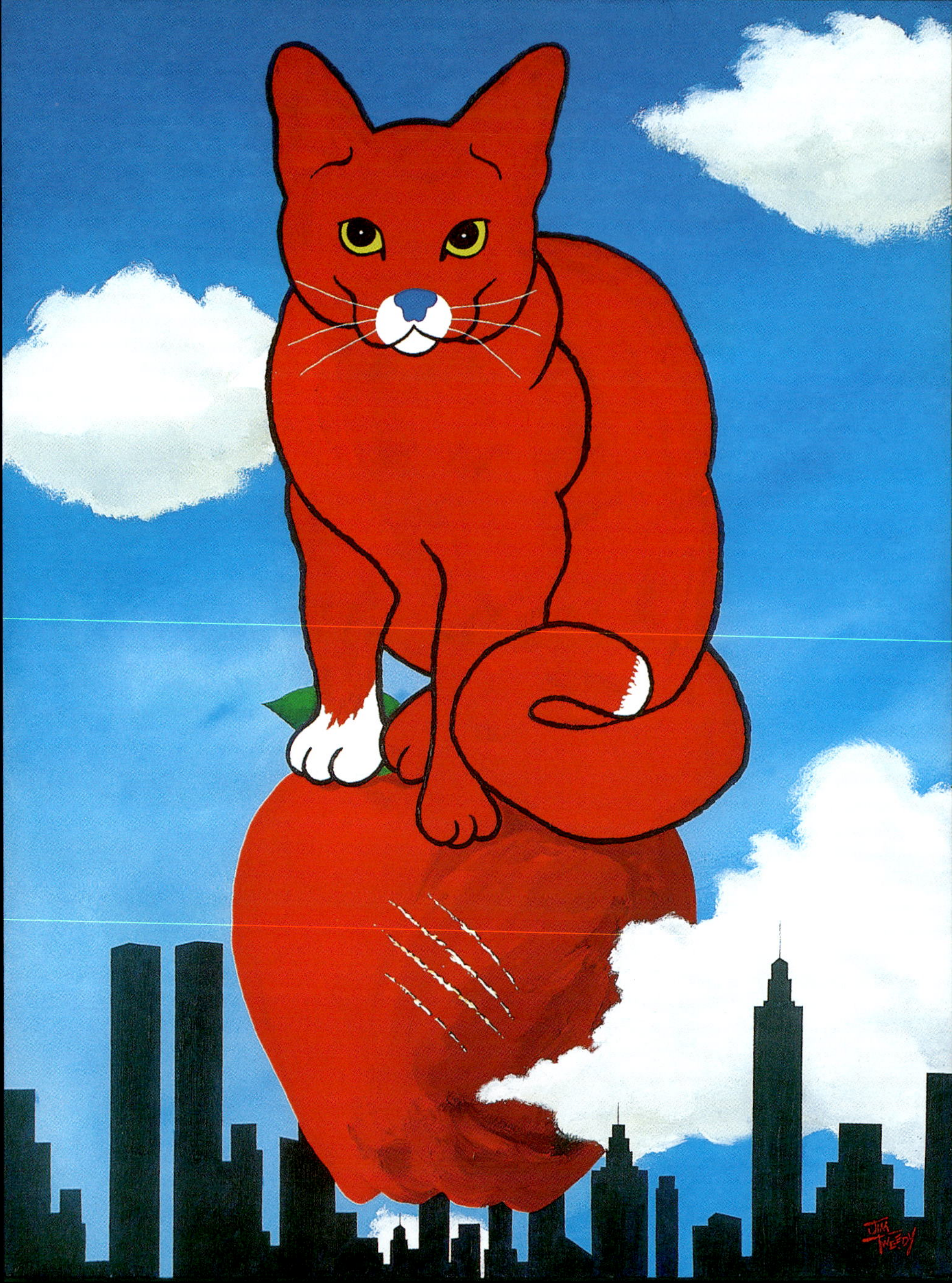

Charlie Takes New York

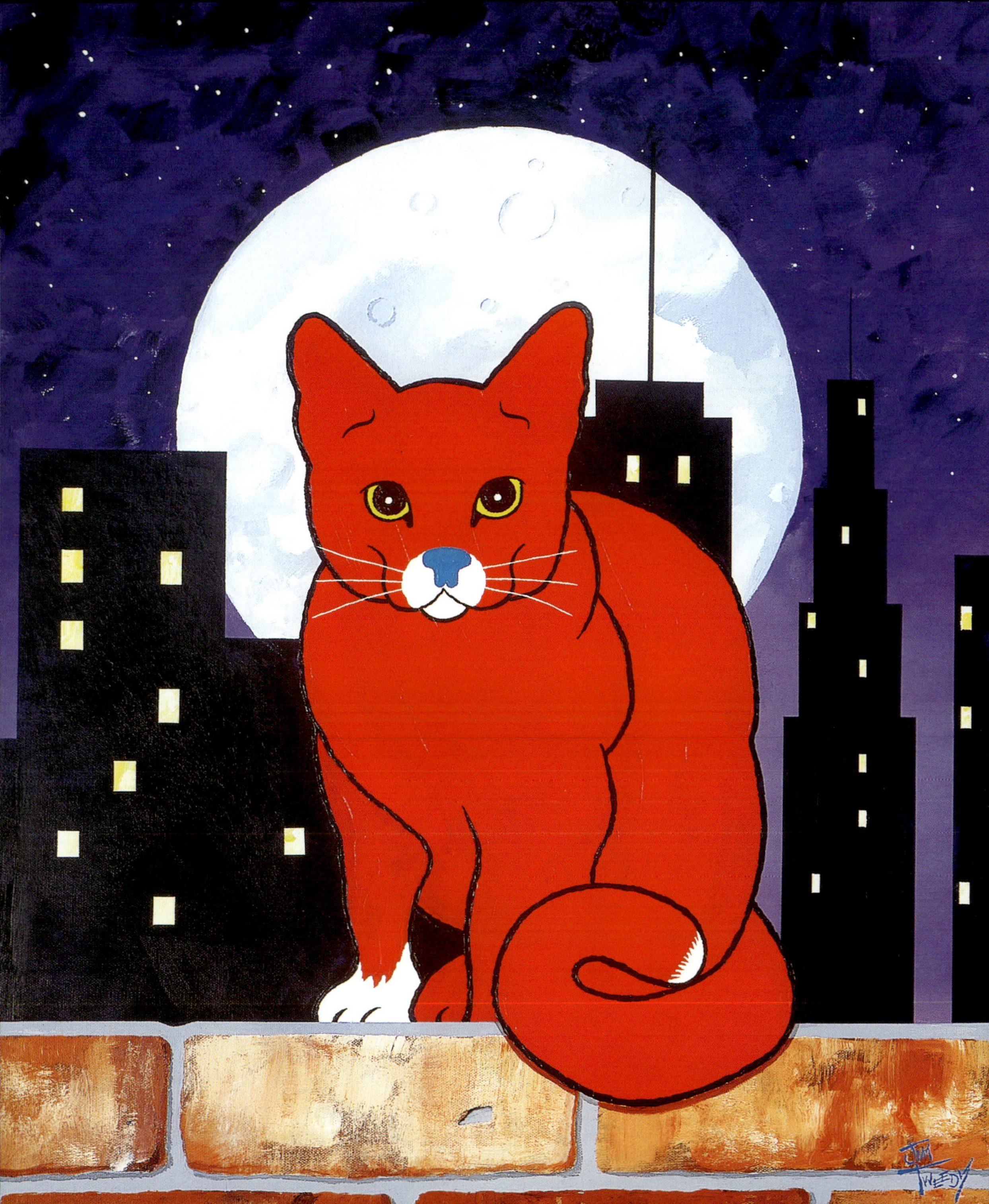

… as he performs "The Midnight Catboy" on Broadway.

"Always ready to belt out a little tune," is Charlie's motto. This was our proposal to a major record producer for the cover of Charlie's first CD entitled "Born to Nap." So far there are no takers among the music guys, but Charlie continues to hone his skills nightly. We know people love his singing because every night when he goes out people toss him valuable things like tomatoes, old shoes, and eggs.

The Midnight Catboy

On Tuesday, Charlie goes to England for a command performance …

This piece was an important part of the "Charlie's World Tour" series. Charlie was more than a little concerned about the weather over there. The rain and fog made it difficult to keep his crimson coat looking its best for the painting. He demanded that I paint him over and over until he was satisfied. We went through a lot of canvas that day, but I think the results speak for themselves.

There is a movement in Parliament to change the name of that big clock in the background to "Big Red."

Charlie Goes to England

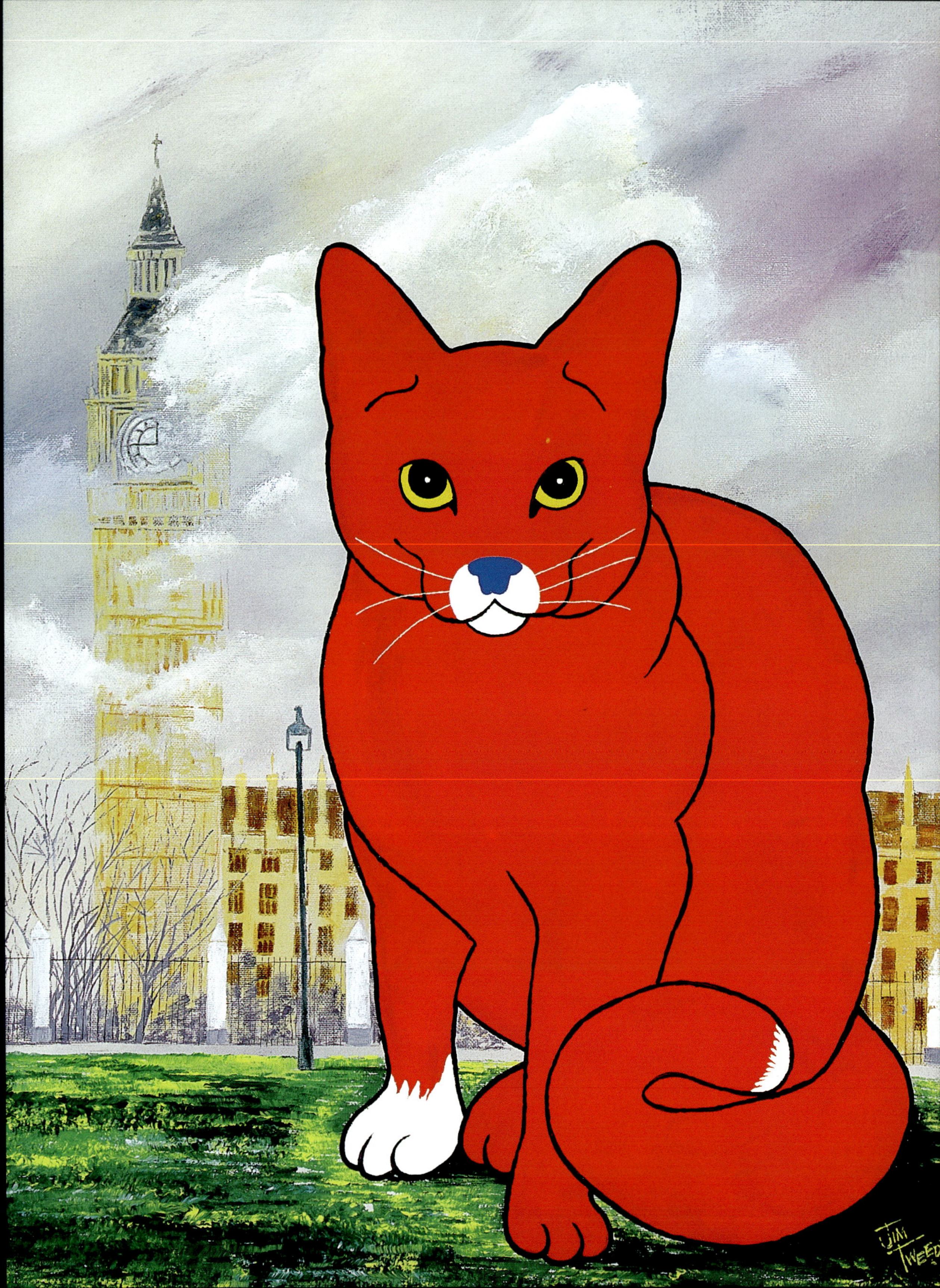

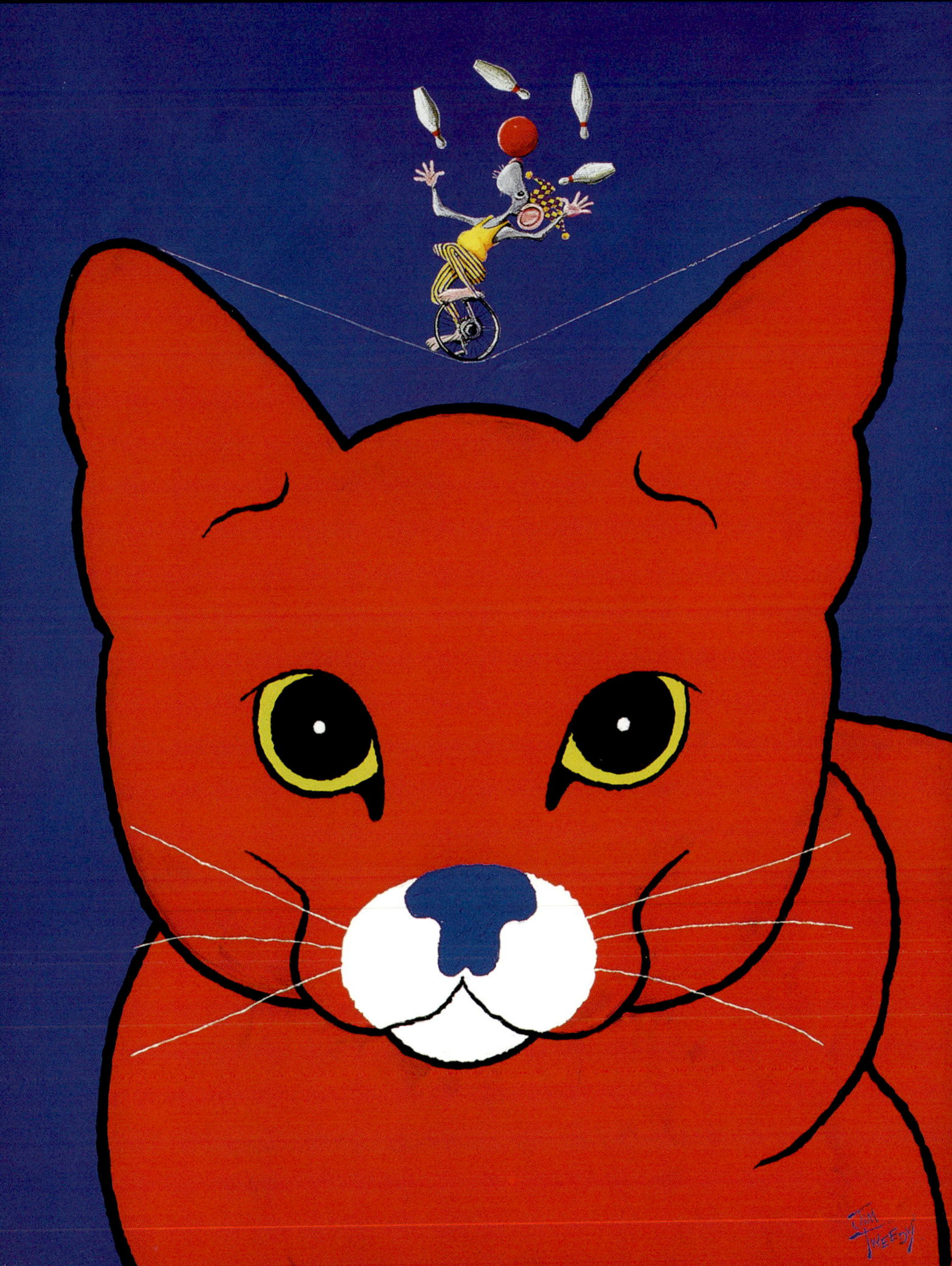

The Cat Jester

... as the cat jester. (It seems the Queen's royal kitty cat doesn't know how to entertain himself.)

You know, some of those kings in medieval times were that way. "Keep me laughing or else."

Too bad they didn't have cable.

On Wednesday, Charlie heads across the channel on his way to France. There's barely time to oui oui there ...

Originally, we were going to do this painting from the top of the Eiffel Tower, but Charlie was afraid he'd get stuck up there just like when he climbed that pine tree back home. We almost didn't go to France at all because he has a real problem with poodles. Charlie believes it's not safe to be around a dog that paints its toenails.

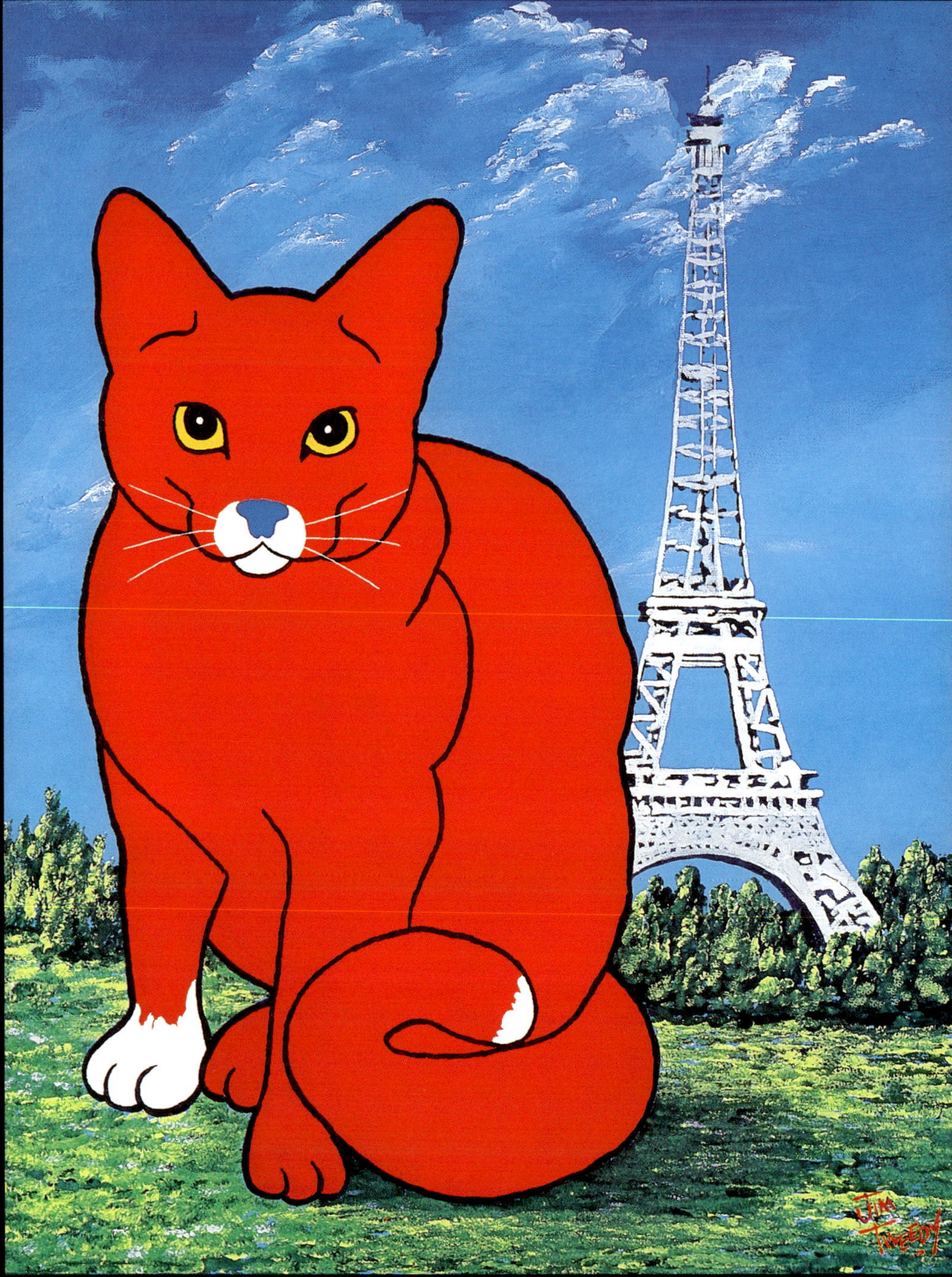

Charlie Goes to France

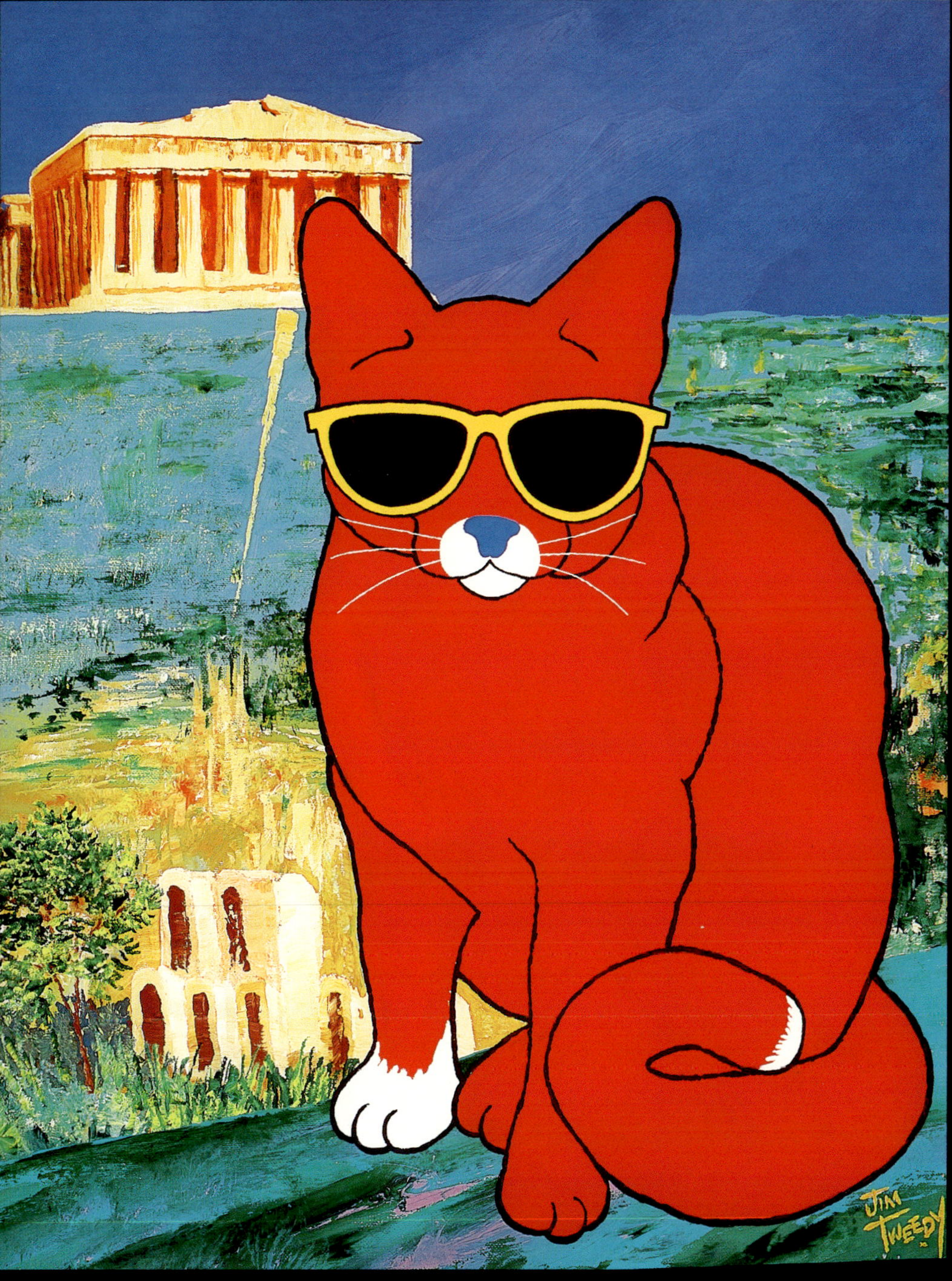

Charlie Goes to Greece

... before Charlie goes to Greece.

The food in Greece was a big disappointment for Charlie, though you would never know it from the expression on his face in the painting. The problem stemmed from a big misunderstanding. You see, Charlie is fond of greasy food—not necessarily food from Greece. Oh well, I liked it and that's all that really matters.

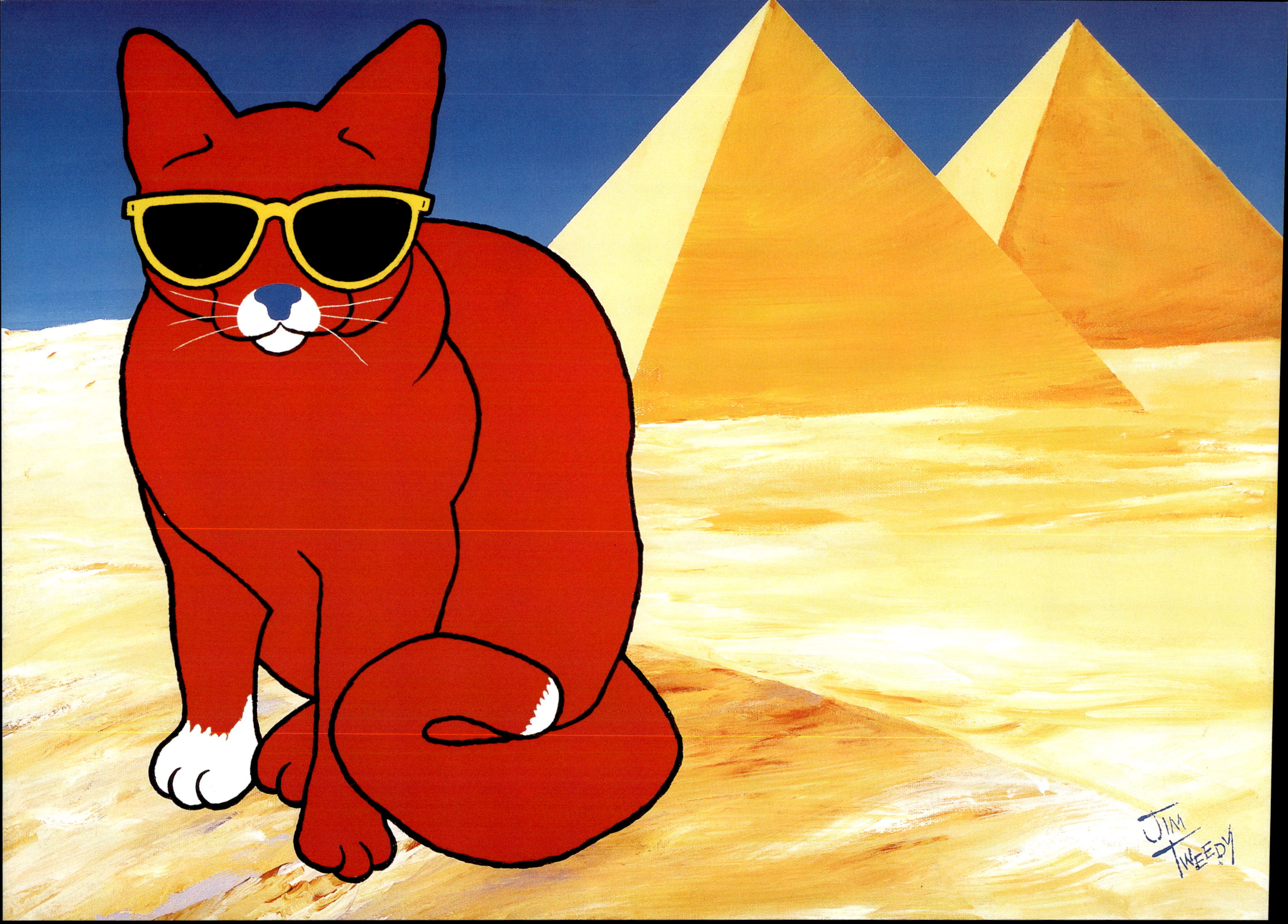

Charlie Goes to Egypt

Next is a brief stop for some pyramid power as Charlie goes to Egypt.

This was one of Charlie's favorite spots for a couple reasons. First, it was hot—hot in the way that all cats prefer. Best of all, the sand was everywhere. That meant no waiting in long lines for the restrooms like we did in Paris.

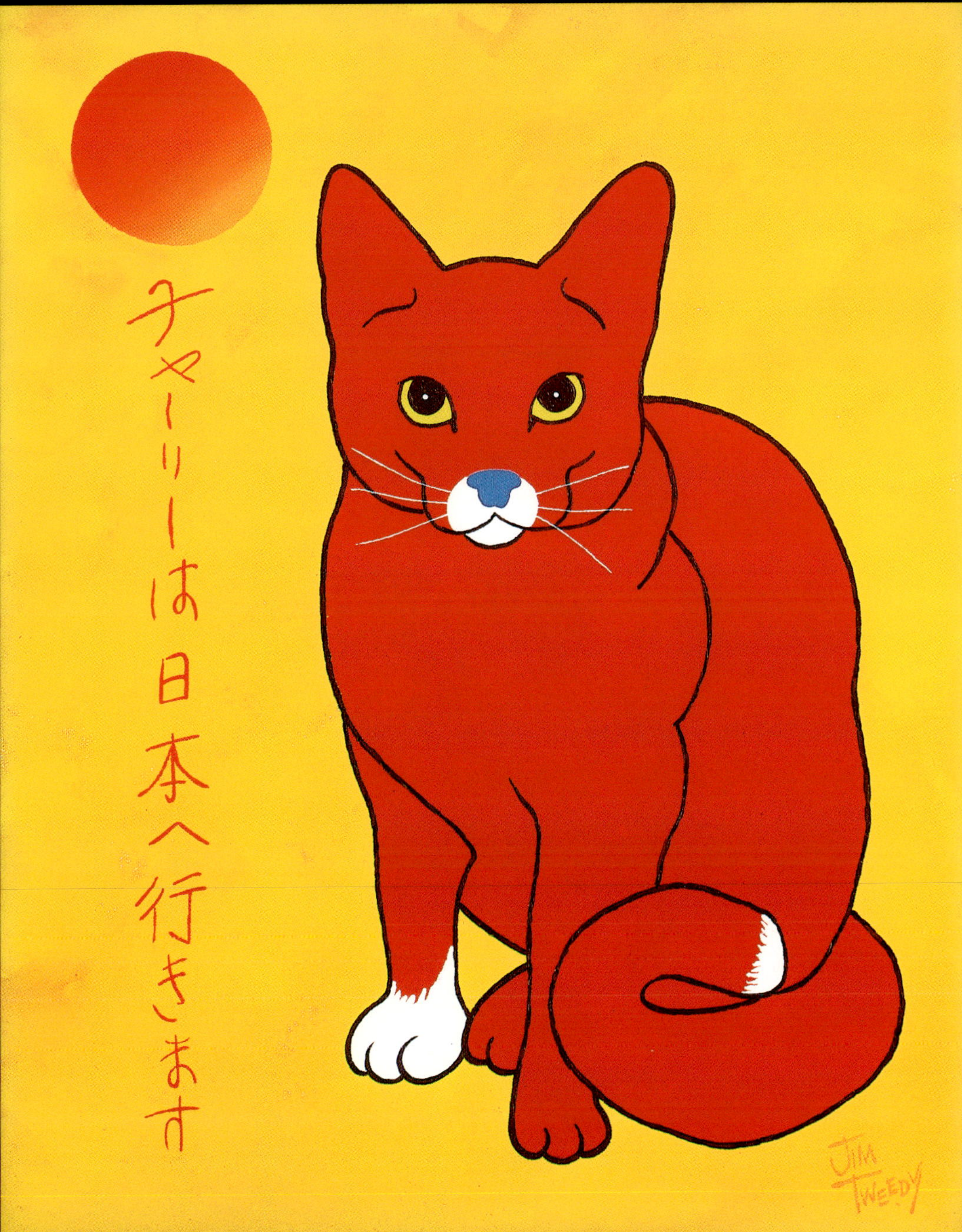

Charlie Goes to Japan

On Thursday, Charlie goes to Japan in time to catch the rising sun.

The land of the rising sun was fantastic. A very old Japanese woman helped me with the lettering on this painting. It is supposed to read: "Charlie Goes to Japan." I can only hope she wasn't telling me something I shouldn't be saying. Charlie became hooked on sushi while we were there, and for once we agreed on something.

riday he relaxes in beautiful Meowii. But wait!

Meow *is actually a Hawaiian word. It means brave, intelligent, handsome, and red.*

It's no wonder that during Charlie's World Tour he was treated like royalty while I still had litterbox duty.

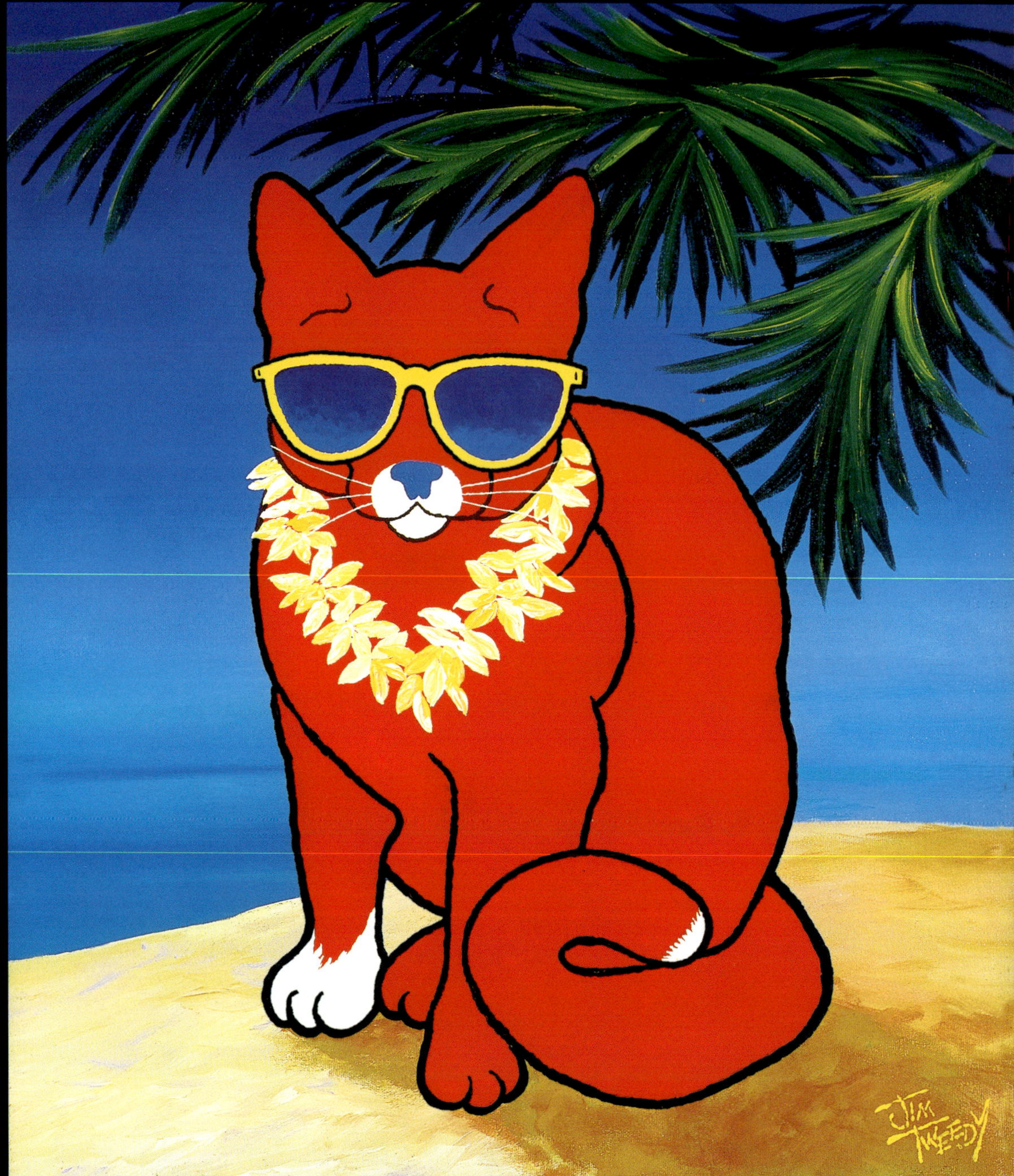

Meowii

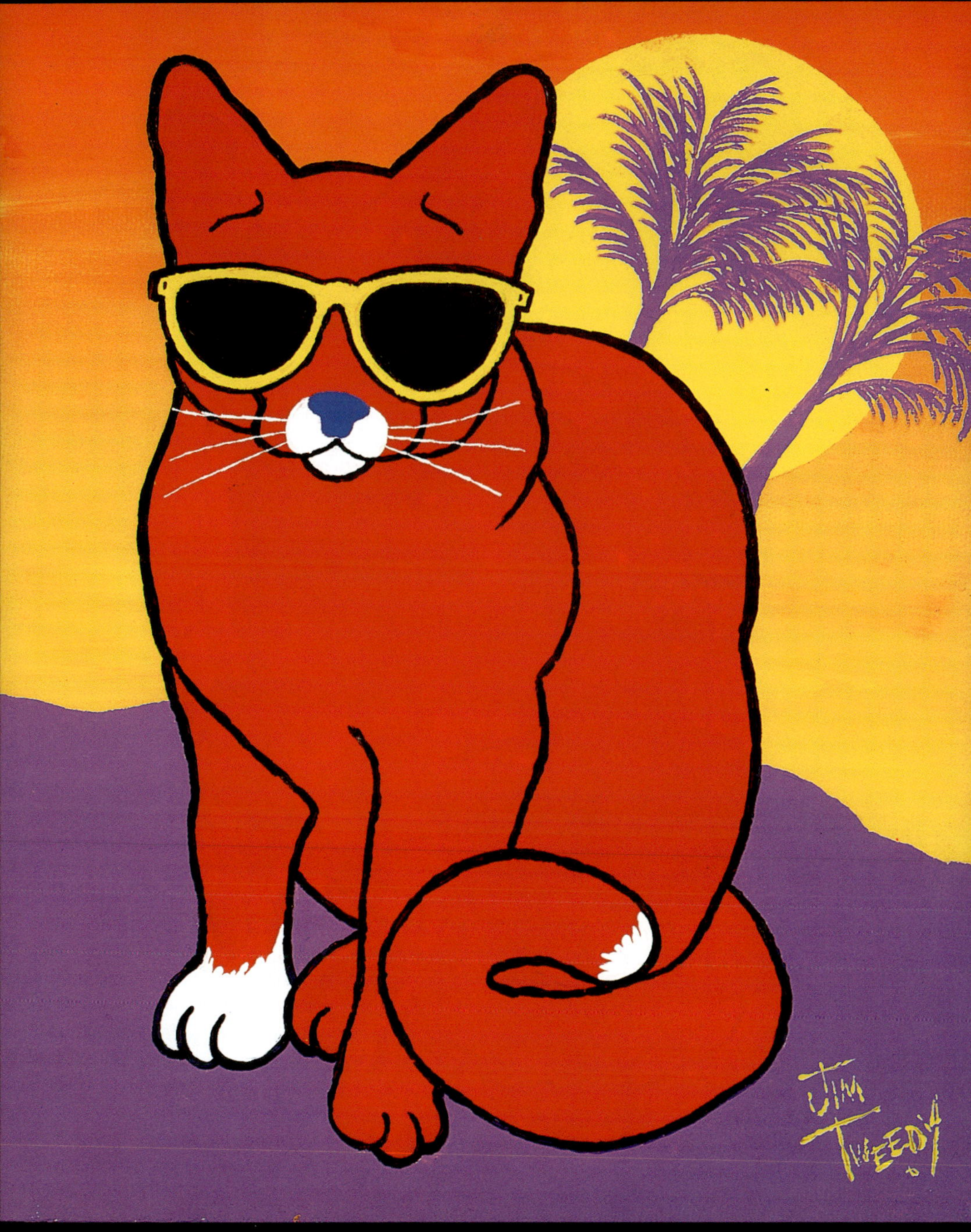

Caribbean Cat

More island hopping is in store as the Caribbean Cat basks on the beach.

Warm sunshine greeted Charlie and me on this final leg of the World Tour. This location led to the inspiration for his first swimsuit calendar and allowed valuable time for Charlie to work on his red.

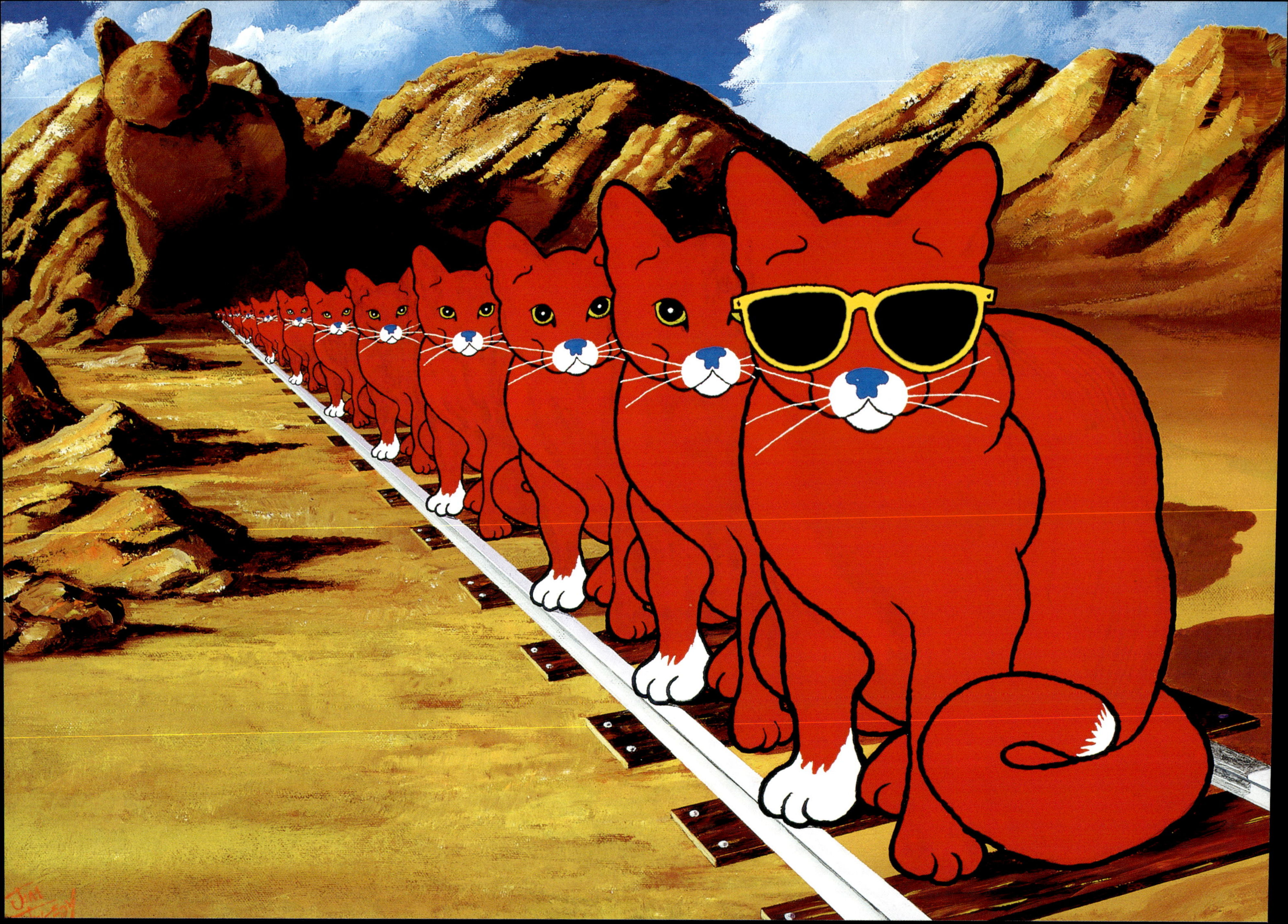

RedCat Express

Saturday, at long last, finds Charlie back on the mainland as he boards the RedCat Express.

The so-called "iron horse" that conquered the West was a myth perpetuated by some western historian who didn't like cats.

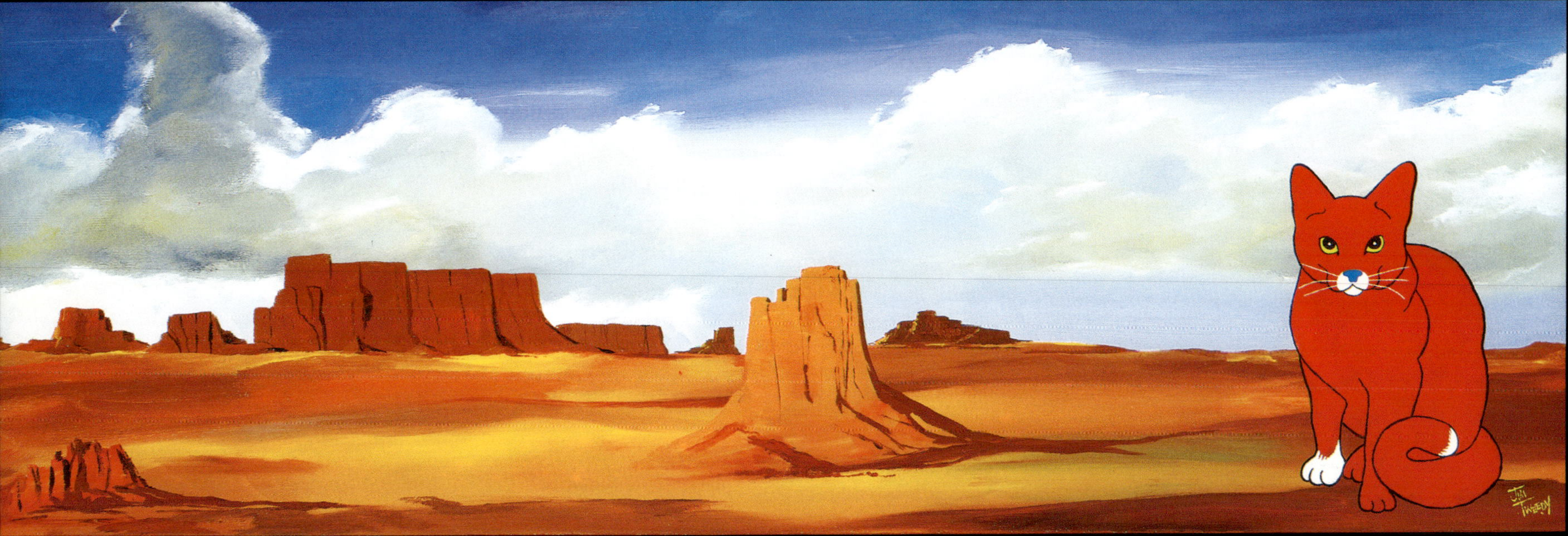

Southwest Charlie

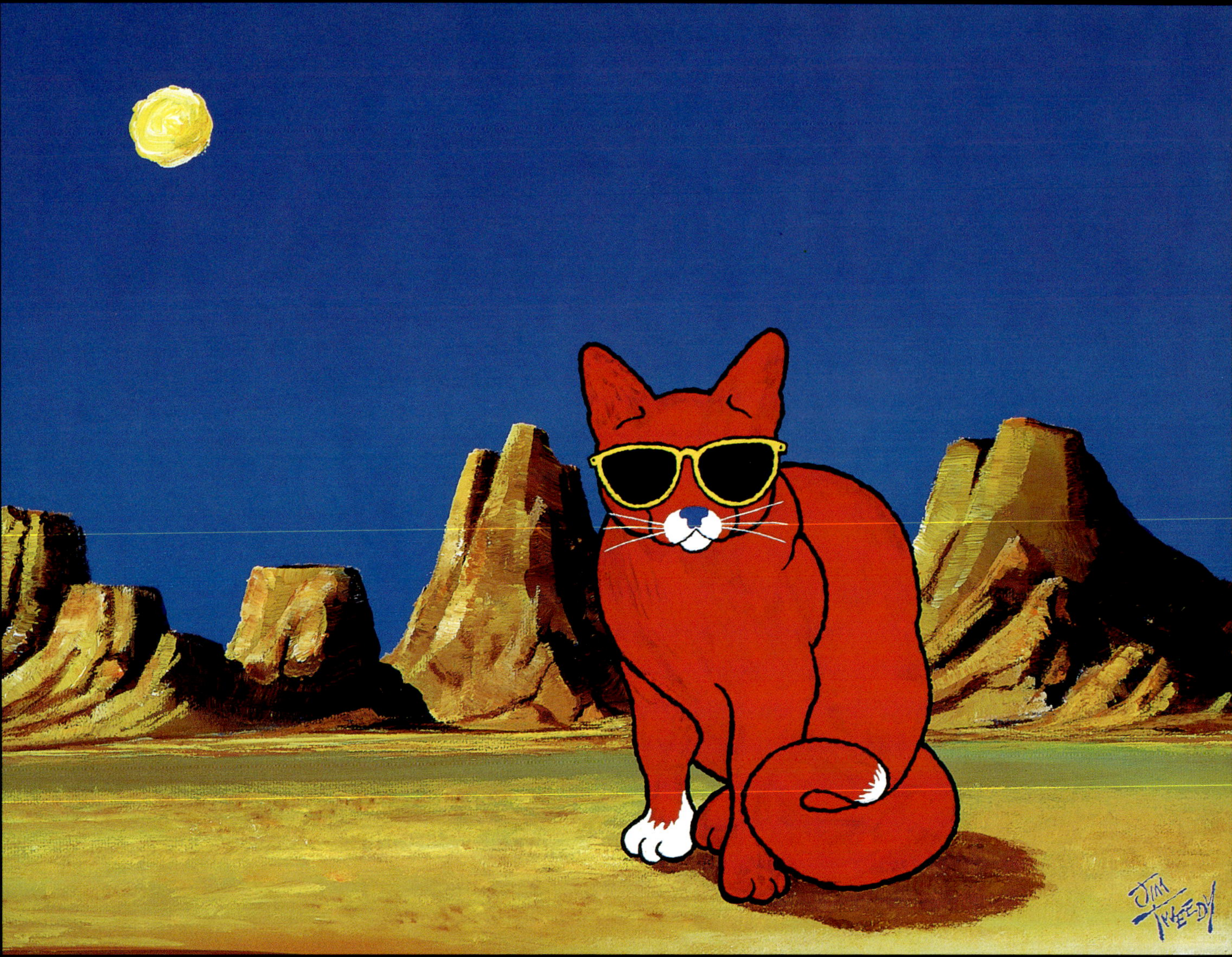

"It's hot out here," Charlie says.

"Turn up the heat" is every cat's battle cry. When you're as cool as Charlie is even the Arizona sun is a breeze. On this little excursion Charlie insisted on sleeping on the hood of our taxicab in the desert sun after eating a jalapeño sandwich with pepper sauce on it. That's way cool.

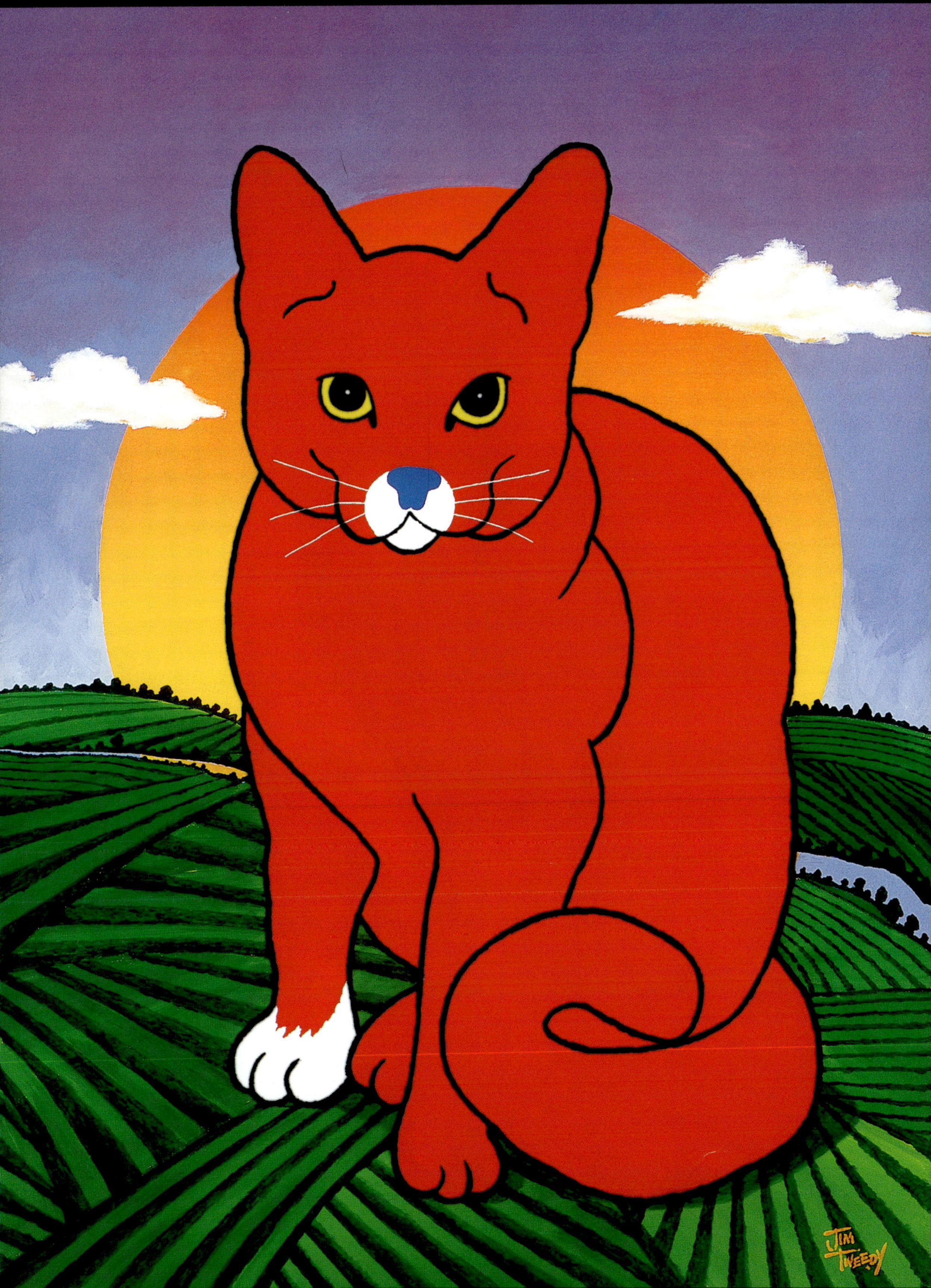

"It was easier to catch a catnap in Napa Valley."

When Charlie learned there was such a thing as red wine, he made a beeline for a glass of what he expected would be feline wine. He was shocked, yes, even appalled to learn it did not exist.

Charlie took his idea straight to Napa Valley, but was tossed out on his tail. That was even more appalling to Charlie. But not to me. You see, Charlie's theory involved having cats smash the grapes for Feline Wine. He claims that since cats have twice as many feet as humans do, they could be smashed in half as much time. Oh, and so could the grapes.

Cat
Napa

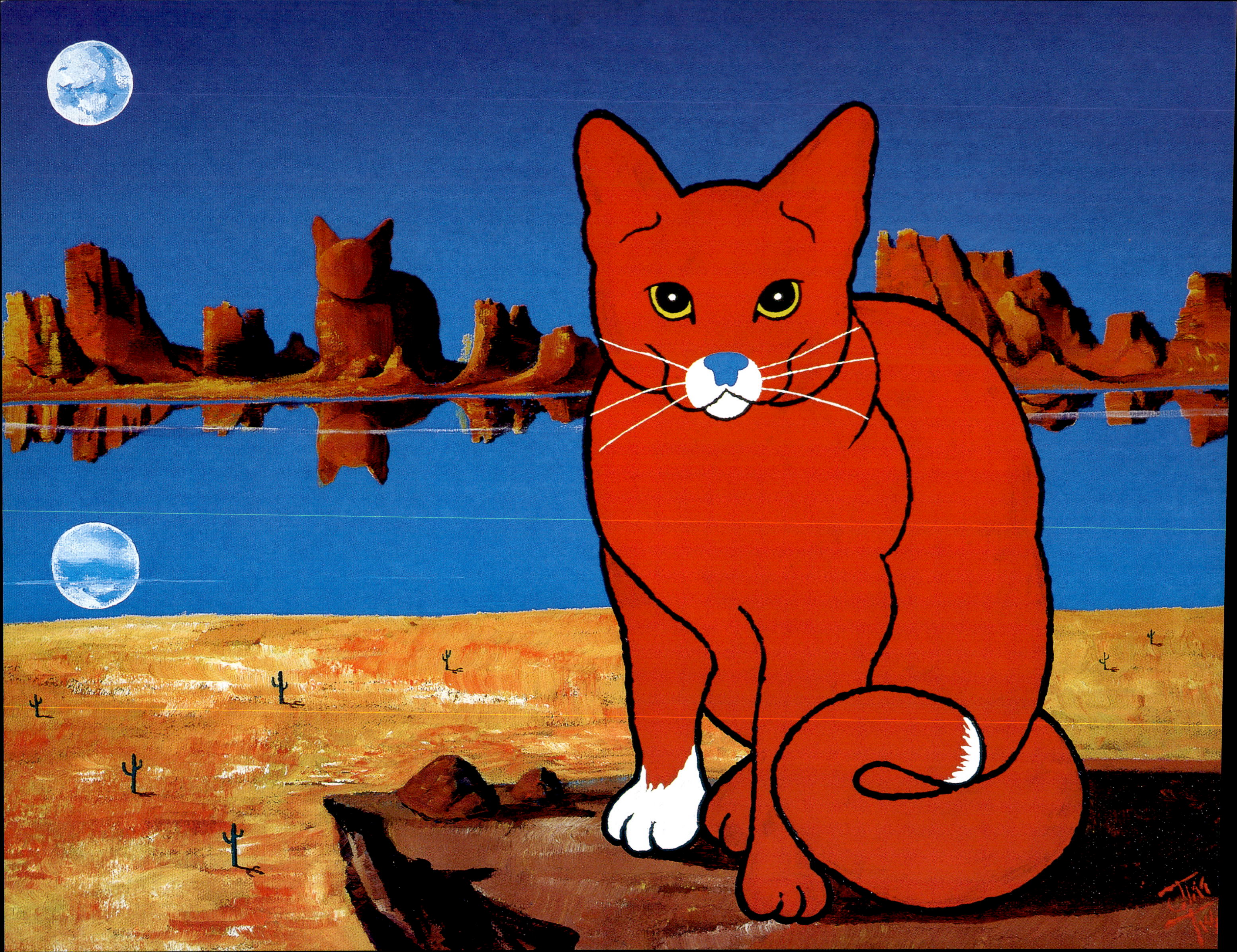

RedCat Rock

After one last look at RedCat Rock ...

This is one of the Seven Wonders of the World. It falls somewhere in between Stevie and catnip.

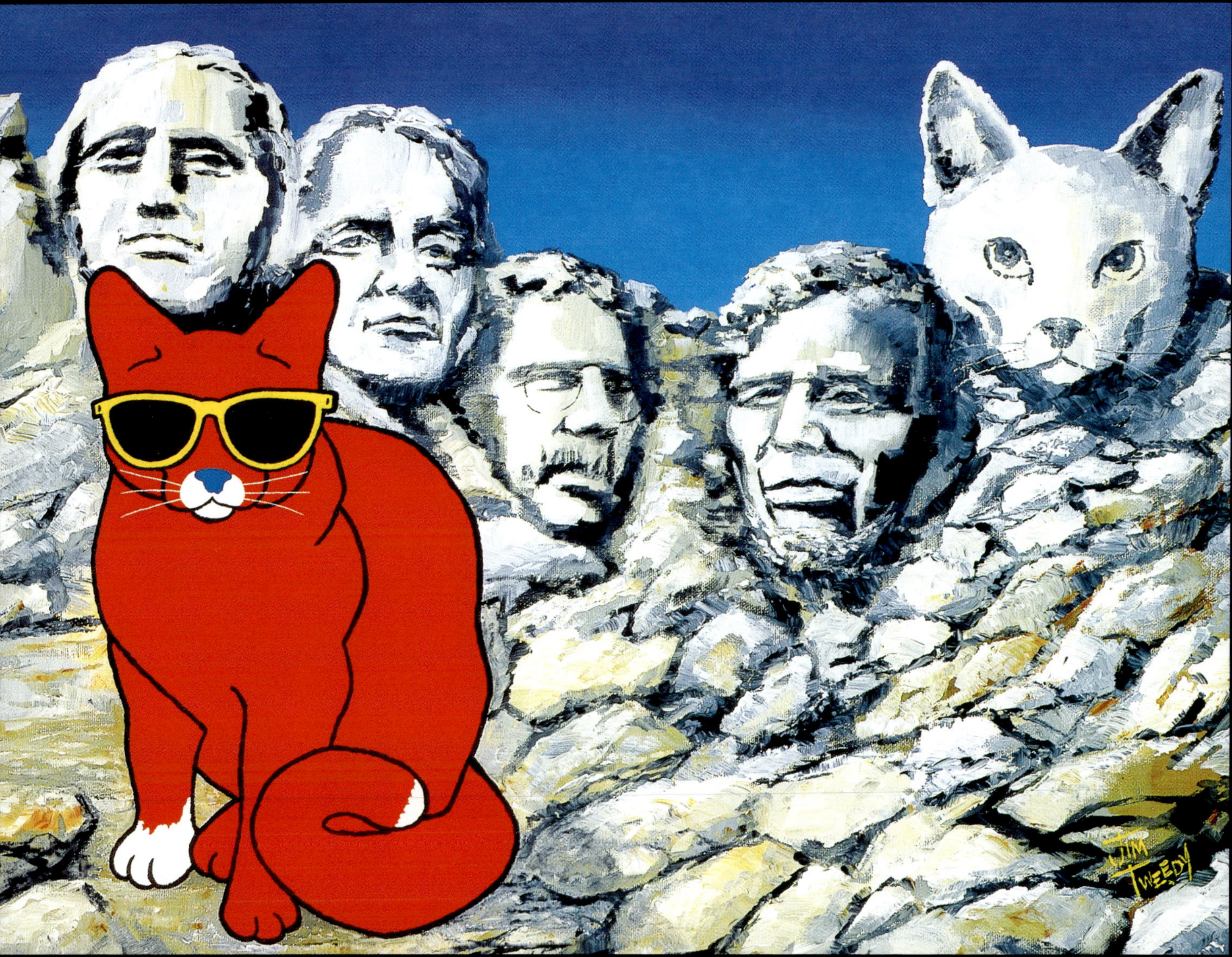

... Charlie heads north to South Dakota to see the breathtaking Mount Charliemore.

This is perhaps the greatest tribute Charlie has ever received.

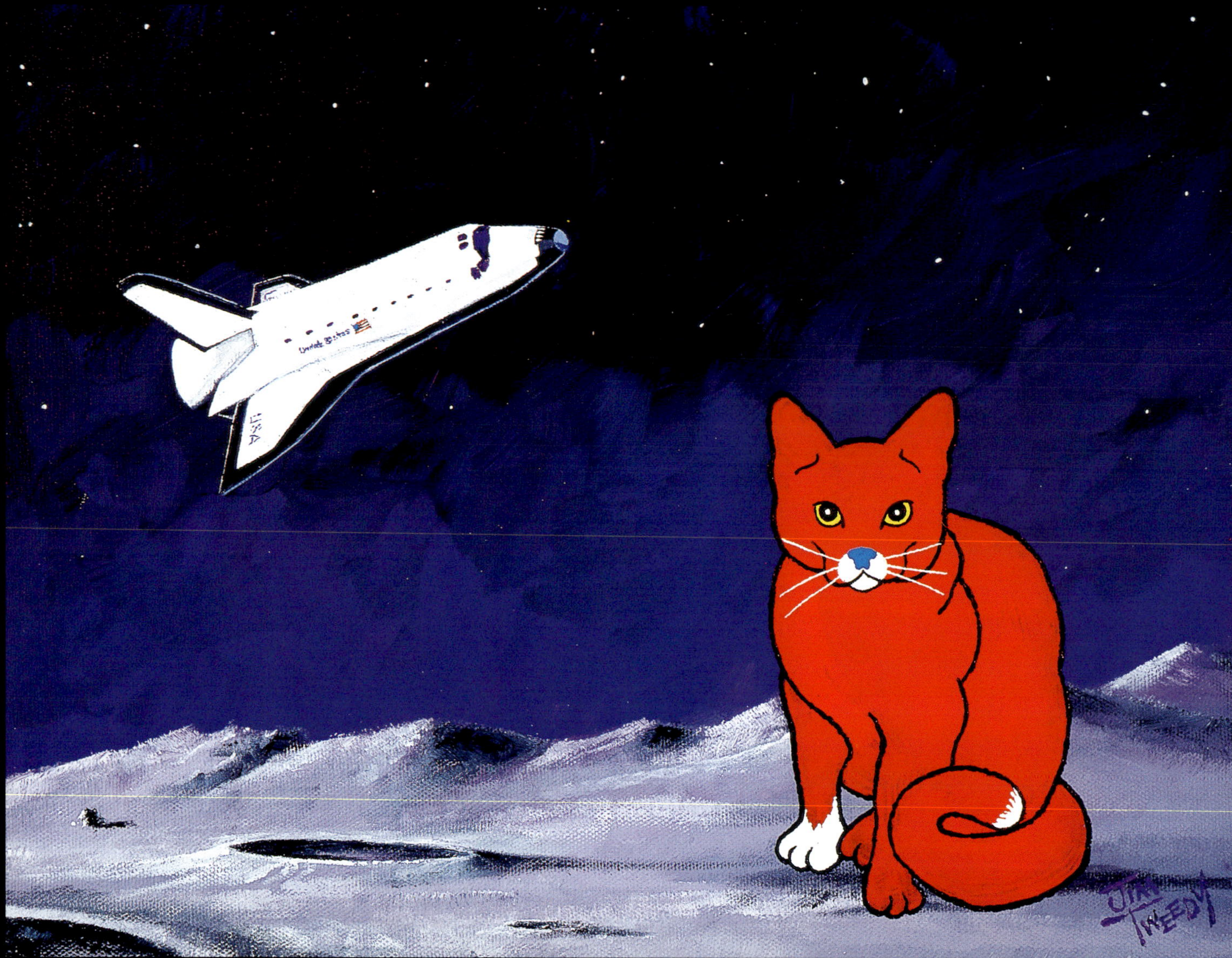

Finally, Sunday is here and Charlie heads for Florida to take an exciting space flight on his namesake space shuttle, Charlie.

Chosen for his courage and ability to always land on his feet, even in zero gravity, Charlie was the original passenger selected for the first space shuttle mission to land on the Moon. At the time, scientists planned to send up a female cat at a later date so the two could populate the Moon. They anticipated the RedCats would live off the large mouse population that fed on the cheese surface of the moon.

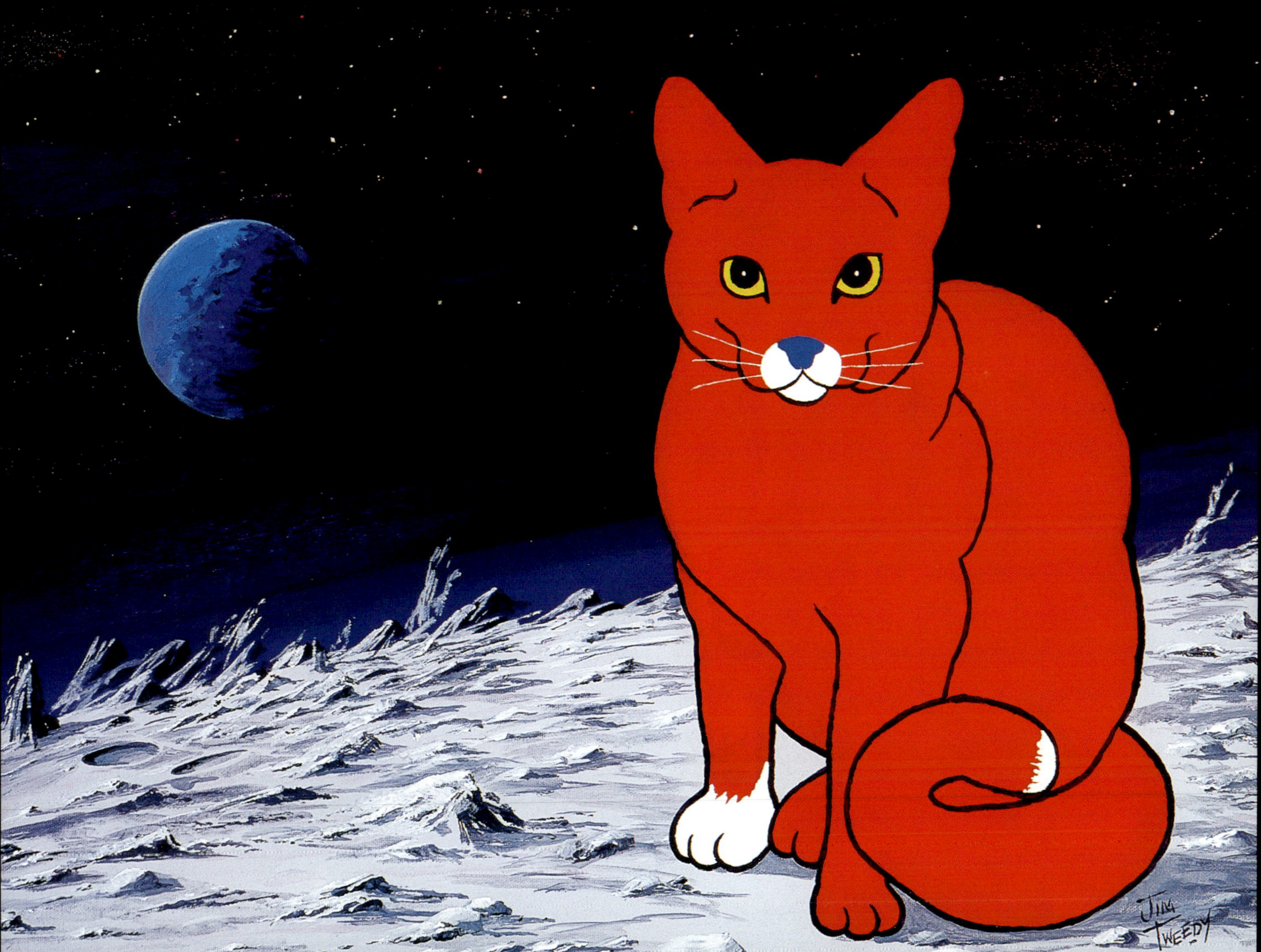

Charlie is apprehensive about spending a day at the moon. However, as Charlie leaves Earth's atmosphere and the world becomes a distant speck in the window, he has time to reflect on all that is good about being a RedCat.

That's four small steps for RedCat. One giant leap for catkind.

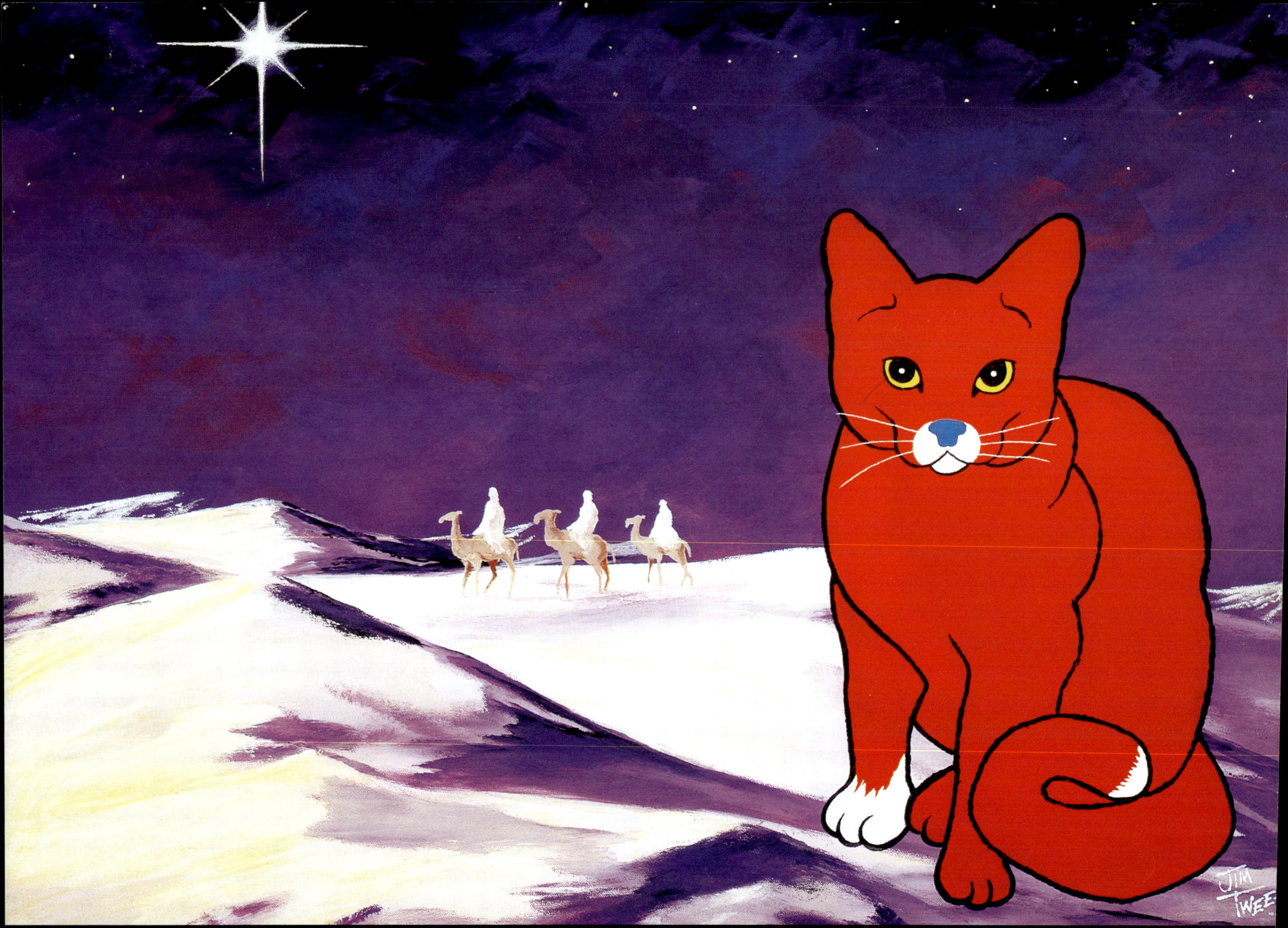

In His Wisdom He Made Them All, Every Creature Both Great and Small … and Red Ones, Too

With a tiny tear in his eye, Charlie the RedCat quietly purrs these words: "In His wisdom He made them all, every creature both great and small … and Red ones, too."